Hotel Maintenance: Security Safety and First Aid

HOTEL MAINTENANCE: SECURITY SAFETY AND FIRST AID

Suwarna Deshmukh

NAMAN PUBLISHER & DISTRIBUTORS
NEW DELHI

Published by
Sangeeta Jain for Naman Publisher & Distributors
7360-B, Prem Nagar,
Gali No.1, Shakti Nagar,
Delhi-110007
PH: 23823642, MOB.: 09013478302
E-mail: rajivjain72@ymail.com

First Published – 2011

ISBN–978-81–920935–5-0

Published in an association with **HLDC**, Agra.

SOLE DISTRIBUTOR
JINDAL BOOK SERVICES
LG-4A, Ganpati Bhawan,
4675-B/21, Ansari Road,
Darya Ganj, Delhi - 110002

Jacket Designed by :
S.M. Graphics

Printed by:
Sachin Printers, Delhi, India

Preface

Most hotels and motels are concerned with security and have measures in place to prevent crimes against patrons. At the same time, however, hotels and motels continue to be targeted by criminal elements. Security in the lodging environment presents a wide range of challenges if only because the lodging business is in operation every hour of the day, every day of the year.

Inexpensive safeguards can usually be implemented at a budget motel, but the more significant and costly safeguards tend to be put on the back burner. Unfortunately, it is the absence of the significant safeguards that leads to litigation. On the one hand, budget motel management may recognise the need to upgrade security and appreciate the attendant liability risk, but on the other hand, may lack the financial resources to do anything about it.

The public has become more educated concerning personal safety. In an overbuilt lodging market with heavy competition and fewer people travelling, hotel and motel owners are responding to their customers' concerns about personal safety.

Unlike other security specialists, the lodging security manager operates in an environment where the protected group is nearly always changing. With the exception of the employees working on the property, the guest population changes nearly everyday. A wide spectrum of society is represented in the guest population; also represented are the problems the guests bring with them. As with any facility security programme, the security manager will develop a loss prevention plan and programme based on the results of a survey. Ideally, although seldom the case, the survey will occur prior to the facility being constructed.

The book contains 10 chapter on variours aspects, i.e., Lodging Security Issues, Hotel Buildings, Electronic Wiring in Hotels, Refrigeration and Air Conditioning, Hotel Communication Systems, Accidents and First Aids, Fire Protection, Water and Sanitation, Hotel Security Design, Guest Protection and Safety Management.

This book is designed and presented in an easy to read and easy to understand format. It will be beneficial to both aspiring professionals and those already in the industry.

We hope this text book meets its intended purpose as a practical resource, and serve as a vehicle for promoting the professionalism of this important segment of the Hospitality Industry.

SUWARNA DESHMUKH

HERITAGE

LEARNING & DEVELOPMENT CENTER

Heritage Learning and Development Centre (HLDC) is an extended arm of Heritage Institute of Hotel & Tourism (HIHT). Heritage Institute of Hotel & Tourism is an Institute of excellence of the upcoming chain of Management Institutes, founded by D. K. Singh, President. At HIHT, our endeavour is to take education to the higher domains of never ending success. Heritage Institute of Hotel & Tourism provides the best possible infrastructure for pursuing best quality Hotel Management Education. HIHT has three campuses Agra, Shimla and Goa and proposed campuses at Kolkata, Pune, and Singapore.

In the modern era, Hospitality Industry is a reality, fighting for extremely challenging phase and getting into a stability mode. There are SMILES everywhere and this is relatively controlled and guarded, a sign of maturing and learning of Hospitality, which is cyclic in nature. The Hospitality Industry reflects a bright future. Earlier days, hospitality was synonymous with only hotel industry, but today this industry holds its important place with tourism. Hospitality academic in India is still in its nascent stage when compared to the west.

HLDC has been developed through the inputs from the industry and experts from the academics. This panel of experts have gone through the book and made suggestions which were incorporated. Every attempt has been made to thoroughly cover the day to day problems faced in the profession. In this field, as in most any other, it is prudent to remember the old adage, actions speak louder than words. The information given in this book makes the students fit for the industry. It provides about technical skills, personality and soft skills and ability to think and make decision.

This book is designed and presented in an easy to read and easy to understand format. It will be beneficial to both aspiring professionals and those already in the industry.

We hope this text book meets its intended purpose as a practical resource, and serve as a vehicle for promoting the professionalism of this important segment of the Hospitality Industry.

Contents

Contents

[illegible]

1

Lodging Security Issues

Most hotels and motels are concerned with security and have measures in place to prevent crimes against patrons. At the same time, however, hotels and motels continue to be targeted by criminal elements. Security in the lodging environment presents a wide range of challenges if only because the lodging business is in operation every hour of the day, every day of the year.

Inexpensive safeguards can usually be implemented at a budget motel, but the more significant and costly safeguards tend to be put on the back burner. Unfortunately, it is the absence of the significant safeguards that leads to litigation. On the one hand, budget motel management may recognise the need to upgrade security and appreciate the attendant liability risk, but on the other hand, may lack the financial resources to do anything about it.

Even with new construction or retrofitting for expansion or other non-security purposes, management may be unable to find enough capital to fund needed security improvements. With the exception of safe deposit boxes at the front desk, which limit a motel's exposure to property loss, no codes or laws require a motel to provide physical security. Courts across the nation have mandated that motels must merely take "reasonable" precautions to protect their guests from physical harm.

The public has become more educated concerning personal safety. In an overbuilt lodging market with heavy competition and fewer people travelling, hotel and motel owners are responding to their customers' concerns about personal safety.

Six very fundamental security steps that involve time but little cost can be implemented at the budget motel:

— Managing by walking around (MBWA) involves getting into the trenches and seeing what's going on in the business, and getting close to customers and employees. The really small "Mom and Pop" motels practiced MBWA before Tom Peters put a label on the concept. The larger, multi-unit motel chains are often lacking in this valuable practice. MBWA is a caring attitude that is imparted to employees and guests alike.

  Many security professionals emphasise having a written policy and programme, and although written materials can be helpful, they cannot engender the caring attitude and genuine concern that must be projected for security to succeed.

— A background investigation that includes contacting prior employers and making criminal records checks should be conducted before employees are hired. This is the second step. This is important because applicants may falsify prior employment information in order to conceal personal defects that make them unsuitable for assignment to high-trust jobs.

  The value of background checking is apparent at the budget motel where only one or two employees are present in the evening hours. At stake are the care and custody of the motel and its assets, and the protection of the patrons and their valuables. These are awesome responsibilities that cannot be placed into the hands of people about whom little is known.

— Employees need to be involved in security. One way to promote involvement is to make employees aware of security risks, how the risks affect the motel, the staff and the patrons, and what the staff can do to offset risks. The American Hotel & Motel Association offers a series of training video workshops on the basics of lodging security. Workshops cover everything from awareness to handling disturbances. Another consideration is to motivate employees to carry out their security responsibilities, especially with respect to emergency response procedures.

Programmes that provide rewards, such as a deserved thank-you from a supervisor, a certificate of appreciation, recognition by co-workers, a day off or a merit bonus, can go a long way to building a security programme. It is not unusual in the lodging industry for an employer to pay for performance as opposed to paying for time spent on the job. The quality and quantity of work, especially work that is central and essential to the business, is recognised as having a higher value than hours spent at the workplace. Incentive programmes can include financial rewards for excellence in security.

— Having a liaison with local law enforcement is crucial to the small property operator. Without adequate police protection, the budget motel is at extreme risk. The property management can contact the local crime prevention unit to identify the criminal threats confronting the motel and to learn what the police and the management can do to improve security at the property.

At a minimum, the local management needs to know the nature of the police services that are available, the manner in which those services are performed, and the officers who deliver the services.

— The motel manager needs to communicate with neighbours. The idea is to share information about crime in the neighbourhood and to look out for each other's interests with respect to spotting and reporting suspicious activity.

Neighbours can also share details of their successes and failures in setting up countermeasures to local crime. These are the kinds of activities that defend against allegations that the motel management was negligent by not recognising crime risks that can impact its patrons and by not having a security programme at least equal to that of nearby competitors. The motel manager should be active in the local business organisations, especially with organisations that serve the lodging industry, such as the local chapter of the American Hotel & Motel Association. The contacts and information obtained through networking can be invaluable.

— Patrolling of the premises should be done during the hours of darkness and whenever crime presents a threat to property or people. Patrolling can be handled on a proprietary basis by designating in-house employees to perform the patrol (as full-time or add-on duties) or patrolling services can be handled on a contract basis with a security guard company.

Whatever the approach, four considerations are important.

First, screen the persons to be selected for patrolling. Ensure they are drug-free, psychologically stable, trustworthy, and possess the physical ability to meet the rigours of constant movement in an outdoor environment.

Second, provide the selected persons with the knowledge and skill to do their jobs effectively. Teach them how to look for the indicators of crime and hazardous conditions, and how to respond when the indicators are present; make sure they understand the limits of their lawful authority; and motivate them to convey an interested and caring attitude in their dealings with people.

Third, give them the proper tools to carry out their jobs. Distinctive uniforms, inclement weather gear, flashlights, and a means of communication are essential.

Fourth, give them plenty of supervision and lots of positive guidance.

Unlike other security specialists, the lodging security manager operates in an environment where the protected group is nearly always changing. With the exception of the employees working on the property, the guest population changes nearly everyday. A wide spectrum of society is represented in the guest population; also represented are the problems the guests bring with them. As with any facility security programme, the security manager will develop a loss prevention plan and programme based on the results of a survey. Ideally, although seldom the case, the survey will occur prior to the facility being constructed.

The survey of a hotel is similar to that of a survey for any other facility, except possibly that more attention must be paid to the surrounding area. The foreseeability of crimes is a concept that has great significance at lodging facilities, requiring careful analysis and formulation of effective countermeasures. Lodging operators have been placed on notice by the courts that the owner/operator "may be liable for failure to warn guests and to prevent criminal assault where prior criminal activity in the area should have made the attack on the hotel guest foreseeable to the owner/ operator". Lodging industry professionals are clearly faced with a duty to act to protect guests. The security survey is an element in meeting the duty.

Zone Approach

In this approach, the facility, the land it sits on, and the surrounding neighbourhood are compartmented in four zones.

Zone 1 is the neighbourhood immediately surrounding the property. Obviously, if the hotel staff is afraid to walk the sidewalk in front of the property after sunset, there is a real problem. While the hotel staff may be aware of crime in the immediate area and may in fact have developed personal strategies for dealing with it, the guests will have no awareness, no warning, and no personal defence mechanisms at hand.

A good way for the security manager to begin to appreciate the crime problem is to walk the area during various times of the day and week, and determine first-hand the types of activities occurring on the fringes of the property. A next step for the security manager is to establish working relationships with officers in local, county, and state law enforcement agencies. These may be the supervisors of patrol operations in the neighbourhood, vice squad officers, and robbery and burglary detectives. The security manager can learn from them the types and frequencies of crimes, the criminal methods of operation, and the nature of the criminal threats, e.g., whether the criminals act individually, in small teams, or as large gangs.

Printouts of crime statistics relating to the neighbourhood should be obtained and studied, along with the Federal Bureau of Investigation's (FBI's) Uniform Crime Report. Notes should be made of these liaison activities and held for possible use in defending against litigation that may later arise. The analysis of information collected through personal observation, interviews of knowledgeable law enforcement professionals, and crime statistics will help the security manager during the remainder of the survey to focus on vulnerabilities that may be exploited by the crime threat.

The security manager will follow a logical progression from analysis of threat to analysis of vulnerability to formulation of countermeasures. This is also another way of describing how the security manager will construct an overall protective programme. As a small example: in a walk-through of the neighbourhood the security manager observes gang activity (threat); joggers make up a good percentage of the clientele (vulnerability); the security manager asks for increased police patrol presence along the jogging route.

Zone 2 begins at the property boundary and extends to the wall of the first building. In nearly all cases, this area will include parking areas. The swimming pool, tennis courts, and other outdoor recreational facilities might also be in this area. The zone 1 analysis will provide clues to the types of security problems that can be anticipated in zone 2. Other factors requiring consideration are: the perimeter, parking areas, exterior lighting, recreational areas, and the exterior walls of the lodging facility.

The security manager should examine the boundaries of the property to determine needs for psychological deterrents and physical barriers. It may be possible to inexpensively create boundaries by linking a natural barrier, such as a stream, with a hedge row, or by installing a short fence that extends from a fence or structure on neighbouring property. Lodging facilities are often constructed amid shrubbery and trees. Although aesthetically pleasing, these offer concealment to criminals who would prey on unsuspecting guests walking on the grounds or moving to and from their vehicles in the parking areas.

Parking schemes for guests vary widely in the lodging industry. There is close-in parking, in which the motel guest's vehicle is parked within a few feet of the guest's room, garage parking, valet parking, on-street parking, parking lots in walking distance, and parking lots with shuttles to the facility. Within the limitations imposed by the type and configuration of parking areas, the security manager must set up safeguards that primarily protect the guests and secondarily protect their vehicles.

Good lighting is both a deterrent to crime and an aid in detecting and apprehending criminals. Lighting is a basic security tool that can also be pleasing to the eye; for example, when it is artfully integrated with foliage and water. Security lighting in a parking area is essential. Unfortunately, a parking area is sometimes not lit properly because management wants to avoid projecting an image that the lodging facility is in a high crime area. In open general parking areas it is recommended that between 0.9 footcandles and 0.6 footcandles be maintained on the pavement. Lighting may go as low as 0.2 footcandles when there is a low level of night-time activity. In covered parking facilities, the recommended illumination levels increase to 5 footcandles for general parking and pedestrian areas; 10 footcandles for ramps and corners; and 50 footcandles at entrance areas.

The security manager must consider the routes and means of transportation utilised by guests going to and from outlying recreational areas; the times of utilisation; the types of guests; and the valuables they may be carrying with them. These considerations will aid the security manager in assessing the security risks involved. The nature of the recreational activity is also a consideration. A swimming pool, for example, may be used at all hours of the day or night when it is fenced or inside a locked building/area where entry is controlled, and where some degree of staff attention is given to the safety and security of guests while using the pool.

However, if the pool is near an unfenced/unprotected perimeter, the relative security of the using guests may drop to a level that would require either closing the pool during high-risk hours or increasing the protection. Hiking, walking, jogging, and biking on unattended trails present similar risks.

The innermost line of defence in zone 2 is the exterior of the lodging facility. Passage through the walls can be made by guests and trades people at any number of entrances. The control of access through the entrances is typically by lodging staff whose training and experience permit them to discriminate between authorised persons and unwelcome visitors. During late evening hours when traffic into the lodging facility is minimal, many or all of the remote entrances can be secured, requiring persons to enter through one or a few entrances that are under the direct observation of staff.

Unwelcome visitors who are able to pass through an entrance unchallenged or by subterfuge would be confronted with the safeguards of zone 3. The term unwelcome visitor is substituted for the term intruder because zones 2 and 3 are essentially public areas. It is not the movement of people through public entrances that is of greatest concern to the security manager—it is the movement of criminals through exterior doors and windows that lead directly into guest rooms or into areas containing the lodging operator's assets.

Zone 3 consists of public space that may include restaurants, lounges, shops, rest rooms, and reading areas. Guest room corridors and fire exit stairwells are technically public but from a practical standpoint the security manager will insist that the lodging staff be alert to suspicious persons in these areas. The main thrust of security with respect to zone 3 is not to keep people out but to exercise subtle controls over human activity inside the zone.

Security awareness should be second nature for all employees. It means being aware of the methods that criminals use, being able to spot suspicious persons and activities, and knowing what to do when the indicators are present. An awareness technique that incorporates both courtesy and attentiveness is for staff to greet persons who are on the premises and to offer assistance when it appears they are not sure of their bearings.

To the guest, the employee making the greeting is seen as a helpful person; to a criminal looking for the opportunity to commit a crime, the employee is seen as a potential adversary and witness.

Robberies at motels, motor lodges, and hotels occur more frequently than property owners care to admit. The foreseeability issue is strongly connected to robberies because of the potential for injury or death to guests and employees. Data gathered in the zone 1 analysis will indicate the probable nature of the robbery threat.

Employees should not be permitted to congregate in the lobby for two reasons. First, an unprofessional image is presented to arriving guests by the appearance of too many employees. Second, the security manager will be concerned that a dishonest employee will have the opportunity to observe guests entering with expensive valuables and act upon this information or pass the information to a confederate. On the latter point, thieves who specialise in victimising lodgers will wait near the registration desk looking for a prospective victim (the "mark") as he or she checks in and hoping to overhear the registration clerk mention the assigned room number. Registration clerks should be trained to simply point to the room number on the registration card when checking guests in.

Zone 4 comprises the guest-rooms within the facility. The guest-room is the traveller's home away from home; a sanctuary from the rest of the world. The major separating point between the sanctuary and outsiders is the guest-room door. The door should be a solid wood or steel door. In most areas, local building codes and/or fire codes will specify doors with a specific fire rating. Hollow core doors should never be used at the entry point to a guest-room. The door should be equipped with at least one viewing port or peep hole.

With the recent enactment of the Americans with Disabilities Act (ADA) serious consideration should be given to providing two peep holes in every door: one at a standard height and one at wheelchair level to accommodate guests in wheelchairs. These view ports or peep-holes should provide the guest with a 180-degree view of the corridor outside of the room.

The door lock is another important element. Whenever possible electronic locking systems should be employed that permit a "key/lock change" with every guest's arrival and departure. Electronic locks also make it possible to determine which key card was used to open a door at a particular time. This audit trail feature can aid investigations that involve unauthorised entries to guest rooms. It is not uncommon, however, to find smaller properties continuing to use the standard lock-in-knob arrangement, which is well known for problems associated with key control.

Even the best hardware can be defeated when a key has been stolen or duplicated. The worst thing that can happen is for a master key to be compromised. Professional thieves are always on the lookout for lodging employees who will sell or rent master keys. It is absolutely essential that mechanical locks be changed immediately whenever a key is missing. This includes keys that the guest forgets to turn in. The guest-room should not be sold to another guest until the locks have been changed. Each employee must turn in at the end of the work shift any lodging facility keys. It should be policy that only a responsible manager, such as the general manager, chief engineer, or manager of security, will be permitted to take keys off of the property.

The door should be equipped with a deadbolt with at least a one-inch throw and self-closing hinges that cause the door to swing into a closed-and-locked position. The self-closing feature must be reliable because guests will expect the doors to always and perfectly close behind them; if the feature fails, resulting in a loss or injury to the guest, the management can expect a claim for damages. The sliding glass or patio door often used in resort properties must be capable of resisting forced entry, including the technique of lifting a door panel out of its sliding track. The rule of thumb is to augment the locking capability of a sliding glass door with the use of a secondary device, such as a charley bar.

Consideration must also be given to where a guest will store valuables. Nearly all states have some version of an innkeeper's law requiring the lodging operator to provide safe deposit boxes for guests. Consideration should also be given to providing a guest with an in-room safe. The survey should determine why and how often employees enter guest rooms. Entry is usually related to the need to make heating, ventilation, and air conditioning (HVAC), mechanical, and plumbing checks, but includes also the need to determine damage to or theft from rooms.

More important, these checks make it possible to discover if a guest inside a room is ill or injured. The standard practice is to conduct a check of each room in every 24-hour period. Unlike office building security, where the office population is generally stable, the lodging security approach is tailored to address the unique problems of an unstable, ever-changing guest population.

In coming to grips with these unique problems, the lodging security professional must take into account the diversity and the changing nature of the clientele. The relatively young lodging guests, those in their 30's and

40's, have different values and expectations than guests who are younger or older. The security manager must be able to balance the need for security, the guest's desire for privacy, and the organisation's need to reduce liability and losses.

SELECTION OF SECURITY PERSONNEL

The selection of security personnel must receive 100 per cent attention from the manager and/or assistant. It is essential for all security personnel to be hired directly by the security department managers and not by the human resources department. In most cases hotels will hire personnel based on their immediate need, forcing themselves to hire the next available applicant. It has been a common practice for hotels to hire retired police officers and would-be police officers who for some reason have not been accepted onto the force and so work in security. There are clear pros and cons to this approach related to hiring managers, supervisors, or officers.

Many security managers are hired because they have a work history that includes experience such as law enforcement for a municipality or a federal agency. Traditional management thinking has been that this type of candidate has had extensive experience handling crime-related problems, is usually trained, and has many contacts within the police force or city/state government. For these three reasons, such a choice would seem reasonable and appropriate.

Senior management must consider, however, the actual needs of their hotel. Not all properties are inundated with crime and seldom is the job of security solely focused on crime. Furthermore, it is far more cost-effective to deter crime through broad-based prevention programmes than to expend resources trying to apprehend and prosecute criminals. Another drawback frequently encountered by hiring the retired local, state, or government employee is his or her view that the lodging security job is only a second source of income and, hence, not that important. These comments are not meant to say that no former police officers or government agents can succeed as security managers, because many have, but simply to point out the problems associated with their basic orientations, lack of management skills, and, perhaps, lack of incentive. A preferable candidate for such a position is one who is able to understand and work within a business organisation.

Hotels are more likely to have an emphasis on prevention, management principles, and labour issues, rather than on arrest and prosecution. Thus, a person with well-rounded management skills is far more likely to succeed than one who has a limited sense of the role of security. Security managers are the most important people in the security department because they set the tone of the organisation by their example. However, careful selection of other security personnel should be the second-most important task for security managers filling a department. Lodging security is still a developing profession and, in some people's minds, is subordinate to police work.

Many younger security officers see their positions as interim steps to becoming police officers. This is fine; working in hotel security allows them to develop experience and maturity. Although police officers currently may enjoy a better public image, they are not necessarily better paid, have better training, or have better opportunities for advancement compared to those in the lodging security industry. Still, many people do see lodging security as a path toward public law enforcement. The problem human resources managers, or anyone else involved in the selection process, need to be sensitive to is hiring the frustrated would-be police officer who has been unsuccessful in getting a public sector job. It is one thing, for example, to hire a law enforcement or criminal justice student who wishes to gain experience. It is quite another thing to hire the individual who cannot be a police officer and must settle for the security job.

Promoting from within is a common practice for all types of organisations. The sense that you are getting someone as a supervisor or a manager who has established a track record and who knows the company is more comforting than hiring the unknown candidate. Prior performance, consistency, quality of work product, and reputation are all factors that should be considered.

Past performance usually is a good indicator of future performance, there are some drawbacks to adhering to a strict policy of promoting from within. First, those promoted are likely to reflect the views and values of those above them, and thus this practice will maintain the same types of people throughout the organisation. It may be all right to perpetuate a type of person when it is good for the company, but when the type is not as effective as needed, it could be harmful.

Positive and constructive discipline is training that corrects, moulds, or strengthens an employee in the interest of achieving departmental and hotel goals. Punishment, which is feared and disliked by everyone, is secondary. Any punishment connected with discipline always be a means to an end, and that end should be organisational, not personal. In other words, the effective disciplinary process condemns the act, not the employee. It is also important that discipline should be swift. Whatever the nature of the problem, be it simple tardiness or careless oversight, the long-range effect of coming to grips with problems immediately is better than putting off what probably will have to be faced later.

The real essence and secret of constructive discipline is its preventive nature. To train, mould, and correct now reduces the need for more difficult training, moulding, and correction later. Discipline is a responsibility that rests squarely on the supervisor's shoulders. It cannot be passed to a higher supervisor and should not be passed to human resources. Some weak supervisors shirk their responsibility with the idea that enforcing the regulations will hurt their relations with their subordinates. The supervisor who is fair and consistent in his or her treatment of employees will gain rather than lose respect through being firm and expecting conformity to the rules. Some make the mistake of believing that discipline is only directed at the inefficient worker.

All employees require constructive discipline. Most employees want to do a good job. If care is taken in giving assignments, there will be fewer failures and fewer disciplinary problems resulting from failures. However, there are six fundamental rules in the disciplinary process that have universal applicability. As presented by Sennewald, these are:

— Rule #1: Put rules in writing. Make certain that employees understand the rules. No rule should be assumed. If a rule is worth having, it is worth writing down.

— Rule #2: Discipline in the privacy of an office. To the employee, being corrected for deficiencies in conduct or performance is a sensitive and frequently embarrassing experience. Being corrected in the presence of others is considered degrading, and the end result of that approach is seething resentment and angry embarrassment—emotions that are counterproductive to the true disciplinary goal.

— Rule #3: Be objective and consistent. Effective discipline condemns the act, not the person. This approach is obviously objective; personalities are not the issue, or at least should not be.

— Rule #4: Educate, do not humiliate. The concept here is to help, not hurt an employee who has failed to meet standards of conduct or performance. If the disciplinary action truly corrects, trains, or moulds the individual to meet standards, they come away from the experience with better insight into themselves and what the company expects. They come away educated.

— Rule #5: Keep a file on all employee infractions. Documented incidents of past failures are a necessary and useful reference for repeated incidents.

— Rule #6: Exercise discipline promptly. As time passes the infraction, whatever magnitude it may have, becomes vague and almost controversial.

No company likes to discipline its employees or separate them from its employment. However, disciplinary action must be taken whenever an employee violates any rule of the hotel, fails to adhere to any policies and procedures, or fails to uphold the spirit of the hotel's mission.

A hotel's reputation as a safe, well-run, clean, and comfortable establishment is essential for its success. The same argument can be made for the reputation of the security department and, certainly, the hotel's reputation will depend in good measure upon the success of the security programme. That programme's success is tied directly to the reputation and image of the department in the opinion of the hotel's employees, its guests, and the general public.

Capable and effective from the employees' perspective, the members of the security department and the manager, in particular, must project a positive image. Image is affected by a variety of factors, including outward appearance—grooming, demeanour and attire, personality (friendly and caring but professional at all times), consistency in treatment of employees in situations requiring security intervention, and emphasis on the positive aspect of services provided to fellow employees. It is a popular trend, for example, to eliminate the traditional security uniform and replace it with business attire.

The security manager sets the tone for the organisation and should maintain positive interaction with all levels of employees, never using authority as a means of exerting influence or pressure on the employees. From the guest's point of view, image and reputation will be determined primarily by the nature of the guest's contact, if any, with security while staying at the hotel. Most guests do not have any direct contact with security, and those who do will generally have it under adverse conditions, such as a theft of property or some other negative situation.

Any victim, regardless of the seriousness of the loss or inconvenience, will behave in a fairly predictable manner, frequently blaming the security officer for not doing his or her job. It is essential that security personnel recognise that the guest's response is a normal reaction to stress. Furthermore, most victims know that it is unlikely that the harm they suffered cannot be undone and, therefore, really only look to the officer for some compassion and information.

Most victims simply want someone to listen to their plight, which suggests that the security officers must have developed good listening skills. To the outside world, the public at large, the reputation of a hotel's security department will depend on all the factors cited above, and the relationship the department and its members—especially the manager—have established in the community. That community includes other hotels, the local police, the courts, the general public, visiting travellers, and criminals themselves, who have been known to have their own information system. Prostitutes, for example, know which hotels are easy to work in and which ones are not.

The security manager should make every effort to become involved in community activities related to crime and the hotel's business. As mentioned, relations with local police are extremely important, especially in times of limited staffing in police departments. Problems of crime will occasionally be so serious that police assistance will become necessary. A poor relationship with the local law enforcement authorities will impede solving such problems. Security personnel must be considered thorough and competent by the general public or the hotel security department will acquire a rent-a-cop image.

Function of Security

The most basic function for the security personnel in any hotel is to perform regular patrols of the property, both inside and outside. There are three different types of security patrolling that have been utilised in hotels for decades, yet continue to serve the needs of guests, employees, and the property in general: random routine patrol, lobby patrol, and basic rounds. In random routine patrol, the security officer walks, or in some cases drives, around the property on a random basis to check for irregularities, suspicious circumstances, and intruders.

There are two objectives achieved by this type of patrol. First, any irregularity or suspicious circumstance hopefully will be discovered before a major problem develops. For example, there may be a leaking roof, broken pipes, dark hallways or stairways, and other unsafe conditions that may cause injury to a guest or employee. The second objective is crime prevention. By patrolling in a randomised fashion, potential assailants or other wrongdoers can be detected or deterred from committing their acts. It is essential that this form of patrol not become too methodical or predictable. The officer should never patrol a site in a fixed schedule or pattern; however, it is critical to have key checkpoints throughout the patrol.

The second form of security patrol commonly employed in a hotel is lobby duty or surveillance. Any area of the hotel open to the general public requires a different type of patrol. The officer who is assigned to a public area, such as the lobby, must stay in one general location for extended periods of time to fulfil his or her duty. There are three benefits or purposes filled by this type of security presence: observance of undesirable persons or behaviour; assisting guests or others; and, deterring crime as a visible presence.

The third and most traditional form of security patrol is the fire watch. It differs from randomised patrol, although both may be accomplished simultaneously. On a fire watch, the officer patrols every floor and section of the building, including locked areas, in hopes of discovering any potential fire hazard, smoke, or actual fire. It is a common practice to utilise some type of watch clock, checklists, or an electronic wand to record what items or areas were checked and at what time. Caution should be taken by security managers to control the keys and discs that are imprinted from this equipment to prevent tampering and destruction. Accurate records should be maintained with the daily log books and incident reports, mostly for insurance purposes but for legal purposes also.

A contemporary version of the watch clock is an electronic device that reads barcodes similar to those used in grocery stores. The officer carries the device, which is about the size of a hand-held calculator, and passes it by a code placed on a tag at the location to be checked. At the end of the shift, the officer can insert the device into a recorder, which will read all rounds made, critical areas missed, and so on, and generate a hardcopy printout. Any of these measures is helpful to enhance the level of watchfulness necessary during late night hours.

An important aspect of patrolling for all security personnel is the awareness of arson signs. Arsonists are known to use hotels as avenues for committing theft by setting fire to one location and, while everyone evacuates, stealing the guests' or hotel's property. Other arsonists like to watch people evacuate from buildings and will usually blend in with the crowd watching the scene. The typical arsonist has little concern for a facility's occupants or the firefighting personnel. Arsonists, particularly a professional "torch", will use flammable liquid in quantity. Look for liquid containers that may hold accelerants that can turn a small fire into a major fire in a short time.

One accelerant of which most people are unaware is the basic corrugated cardboard; it will burn intensely. Other items to be noted and acted upon include: dynamite charges connected with primer cord; hydrants or sprinkler valves that have been shut down or have deliberately damaged threads to prevent hose hook-ups; and unusual odours such as gasoline, kerosene, or fuel oil. For further information on arsonists and arsonist methods, security managers should contact their local chapter of the International Association of Arson Investigators.

Documentation is essential to the proper operation of a security department in any environment. Reports usually generated by a hotel security department include incident reports, activity or shift reports, and safety rules violations. Well-written, typed, and accurate record keeping is very important and helpful to the future planning of the hotel in general and of security specifically. A security manager should be able to review the previous year or more of reports and identify patterns of activity that will help direct available resources in the security programme.

Security reports are important as records for insurance or prosecution purposes; they should be thought of as important management tools, not locked away in a storage room or discarded. It is easier to maintain and research incident reports if they are kept chronologically. Caution should be used when storing these records; a fire file safe is recommended. Be sure to check the state statute of limitations for civil action suits and keep all records for the required time, as well as keeping records for specific pending cases until the cases are completely settled; check with your legal department.

Hotels offer a wide variety of services to guests, and like most other businesses they also maintain a lost-and-found department. The number of found items a hotel can accumulate varies with the size of the hotel and the volume of business within the hotel. Property that is turned in to security can potentially belong to a guest, patron, employee, or someone passing by the hotel. For ethical reasons as well as ensuring that all found property is secure, all lost-and- found items should be turned in to the security department daily. The property should be logged in and only given to its rightful owner on request. Lost-and-found sheets are critical, as well as a lost-and-found log book tracking the property chronologically.

Hotel Protection

As protection management is the one of the most important factors in the lodging industry, one must learn to integrate guest protection techniques and practices into the normal management approaches. The guests expect protection; the courts have decreed that we must provide protection; we cannot survive unless we do provide protection.

However, a major question among those forward-thinking hoteliers who recognise the requirement to provide guest protection has not been whether to provide such care but how to provide it. We strive to be the perfect host. By word, act, appearance, and design we attempt to send the message to our patrons that they are, indeed, like guests in our homes. We strive to provide easy and friendly access to our properties. How can we succeed at that and at the same time limit or deny access to those we wish to exclude? We design our rooms to be comfortable, inviting and attractive. Isn't it a seeming contradiction to transpose such a welcoming room into one which is bedecked with locks, safety devices and protection equipment? How can we present the friendly, open and inviting atmosphere which the perfect host portrays?

Hotel protection management consists of an integrated management model and series of approaches which, when properly applied, allow for the establishment and maintenance of an acceptable level of protection. And at the same time the image of hospitality is maintained.

Major steps involved in the development of the hotel protection model are the following:

— Identifying and evaluating assets which must be protected.

— Identifying and evaluating the threats which exist to those assets.

— Employing a series of countermeasures designed to minimise those threats.

— Developing a protection profile system from the above listed property-unique aspects and applying accepted management-science techniques thereto.

This methodology has evolved from the totality of the three factors: hotel, protection, and management.

Travellers not only do have virtually an unlimited choice of means of travel, but also have an exceptionally broad choice of accommodations when they reach their destination. A traveller might have some of the following choices when he reaches the hotel.

— A luxury full-service hotel

— A modest hotel offering limited service

— A roadside motel

— A bed-and-breakfast establishment

— A time-sharing establishment

— A resort

— An apartment hotel

— A campsite

The list choices go on from modest to luxurious, from full-service to virtually do-it-yourself. From casino resorts to private clubs, the traveller has never had such a selection from which to choose. Further, the traveller can avail himself of a property which functions as a multi-operation facility, at the same time offering long-term accommodations to some (an apartment), both room and food to others (a boarding house), and finally supplying the basic needs of an overnight guest (a traditional hotel.)

For all practical purposes, there is little legal difference between any of these types of facilities when it comes to hotel protection management. The legal definition of inns and hotels can be traced to several legal decisions dating from the late 16th century. These early legal definitions vary to such a degree that it is difficult for a lay person to derive a common definition.

However, in Juengel vs. City of Glendale (Mo. 1942) non-legally trained hoteliers can get more definitive and useful legal definition. It denies hotel as a house which is held out to the public as a place where all transient persons who come will be received and entertained as guests for business, with food and lodging while on their journey; or a house where travellers are furnished with everything which they have occasion for while upon their way; or a place where transient guests are admitted to lodge, as well as one where they are fed and lodged.

These general descriptions seem to fit our common perception of hotels and inns. Further, the terms innkeeper, hotel-keeper, and hotelier are used interchangeably. Likewise, the term motel, for all practical purposes, may be used as synonymous with hotel and inn. For the purposes of this text, we should consider all these various forms of accommodations as hotel.

Lodging managers have been besieged with a multiplicity of terms which seem to surround the subject of guest protection. These terms, in and of themselves, seem ill-defined, perhaps non-defined, and certainly confusing. The following terms are bandied around constantly. They may be separate and distinct to the professional who deals with protection on a full time basis, to the average lodging manager. They are given below.

— Security
— Risk control
— Safety
— Life-safety
— Loss prevention
— Asset protection
— Loss control
— Loss reduction
— Crime prevention

The hotel industry is well advised to adopt a single, descriptive and extremely useful term protection to replace all the ill-defined terms used above. Protection is defined as the state of being protected—the covering or shielding from harm, injury or destruction. Shielding from harm seems to imply that the acts of protecting must, by definition, be proactive. If one is shielded from harm, then it seems evident that the harm will not be allowed to reach the person being protected.

A barrier, or protective shield, or line of defence has been established which decreases the possibility and probability of the danger ever reaching and harming or causing loss to the one being protected. Such action does not prevent the loss by attacking the potential doer of the harm. Rather, by surrounding the intended victim of the harm, it has the effect of reducing the possibility of the harm being inflicted. It does not, in the case of the threat of crime, claim to prevent. Rather it aims to deter the criminal act from ever reaching the target victim.

By definition, by design, and by necessity, protection is proactive. As such, the shield or barrier or protective techniques which act as the deterrent must be in place prior to the threat ever occurring. As it is proactive rather than reactive so it differs from the traditional role of the police. Police devote an extraordinary amount of time to an event after it occurs. We in the private sector must do just the opposite. We must provide protection, not simply what is considered security, before the event occurs.

The term security can be a problem in and of itself, and its usefulness as the term to define protection may have run its course. The term causes a mis-focus and should not be used in a modern proactive, management-science-based property protection programme. There are several reasons for this assertion, not the least of which is the fact that the term security conjures visions of a security officer, private police or a security department. The responsibility of guest protection is limited to those security individuals and security departments, and worse yet, that such care is their exclusive responsibility. This perception is both invalid and dangerous.

Management

Management is art of managing, directing, facilitating or

ascertaining the successful accomplishment of tasks or the attainment of stated objectives. In its simplest form management can best be described as that discipline designed and used to get tasks accomplished. This simple definition denigrates the fact that much of today's modern management theory is steeped in and has been developed from theories which were initially university-based. From the early university psychologist/ educators, the science of management has been strongly influenced by academic.

From McGregor's Theory X, Theory Y to behavioural sciences and quantitative approaches, virtually all management approaches have their roots in the university setting. The lodging management student should not consider his undergraduate or graduate studies complete without a thorough investigation of various management theories and approaches.

A model hotel manager's tools are the same tools every manager has to some degree. They are called the "M" tools and they are the tools he uses to accomplish tasks. The four "Ms" represent Money, Methods, Machinery and Manpower. To one extent or another, these are the tools which every manager has as he strives to accomplish his objectives. He learns to influence and motivate and make most productive his "Manpower" tools and leads. He learns to develop, adjust and maintain ways and means of getting tasks done reasonably by his tool labelled "Methods". He learns to understand and utilise mechanical and electrical technology which has been developed over the years and his "Machinery" tools come into play. He learns to make the best use of his fiscal resources, and for how to spend and invest and budget them most efficiently his "Money" tools are used. Each of the four "M" tools, individually utilised and manipulated in concert with the other three, provides the manager with the ability to become effective.

This book elaboratively describes how to provide to the lodging professional management-science techniques, methods and procedures which allow a systems approach to guest protection and reasonable care. This approach, when properly applied, not only protects the guests but significantly reduces costs, increases staff morale and facilitates enhanced property-wide departmental management. It also describes how to change the face of security. In the minds of most hoteliers, security conjures visions of a cigar-smoking, perhaps overweight, retired police officer whose career has been one of reacting to a call. It is designed to change that image to one of a proactive, property-wide management programme which can provide virtual certainty of reasonable care.

2

Hotel Buildings

A building as a shelter represents a physical division of the human habitat into the inside and the outside. Humans have a remarkable drive to reflect on their lives and express themselves through art. Ever since the first cave paintings, buildings have become objects of artistic expression.

Commercial buildings are for business use, e.g., for offices and sales. Industrial buildings include manufacturing and warehousing functions, for example. Institutional buildings, such as governmental and military hospitals, colleges, and administration buildings are normally built for longer lives.

Residential buildings are called houses. Single family and multi-family dwellings are typically built as shelter and living space. These building types may range from one-room wood-framed, masonry, or adobe dwellings to multi-million dollar high-rise buildings able to house thousands of people. The definition of a low-rise vs. a high-rise residential building is being debated, but generally three stories or less is considered low-rise. A multi-story building (American English, Multi-storey Building British English) is a building that has multiple floors (stories (storeys in British)) above ground in the building.

Multi-story buildings aim to increase the area of the building without increasing the area of the land the building is built on, hence saving land and, in most cases, money (depending on material used and land prices in the area, of course). The practice of designing, constructing, and operating buildings is normally a collective effort of different groups of professionals and trades. Depending on the size, complexity, and purpose of a particular building project, the project team may include:

— A real estate developer who secures funding for the project;

— One or more financial institutions or other investors that provide the funding

— Local planning and code authorities

— A Surveyor who performs an ALTA/ACSM and construction surveys throughout the project;

— Construction managers who coordinate the effort of different groups of project participants;

— Licensed architects and engineers who provide building design and prepare construction documents;

— Landscape architects;

— Interior designers;

— Other consultants;

— Contractors who provide construction services and install building systems such as climate control, · electrical, plumbing, fire protection, security and telecommunications;

— Marketing or leasing agents;

— Facility managers who are responsible for operating the building.

Regardless of their size or intended use, all buildings in the US must comply with zoning ordinances, building codes and other regulations such as fire codes, life safety codes and related standards. Vehicles—such as trailers, caravans, ships and passenger aircraft—are treated as "buildings" for life safety purposes.

Building Construction

In general, there are three types of construction:

— Building construction

— Heavy/highway construction

— Industrial construction

Each type of construction project requires a unique team to plan, design, construct, and maintain the project. Building construction is the process of adding structure to real property. The vast majority of building construction projects are small renovations, such as addition of a room, or renovation of a bathroom. Often, the owner of the property acts as labourer, paymaster, and design team for the entire project. However, all building construction projects include some elements in common - design, financial, and legal considerations. Many projects of varying sizes reach undesirable end results, such as structural collapse, cost overruns, and/or litigatios reason, those with experience in the field make detailed plans and maintain careful oversight during the project to ensure a positive outcome.

Building construction is procured privately or publicly utilising various delivery methodologies, including hard bid, negotiated price, traditional, management contracting, construction management-at-risk, design & build and design-build bridging.

Construction Procurement

Procurement describes the merging of activities undertaken by the client to obtain a building. There are many different methods of construction procurement; however the three most common types of procurement are:

— Traditional (Design-bid-build)

— Design and Build

— Management Contracting

Traditional

This is the most common method of construction procurement and is well established and recognised. In this arrangement, the architect or engineer acts as the project coordinator. His or her role is to design the works, prepare the specifications and produce construction drawings, administer the contract, tender the works, and manage the works from inception to completion. There are direct contractual links between the architect's client and the main contractor. Any subcontractor will have a direct contractual relationship with the main contractor.

Design and build

This approach has become more common in recent years and includes an entire completed package, including fixtures, fittings and equipment where necessary, to produce a completed fully functional building. In some cases, the Design and Build (D & B) package can also include to find the site, arranging funding and applying for all necessary statutory consents.

The client/ owner will produce a list of 'clients requirements' for a project, for which the D & B contractor will translate into a set of 'contactors proposals'. The latter will then be altered and adapted until the client is satisfied that the D & B contractor knows exactly what the client wants from his or her completed building. D & B is usually used for less complicated projects such as office or industrial buildings, although its use on large, complicated projects has become more common in recent years. The potential advantage D & B offers over other methods of construction procurement is that it can lead to greater certainty for costs and schedule. In this arrangement, the client typically has direct contractual relationship with the D & B contractor only.

Management procurement systems

In this arrangement the client plays an active role in the procurement system by entering into separate contracts with the designer (architect or engineer), the construction manager, and individual trade contractors. The client takes on the contractual role, while the construction or project manager provides the active role of managing the separate trade contracts, and ensuring that they all work smoothly and effectively together.

Management procurement systems are often used to speed up the procurement processes, allow the client greater flexibility in design variation throughout the contract, the ability to appoint individual work contractors, separate contractual responsibility on each individual throughout the contract, and to provide greater client control.

Residential construction

More and more families are looking into building their own homes, or contracting to have them built.

Construction practices, technologies, and resources conform to state and local building codes.

Highway construction

Heavy/highway construction is the process adding infrastructure to our built environment. Owners of these projects are usually government agencies, either at the national or local level. As in building construction, heavy/highway construction has design, financial, and legal considerations, however these projects are not usually undertaken for-profit, but to service the public interest. However, heavy/highway construction projects are also undertaken by large private corporations, including, among others, the golf courses, harbours, power companies, railroads, and mines, who undertake the construction of access roads, dams, railroads, general site grading, and massive earthwork projects. As in building construction, the owner will assemble a team to create an overall plan to ensure that the goals of the project are met.

Authority having jurisdiction (AHJ)

In construction, the authority having jurisdiction (AHJ) is the governmental agency or subagency which regulates the construction process. In most cases, this is the municipality in which the building is located. However, construction performed for supra-municipal authorities are usually regulated directly by the owning authority, which becomes the AHJ.

During the planning of a building, the zoning and planning boards of the AHJ will review the overall compliance of the proposed building with the municipal General Plan and zoning regulations. Once the proposed building has been approved, detailed civil, architectural, and structural plans must be submitted to the municipal building department (and sometimes the public works department) to determine compliance with the building code and sometimes for fit with existing infrastructure. Often, the municipal fire department will review the plans for compliance with fire-safety ordinances and regulations.

Before the foundation can be dug, contractors are typically required to notify utility companies, either directly or through a company such as Dig Safe to ensure that underground utility lines can be marked. This lessens the likelihood of damage to the existing electrical, water, sewage, phone, and cable facilities, which could cause outages and potentially hazardous situations. During the construction of a building, the municipal building inspector inspects the building periodically to ensure that the construction adheres to the approved plans and the local building code. Once construction is complete and a final inspection has been passed, an occupancy permit may be issued.

An operating building must remain in compliance with the fire code. The fire code is enforced by the local fire department. Any changes made to a building including its use, expansion, its structural integrity, and fire protection items, require acceptance by the AHJ. Anything affecting basic safety functions, no matter how small they may appear, may require the owner to apply for a building permit, to ensure proper review of the contemplated changes against the building code.

Industrial construction

Industrial construction, though a relatively small part of

the entire construction industry, is a very important component. Owners of these projects are usually large, for-profit, industrial corporations. These corporations can be found in such industries as medicine, petroleum, chemical, power generation, manufacturing, etc. Processes in these industries require highly specialised expertise in planning, design, and construction. As in building and heavy/highway construction, this type of construction requires a team of individuals to ensure a successful project.

In the modern industrialised world, construction usually involves the translation of paper or computer based designs into reality. A formal design team may be assembled to plan the physical proceedings, and to integrate those proceedings with the other parts. The design usually consists of drawings and specifications, usually prepared by a design team including architects, interior designers, surveyors, civil engineers, cost engineers (or quantity surveyors), mechanical engineers, electrical engineers, structural engineers, and fire protection engineers.

The design team is most commonly employed by (i.e. in contract with) the property owner. Under this system, once the design is completed by the design team, a number of construction companies or construction management companies may then be asked to make a bid for the work, either based directly on the design, or on the basis of drawings and a bill of quantities provided by a quantity surveyor. Following evaluation of bids, the owner will typically award a contract to the lowest responsible bidder.

The modern trend in design is toward integration of previously separated specialties, especially among large firms. In the past, architects, interior designers, engineers, developers, construction managers, and general contractors were more likely to be entirely separate companies, even in the larger firms. Presently, a firm that is nominally an "architecture" or "construction management" firm may have experts from all related fields as employees, or to have an associated company that provides each necessary skill. Thus, each such firm may offer itself as "one-stop shopping" for a construction project, from beginning to end. This is designated as a "design Build" contract where the contractor is given a performance specification, and must undertake the project from design to construction, while adhering to the performance specifications.

Several project structures can assist the owner in this integration, including design-build, partnering, and construction management. In general, each of these project structures allows the owner to integrate the services of architects, interior designers, engineers, and constructors throughout design and construction. In response, many companies are growing beyond traditional offerings of design or construction services alone, and are placing more emphasis on establishing relationships with other necessary participants through the design-build process.

The increasing complexity of construction projects creates the need for design professionals trained in all phases of the project's life-cycle and develop an appreciation of the building as an advanced technological system requiring close integration of many sub-systems and their individual components, including sustainability. Building engineering is an emerging discipline that attempts to meet this new challenge.

Role of Financial Advisors

Many construction projects suffer from preventable financial problems. Underbids ask for too little money to complete the project. Cash flow problems exist when the present amount of funding cannot cover the current costs for labour and materials, and because they are a matter of having sufficient funds at a specific time, can arise even when the overall total is enough. Fraud is a problem in many fields, but is notoriously prevalent in the construction field. Financial planning for the project is intended to ensure that a solid plan, with adequate safeguards and contingency plans, is in place before the project is started, and is required to ensure that the plan is properly executed over the life of the project.

Mortgage bankers, accountants, and cost engineers are likely participants in creating an overall plan for the financial management of the building construction project. The presence of the mortgage banker is highly likely even in relatively small projects, since the owner's equity in the property is the most obvious source of funding for a building project. Accountants act to study the expected monetary flow over the life of the project, and to monitor the payouts throughout the process.

Cost engineers apply expertise to relate the work and materials involved to a proper valuation. Cost overruns with government projects have occurred when the contractor was able to identify change orders or changes in the project resulting in large increases in cost, which are not subject to competition by other firm as they have already been eliminated from consideration after the initial bid.

Large projects can involve highly complex financial plans. As portions of a project are completed, they may be sold, supplanting one lender or owner for another, while the logistical requirements of having the right trades and materials available for each stage of the building construction project carries forward. In many English speaking countries, but not the United States, projects typically use quantity surveyors.

Autonomous Building

An autonomous building is a building designed to be operated independently from infrastructural support services such as the electric power grid, municipal water systems, sewage treatment systems, storm drains, communication services, and in some cases public roads.

Advocates of autonomous building describe advantages that include reduced environmental impacts, increased security, and cost efficiencies. Some cited advantages satisfy tenets of green building, not independence per se. Off-grid buildings often rely very little on civil services and are therefore safer and more comfortable during civil disaster or military attacks.

As an architect or engineer becomes more concerned with the disadvantages of transportation networks, and dependence on distant resources, their designs tend to include more autonomous elements. The historic path to autonomy was a concern for secure sources of heat, power, water and food. A nearly parallel path toward autonomy has been to start with a concern for environmental impacts, which cause disadvantages.

Autonomous buildings can increase security and reduce environmental impacts by using on-site resources (such as sunlight and rain) that would otherwise be wasted. Autonomy often dramatically reduces the costs and impacts of networks that serve the building, because autonomy short-circuits the multiplying inefficiencies of collecting and transporting resources. Other impacted resources, such as oil reserves and the retention of the local watershed, can often be cheaply conserved by thoughtful designs.

Autonomous buildings are usually energy-efficient in operation, and therefore cost-efficient, for the obvious reason that smaller energy needs are easier to satisfy off-grid. But they may substitute energy production or other techniques to avoid diminishing returns in extreme conservation.

An autonomous structure is not always environmentally friendly. The goal of independence from support systems is associated with, but not identical to, other goals of environmentally responsible green building. However, autonomous buildings also usually include some degree of sustainability through the use of renewable energy and other renewable resources, producing no more greenhouse gases than they consume, and other measures.

First and fundamentally, independence is a matter of degree. Complete independence is very hard or impossible to attain. For example, eliminating dependence on the electrical grid is one thing, and growing all of your own food is a more demanding and time-consuming proposition.

Living in an autonomous shelter can require one to make sacrifices in one's lifestyle choices, personal behaviour, and social expectations. Even the most comfortable and technologically advanced autonomous houses may require some differences in behaviour. Some persons adjust easily. Others describe the experience as inconvenient, irritating, isolating, or even as an unwanted full-time job. A well-designed building can reduce this issue, but usually at the expense of reduced autonomy.

An autonomous house must be custom-built (or extensively retrofitted) to suit the climate and location. Passive solar techniques, alternative toilet and sewage systems, thermal massing designs, basement battery systems, efficient windowing, and the array of other design tactics require some degree of non-standard construction, added expense, ongoing experimentation and maintenance, and also have an effect on the psychology of the space.

Maintenance Systems

Water

Water is the most important utility, and is fast becoming a scarce resource. There are many methods of collecting and conserving water. Use reduction is cost-effective.

The classic solution with minimal life-style changes is a proven well. However drilling a well is an uncertain activity, and can be expensive. Well water can be contaminated in some areas, and is depleted in others. Also, once drilled, a well-foot requires substantial power. However, advanced well-foots can reduce power usage by twofold or more from older models. The sono arsenic filter eliminates unhealthy arsenic in well water. It is often more economical to design a building to use rain, with supplementary water deliveries in a drought. Rain water makes excellent soft washwater. A small reverse osmosis unit can provide drinking water.

Bottled water for drinking is often inexpensive, taste-tested, premineralised, with controlled mineral and bacterial counts. It harms autonomy, but can dramatically improve health and lifestyle in a home with autonomous water sources.

Greywater systems reuse drained wash water to flush toilets, and water lawns and gardens. Greywater systems can halve the water use of most residential buildings; however, they require the purchase of a sump, greywater pressurisation pump and secondary plumbing. Some builders are installing waterless urinals and even composting toilets that completely eliminate water usage in sewage disposal.

Most desert and temperate climates get at least 250 mm (10 in) of rain per year. This means that a typical one story house with a greywater system can supply its year-round water needs from its roof alone. In the most extremely dry areas, it will require a cistern of 30 m^3 (8400 U.S. gallons). Many areas average 13 mm (0.5 in) of rain per week, and these can use a cistern as small as 10 m^3. It can be convenient to use the cistern as a heat sink or trap for a heat pump or air conditioning system; however this can make cold drinking water warm, and in drier years the efficiency of the HVAC system may decrease.

Cistern design can reduce costs and inconvenience. Gravity tanks on short towers are reliable, so pump repairs are less urgent. The least expensive bulk cistern is a fenced pond or pool at ground level. The size and expense of a cistern can be reduced substantially when supplemented with water deliveries. Many autonomous homes can reduce water use below ten gallons per person per day. In a drought, water can be delivered to the house inexpensively via truck. Self delivery is possible by installing fabric water-tanks that can fit inside the bed of a pick-up truck.

In many areas, it is difficult to keep a roof clean enough to assure that the water collected is clean enough for drinking. Commercial reverse osmosis systems provide good quality drinking water, and some people attach devices to remineralise drinking water afterwards.

Solar stills can efficiently produce drinking water, especially high-efficiency multiple effect humidification designs, which separate the evaporator(s) and condenser(s). New technologies, like reverse osmosis, and Aquosus, can create unlimited amounts of pure water from polluted water, ocean water, and even from humid air. Water makers are available for yachts that convert seawater and electricity into potable water and brine. Atmospheric water generators like the Vapaire extract moisture from dry desert air and filter it to pure water.

Sewerage

The approaches above treat human excrement as a waste rather than a resource. Humanure is composted human excrement, and can return nutrients to a garden. Recycling human excrement requires minimal life-style changes. In the case of composting toilets, units of varying size can be used to naturally decompose human feces into a highly useful odourless and safe compost. Without further research most health authorities forbid use of "humanure" for growing food directly in the compost. The risk is microbial and viral contamination.

State of the art home sewage treatment systems use biological treatment, usually beds of plants and aquaria, that eliminate nutrients and bacteria and convert greywater and sewage to clear water. This odor- and colour-free reclaimed water can be used to flush toilets and water outside plants. When tested, it approaches standards for potable water. In climates that freeze, the plants and aquaria need to be kept in a small greenhouse space. Good systems need about as much care as a large aquarium.

Electric incinerating toilets turn excrement into a small amount of ash. They are cool to the touch, have no water and no pipes, and require an air vent in a wall. They are used in remote areas where access to septic tank resources are limited. NASA's bioreactor is an extremely advanced biological sewage system. It can turn sewage into air and water through microbial action. NASA plans to use it in the manned Mars mission. A big disadvantage of biological sewage treatment systems is that if the house is empty, the sewage system biota starve to death. Another method is NASA's urine-to-water distillation system.

Sewage handling is not attractive, but it is essential for public health. Many diseases are transmitted by poorly functioning sewage systems. The standard system is a tiled leach field combined with a septic tank. The basic idea is to provide a small system with primary sewage treatment. Sludge settles to the bottom of the septic tank, is partially reduced by anaerobic digestion, and fluid is dispersed in the leach field. The leach field is usually under a yard growing grass. Septic tanks can operate entirely by gravity, and if well managed, are reasonably safe.

Septic tanks have to be pumped periodically by a honey wagon to eliminate non reducing solids. Failure to pump a septic tank can cause overflow that damages the leach field, and contaminates ground water. Septic tanks may also require some lifestyle changes, such as not using garbage disposals, minimizing fluids flushed into the tank, and minimizing nondigestible solids flushed into the tank. For example, septic safe toilet paper is recommended.

However, septic tanks remain popular because they permit standard plumbing fixtures, and require few or no lifestyle sacrifices. Composting or packaging toilets make it economical and sanitary to throw away sewage as part of the normal garbage collection service. They also reduce water use by half, and eliminate the difficulty and expense of septic tanks. However, they require the local landfill to use sanitary practices.

Incinerator systems are quite practical. The ashes are biologically safe, and less than 1/10 the volume of the original waste, but like all incinerator waste, are usually classified as hazardous waste. Some of the oldest pre-system sewage types are pit toilets, latrines, and outhouses. These are still used in many developing countries.

Storm Drains

Drainage systems are a crucial compromise between human habitability and a secure, sustainable watershed. Paved areas and lawns or turf do not allow much precipitation to filter through the ground to recharge aquifers. They can cause flooding and damage in neighbourhoods, as the water flows over the surface towards a low point.

Typically, elaborate, capital-intensive storm sewer networks are engineered to deal with stormwater. In some cities, such as the Victorian era London sewers or much of the old City of Toronto, the storm water system is combined with the sanitary sewer system. In the event of heavy precipitation, the load on the sewage treatment plant at the end of the pipe becomes too great to handle and raw sewage is dumped into holding tanks, and sometimes into surface water.

Autonomous buildings can address precipitation in a number of ways: If a water absorbing swale for each yard is combined with permeable concrete streets, storm drains can be omitted from the neighbourhood. This can save more than $500 per house (1995) by eliminating storm drains. One way to use the savings is to purchase larger lots, which permits more amenities at the same cost.

Permeable concrete is an established product in warm climates, and in development for freezing climates. In freezing climates, the elimination of storm drains can often still pay for enough land to construct swales (shallow water collecting ditches) or water impeding berms instead. This plan provides more land for homeowners and can offer more interesting topography for landscaping. A green roof captures precipitation and uses the water to grow plants. It can be built into a new building or used to replace an existing roof.

Electricity

Since electricity is an expensive utility, the first step towards conservation is to design a house and lifestyle to reduce demand. Fluorescent lights, laptop computers and gas-powered refrigerators save electricity, although gas-powered refrigerators are not very efficient. There are also superefficient electric refrigerators, such as those produced by the Sun Frost company, some of which use only about half as much electricity as a mass-market energy star-rated refrigerator.

Using a solar roof, solar cells can provide electric power. Solar roofs have the potential to be more cost-effective than retrofitted solar power, because buildings need roofs anyway. Modern solar cells last about 40 years, which makes them a reasonable investment in some areas. Solar cells have only small life-style impacts: The cells must be cleaned a few times per year.

A number of areas that lack sun have wind. To generate power, the average autonomous house needs only one small wind generator, 5 m or less in diameter. On a 30 m high tower, this turbine can provide enough power to supplement solar power on cloudy days. Commercially available wind turbines use sealed, one-moving-part AC generators and passive, self-feathering blades for years of operation without service.

The largest advantage of wind power is that larger wind turbines have a lower per-watt cost than solar cells, provided there is wind. However, location is critical. Just as some locations lack sun for solar cells, some locations lack sufficient wind for an economical turbine installation. Paul Gipe says that in the Great Plains of the United States a 10 m turbine can supply enough energy to heat and cool a well-built all-electric house. Economic use in other areas requires research, and possibly a site-survey.

During times of low demand, excess power can be stored in batteries for future use. However, batteries need to be replaced every few years. In many areas, battery expenses can be eliminated by attaching the building to the electric power grid and operating the power system with net metering. Utility permission is required, but such cooperative generation is legally mandated in some areas (e.g. California). A grid-based building is less autonomous, but more economical and sustainable with fewer lifestyle sacrifices. In rural areas the grid's cost and impacts can be reduced by using single wire earth return systems.

In areas that lack access to the grid, battery size can be reduced by including a generator to recharge the batteries during extended fogs or other low-power conditions. Auxiliary generators are usually run from propane, natural gas, or sometimes diesel. An hour of charging usually provides a day of operation. Modern residential chargers permit the user to set the charging times, so the generator is quiet at night.

Recent advances in passively stable magnetic bearings may someday permit inexpensive storage of power in a flywheel in a vacuum. Well-funded groups like Canada's Ballard Power Systems are also working to develop a "regenerative fuel cell," a device that can generate hydrogen and oxygen when power is available, and combine these efficiently when power is needed. Earth batteries tap electric currents in the earth called telluric current. They can be installed anywhere in the ground. They provide only low voltages and current. They were used to power telegraphs in the 19th century. As appliance efficiencies increase, they may become practical.

Solar Heating

Passive solar heating can heat most buildings in even the coldest climates. In colder climates, extra construction costs can be as little as 15% more than new, conventional buildings. In warm climates, those having less than two weeks of frosty nights per year, there is no cost impact. The basic requirement for passive solar heating is that the solar collectors must face the prevailing sunlight (south in the northern hemisphere, north in the southern hemisphere), and the building must incorporate thermal mass to keep it warm in the night.

The least expensive solar heating systems use the ground beneath a building for thermal mass. Precipitation can carry away the heat, so the ground is shielded with 6 m skirts of plastic insulation. The thermal mass of this system is sufficiently inexpensive and large that it can store enough summer heat to warm a building for the whole winter, and enough winter cold to cool the building in summer. This "passive annual solar heating" is practical even in regions that get little or no sunlight in winter.

In passive annual systems, the solar collector is often separate from (and hotter or colder than) the living space. The building is often constructed from insulation, e.g. Straw-bale construction. Some buildings have been aerodynamically designed so that convection via ducts and interior spaces eliminates any need for electric fans. A more modest "daily solar" design uses windows, R-30 insulation and a smaller thermal mass. Modern krypton- or argon-insulated windows permit normal-looking windows to provide passive solar heat without compromising insulation or structural strength. If a small heater is available for the coldest nights, a slab or basement cistern can inexpensively provide the required thermal mass.

In all systems, a small supplementary heater increases personal security and reduces lifestyle impacts for a small reduction of autonomy. The two most popular heaters for ultra-high-efficiency houses are a small heat pump, which also provides air-conditioning, or a central hydronic (radiator) air heater with water recirculating from the water heater. Earth sheltering and windbreaks can also reduce the absolute amount of heat needed by a building. Several feet below the earth, temperature ranges from 4 °C (40 °F) in North Dakota to 26 °C (80 °F), in Southern Florida. Wind breaks reduce the amount of heat carried away from a building.

An increasing number of commercial buildings use a combined cycle with cogeneration to provide heating, often water heating, from the output of a natural gas reciprocating engine, gas turbine or stirling electric generator. Houses designed to cope with interruptions in civil services generally incorporate a wood stove, or heat from diesel fuel or bottled gas, regardless of their other heating mechanisms. Electric heaters and electric stoves provide pollution-free heat, but use large amounts of electricity. If enough electricity is provided by solar panels, wind turbines, or other means, then electric heaters and stoves become a practical autonomous design.

Water heating

Solar water heaters are widely useful because they can save large amounts of fuel. Also, small changes in lifestyle, such as doing laundry, dishes and bathing on sunny days, can greatly increase their efficiency. To further increase the efficiency of water heating, either with or without solar, hot water heat recycling units recover heat from drainlines thereby increasing water heating capacity and reducing the energy used to heat water.

The basic trick in a solar water heating system is to use a well-insulated holding tank. Some systems are vacuum insulated, acting something like large Thermos bottles. The tank is filled with hot water on sunny days, and made available at all times. Unlike a conventional tank water heater, the tank is filled only when there is sunlight. Good storage makes a smaller, higher-technology collector feasible. Such collectors can use relatively exotic technologies, such as vacuum insulation, and reflective concentration of sunlight.

Current practical, comfortable water-heating systems combine the solar heating system with a thermostatic gas-powered flow-through heater, so that the temperature of the water is consistent, and the amount is unlimited. This again reduces life-style impacts at some cost in autonomy. However, this compromise can still save 50-75% of the gas otherwise used, and the resulting system is redundantly reliable. If either system fails, the other can continue to provide hot water until the equipment is repaired, fuel or sunlight becomes available, etc.

Some authorities advocate that natural gas be replaced by methane digesters, fuelled by composting human excrement and kitchen scraps. However, the biowaste of single family is usually insufficient to produce enough methane for anything more than cooking. If enough land is available, biodiesel "co-gen" can produce both electricity and hot water from oil crops grown on-site.

Cooling Costs

Earth sheltering or annualised passive solar systems substantially reduce the cooling needed by a building. In temperate climates several feet below the earth the average temperature ranges from 4 °C (40 °F) in North Dakota to 26 °C (80 °F), in Southern Florida. Annualised passive solar buildings often have buried, sloped water-tight skirts of insulation that extend 6 m (20 ft) from the foundations, to prevent heat leakage between the earth used as thermal mass, and the surface. Less dramatic improvements are possible. Windows can be shaded in summer. Eaves can be overhung to provide the necessary shade. These also shade the walls of the house, reducing cooling costs.

Another trick is to cool the building's thermal mass at night, and then cool the building from the thermal mass during the day. It helps to be able to route cold air from a sky facing radiator (perhaps an air heating solar collector with an alternate purpose) or evaporative cooler directly through the thermal mass. On clear nights, even in tropical areas, sky facing radiators can cool below freezing.

If a circular building is aerodynamically smooth, and cooler than the ground, it can be passively cooled by the "dome effect." Many installations have reported that a reflective or light coloured dome induces a local vertical heat driven vortex that sucks cooler overhead air downward into a dome if the dome is vented properly (a single overhead vent, and peripheral vents). Some persons have reported a temperature differential as high as 8 °C (15 °F) between the inside of the dome and the outside. Buckminster Fuller discovered this effect with a simple house design adapted from a grain silo, and adapted his Dymaxion house and geodesic domes to use it.

Refrigerators and air conditioners operating from the waste heat of a diesel engine exhaust, heater flue or solar collector are entering use. These use the same principles as a gas refrigerator. Normally, the heat from a flue powers an "absorptive chiller." The cold water or brine from the chiller is used to cool air or a refrigerated space. Cogeneration is popular in new commercial buildings. In current cogeneration systems small gas turbines or stirling engines powered from natural gas produce electricity and their exhaust drives an absorptive chiller, heats water.

A truck trailer refrigerator operating from the waste heat of a tractor's diesel exhaust was demonstrated by

NRG Solutions, Inc. NRG developed a hydronic ammonia gas heat exchanger and vaporizer, the two essential new, not commercially available components of a waste heat driven refrigerator.

A similar scheme (multiphase cooling) can be by a multistage evaporative cooler. The air is passed through a spray of salt solution to dehumidify it, then through a spray of water solution to cool it, then another salt solution to dehumidify it again. The brine has to be regenerated, and that can be done economically with a low temperature solar still. Multiphase evaporative coolers can lower the air's temperature by 50 F, and still control humidity. If the brine regenerator uses high heat, they also partially sterilise the air.

Food Production

Food production has often been included in historic autonomous projects to provide security. Skilled, intensive gardening can support an adult from as little as 15 square meters of land. Some proven intensive, low-effort food-production systems include hydroponics, and forest gardening.

Communication

Telephone and network service will probably be purchased. A increasing number of activists provide free or very inexpensive web and email services using cooperative computer networks that run wireless ad hoc networks. Network service is provided by a cooperative of neighbors, each operating a router as a household appliance. These minimize wired infrastructure, and its costs and vulnerabilities.

Rural electrical grids can be wired with "optical phase cable", in which one or more of the steel armour wires are replaced with steel tubes containing fiber optics. Satellite Internet access also can provide high speed connectivity to remote locations, but as of 2002, most of these services are limited in which types of network hardware and operating systems they support. They are also not yet on par with the costs of cable modem or DSL service providers.

Use of Paints

Paint is any liquid, liquifiable, or mastic composition which after application to a substrate in a thin layer is converted to an opaque solid film. Paint is used to protect, decorate (such as adding colour), or add functionality to an object or surface by covering it with a pigmented coating. An example of protection is to retard corrosion of metal. An example of decoration is to add festive trim to a room interior. An example of added functionality is to modify light reflection or heat radiation of a surface. Another example of functionality would be the use of colour to identify hazards or function of equipment and pipelines.

As a verb, painting is the application of paint. Someone who paints artistically is usually called a painter or artist, while someone who paints commercially is often referred to as a painter and decorator, or house painter. Paint can be applied to almost any kind of object. It is used, among many other uses, in the production of art, in industrial coating, as a driving aid (road surface marking), or as a barrier to prevent corrosion or water damage. Paint is a semifinished product, or intermediate good as the final product is the painted article itself.

Paint can also be mixed with glaze to create various textures and patterns. This process is referred to as faux finish and is quite popular with discerning homeowners, architects and interior designers. Paint can be applied as a solid, a gaseous suspension (aerosol) or a liquid. Techniques vary depending on the practical or artistic results desired.

As a solid (usually used in industrial and automotive applications), the paint is applied as a very fine powder, then baked at high temperature. This melts the powder and causes it to adhere (stick) to the surface. The reasons for doing this involve the chemistries of the paint, the surface itself, and perhaps even the chemistry of the substrate (the overall object being painted). This is commonly referred to as "powder coating" an object. As a gas or as a gaseous suspension, the paint is suspended in solid or liquid form in a gas that is sprayed on an object. The paint sticks to the object. This is commonly referred to as "spray painting" an object. The reasons for doing this include:

— The application mechanism is air and thus no solid object ever touches the object being painted;

— The distribution of the paint is very uniform so there are no sharp lines

— It is possible to deliver very small amounts of paint or to paint very slowly;

— Stylistic reasons

— A chemical (typically a solvent) can be sprayed along with the paint to dissolve together both the delivered paint and the chemicals on the surface of the object being painted;

— Some chemical reactions in paint involve the orientation of the paint molecules.

In the liquid application, paint can be applied by direct application using brushes, paint rollers, blades, other instruments, or body parts. Examples of body parts include fingerpainting, where the paint is applied by hand, whole-body painting (popular in the 1960s avant-garde movement), and cave painting, in which a pigment (usually finely-ground charcoal) is held in the mouth and spat at a wall.

Paint application by spray is the most popular method in industry. In this, paint is atomised by the force of compressed air or by the action of high pressure compression of the paint itself, which results in the paint being turned into small droplets which travel to the article which is to be painted. Rollers generally have a handle that allows for different lengths of poles which can be attached to allow for painting at different heights. Generally, roller application takes two coats for even colour. A roller with a thicker nap is used to apply paint on uneven surfaces. Edges are often finished with an angled brush.

After liquid paint is applied, there is an interval during which it can be blended with additional painted regions (at the "wet edge") called "open time." The open time of an oil or alkyd-based emulsion paint can be extended by adding white spirit, similar glycols such as Dowanol™ (propylene glycol ether) or commercial open time prolongers. This can also facilitate the mixing of different wet paint layers for aesthetic effect. Latex and acrylic emulsions require the use of drying retardants suitable for water-based coatings.

Paint may also be applied by flipping the paint, dripping, or by dipping an object in paint. Interior/exterior house paint tends to separate when stored, the heavier components settling to the bottom. It should be mixed before use, with a flat wooden stick or a paint mixing accessory; pouring it back and forth between two containers is also an effective manual mixing method. Paint stores have machines for mixing the paint by shaking it vigorously in the can for a few minutes. Water-based paints tend to be the safest, and easiest to clean up after using — the brushes and rollers can be cleaned with soap and water.

It is difficult to reseal the paint container and store the paint well for a long period of time. Store upside down, for a good seal, in a cool dry place. Protect from freezing. Proper disposal of paint is a challenge. Avoid acquiring excess paint. Look for suitable recycled paint before buying more. Try to find recycled uses for your left over paint. Paints of similar chemistry can be mixed to make a larger amount of a uniform colour. Old paint may be usable for a primer coat or an intermediate coat. If you must dispose of paint, small quantities of water based paint can be carefully dried by leaving the lid off until it solidifies, and then disposing with normal trash. But oil based paint should be treated as hazardous waste, and disposed of according to local regulations.

Building Waterproofing

The concept of waterproofing or protecting buildings against the damaging action of water derives from the need to avoid water and humidity related elements that act negatively upon constructions. This negative effect can present itself in several ways, creating health problems, structure deterioration, facility damage and others. Not to mention, that repairing a building damaged by water can be very expensive! Permeability most frequent causes are: porous or flawed material, badly sealed splices, crack existence, building defects and inadequate surface pendant.

However, we can find different kinds of humidity: the one that gets in from the outside (because of rain, different kind of water infiltrations, ground humidity or underground water), building's own humidity (permanent or because of the construction) and the one produced gradually by the building (because of its service as well as due to condensation and water leaks). Basic conditions for waterproofing involve the surface's fitness for treatment and its cleanness. Building waterproofing can be done in a surface with/without the presence of water and with/without previous treatment.

Based on water's origin and effects on buildings and concrete, waterproofing systems have been classified:

— Surface waterproofing: done with coating plates, bituminous emulsions, vinyl pastes, resins and sealants.

— Integral waterproofing: integrated to the mass of concrete, affecting its permeability.

— Hydrophanous waterproofing: integrated to the mixing water or used as curing systems, allow the improvement of concrete's characteristics such as workability, compression resistance, decrease of reinforcement steel corrosion, decrease of fissures and cracks, and extended durability.

3

Electronic Wiring in Hotels

Electrical wiring systems in a single home or duplex, are simple, with relatively low power requirements, infrequent changes to the building structure and layout, usually with dry, moderate temperature, and noncorrosive environmental conditions. In a light commercial environment, more frequent wiring changes can be expected, large apparatus may be installed, and special conditions of heat or moisture may apply. Heavy industries have more demanding wiring requirements, such as very large currents and higher voltages, frequent changes of equipment layout, corrosive, or wet or explosive atmospheres.

Materials for wiring interior electrical systems in buildings vary depending on:

— Intended use and amount of power needed of the circuit

— Type of occupancy and size of the building

— National and local regulations

— Environment in which the wiring must operate.

The very first interior power wiring systems used conductors that were bare or covered with cloth, which were secured by staples to the framing of the building or on running boards. Where conductors went through walls, they were protected with cloth tape. Splices were done similarly to telegraph connections, and soldered for security. Underground conductors were insulated with wrappings of cloth tape soaked in pitch, and laid in wooden troughs which were then buried. Such wiring systems were unsatisfactory due to the danger of electrocution and fire, and due to the high labor cost for such installations.

Knob and Tube Wiring

The earliest standardised method of wiring in buildings, in common use in North America from about 1880 to the 1930s, was knob and tube (K&T) wiring: single conductors ran through cavities between the structural members in walls and ceilings, with ceramic tubes forming protective channels through joists and ceramic knobs attached to the structural members to provide air between the wire and the lumber, and to support the wires.

Since air was free to circulate over the wires, smaller conductors could be used than required in cables. By arranging wires on opposite sides of building structural members, some protection was afforded against short-circuits by driving a nail into both conductors. By the 1940s, the labor cost of installing two conductors rather than one cable resulted in a decline in new knob-and-tube installations.

Metal-sheathed Wires

In the United Kingdom, an early form of insulated cable introduced in 1896 consisted of two impregnated-paper-insulated conductors in an overall lead sheath. Joints were soldered, and special fittings were used for lamp holders and switches. These cables were similar to underground telegraph and telephone cables of the time. Paper-insulated cables proved unsuitable for interior wiring installations because very careful workmanship was required on the lead sheaths to ensure moisture did not affect the insulation.

A later system invented in 1908 in the U.K. employed vulcanised-rubber insulated wire enclosed in a strip metal sheath. The metal sheath was bonded to each metal wiring device to ensure continuity.

Historical Wiring Methods

Other methods of securing wiring that are now obsolete include:

— Re-use of existing gas pipes for electric lighting. Insulated conductors were pulled into the pipes feeding gas lamps.

— Wood moldings with grooves cut for single conductor wires. These were eventually prohibited in North American electrical codes by the 1930s, but may still be permitted in other regions.

Cables

The first polymer-insulated cables for building wiring were introduced in 1922. These were two or more solid copper wires, with rubber insulation, woven cotton cloth over each conductor for protection of the insulation, with an overall woven jacket, usually impregnated with tar as a protection from moisture. Waxed paper was used as fillers and separators.

Rubber-insulated cables become brittle over time due to exposure to oxygen, so they must be handled with care, and should be replaced during renovations. When switches, outlets or light fixtures are replaced, the simple act of tightening connections may cause insulation to flake off the conductors. Rubber was hard to separate from bare copper, so copper was tinned which caused slightly more resistance. From the late 1950s, PVC insulation and jackets were introduced, especially for residential wiring. About the same time, single conductors with a thinner pvc insulation and a thin nylon jacket became common.

Aluminium wire was common in North American residential wiring from the late 1960s to mid 1970s, due to the rising cost of copper. Due to its greater resistivity, aluminium wiring will use larger conductors than with copper - instead of 14 awg for most lighting circuits, aluminium wiring would typically be 12awg on a typical 15 amp circuit, though local building codes may vary.

Aluminium conductors were originally used with wiring devices intended for copper wires. This can cause defective connections unless all devices were designed to address problems with junctions between dissimilar metals, oxidisation on metal surfaces and mechanical effects as differing metals expand with temperature. Due to improper design and installation, some junctions to wiring devices overheated under heavy current load and caused fires. Revised standards for wiring devices were developed to reduce these problems.

Aluminium conductors are still used for power distribution and large feeder circuits because they cost less than copper wiring, especially in large sizes needed for heavy current loads. Aluminum conductors must be installed with compatible connectors. The simplest form of cable is two insulated conductors twisted together to form a unit; such unjacketed cables with two or three conductors are used for low-voltage signal and control applications such as doorbell wiring. In North American practice, an overhead cable from a transformer on a power pole to a residential electrical service consists of three twisted wires, often with one being a bare neutral and the other two being insulated for the line voltage.

Modern Wiring

Modern nonmetallic sheathed cables (NMC), like (US and Canadian) Type NM, consist of two to four thermoplastic insulated wires and a bare wire for grounding (bonding) surrounded by a flexible plastic jacket. Many call this "Romex (tm)" cable since it was the first of its type, by Rome Cable. Rubber-like synthetic polymer insulation is used in industrial cables and power cables installed underground because of its superior moisture resistance.

Insulated cables are rated by their allowable operating voltage and their maximum operating temperature at the conductor surface. A cable may carry multiple usage ratings for applications, for example, one rating for dry installations and another when exposed to moisture or oil. Generally single conductor building wire in small sizes is solid wire, since the wiring is not required to be very flexible. Building wire conductors larger than #10 AWG (or about 6 mm^2) are stranded for flexibility during installation.

Industrial cables for power and control may contain many insulated conductors in an overall jacket, with helical tape steel or aluminum armor, or steel wire armor, and perhaps as well an overall PVC or lead jacket for protection from moisture and physical damage. Cables intended for very flexible service or in marine applications may be protected by woven bronze wires. Power or communications cables that are routed in or through air-handling spaces (plenums) of office buildings are required by model code requirements be either encased in metal conduit, or be rated for low flame and smoke production.

For some industrial uses in steel mills and similar hot environments, no organic material gives satisfactory service. Cables insulated with compressed mica flakes are sometimes used. Another form of high-temperature cable is a mineral insulated cable, with individual conductors placed within a copper tube, and the space filled with magnesium oxide powder. The whole assembly is drawn down to smaller sizes, which compresses the powder. Such cables are have a certified fire resistance rating, and are more costly than non-fire rated cable, and have less flexibility.

Because conductors in a cable cannot dissipate heat as easily as single insulated conductors, those circuits are always rated at a lower "ampacity". Tables in electrical safety codes give the maximum allowable current for a particular size of conductor, for the voltage and temperature rating at the surface of the conductor for a given physical environment, including the insulation type and thickness. The allowable current will be different for wet or dry, for hot (attic) or cool (underground) locations. In a run of cable through several areas, most severe will determine the proper rating of the overall run.

Cables usually are secured by special fittings where they enter electrical apparatus; this may be a simple screw clamp for jacketed cables in a dry location, or a polymer-gasketed cable connector that mechanically engages the armor of an armored cable and provides a water-resistant connection. Special cable fittings may be applied to prevent explosive gases from flowing in the interior of jacketed cables, where the cable passes through areas where flammable gases are present.

To prevent loosening of the connections of individual conductors of a cable, cables must be supported near their entrance to devices and at regular intervals through their length. In tall buildings special designs are required to support the conductors of vertical runs of cable. Usually, only one cable per fitting is allowed unless the fitting is otherwise rated. Special cable constructions and termination techniques are required for cables installed in ocean-going vessels; in addition to electrical safety and fire safety, such cables may also be required to be pressure-resistant where they penetrate bulkheads of a ship.

Raceways between Electrical Devices

Insulated wires may be run in one of several forms of a raceway between electrical devices. This may be a pipe, called a conduit, or in one of several varieties of metal (rigid steel or aluminum) or non-metallic (PVC) tubing. Wires run underground, for example, may be run in plastic tubing encased in concrete, but metal elbows may be used in severe pulls. Wiring in exposed areas, for example factory floors, may be run in cable trays or rectrangular raceways having lids.

Where wiring, or raceways that hold the wiring traverse fire-resistance rated walls and floors, the openings are required by local building codes to be firestopped. In cases where the wiring has to be kept operational during an accidental fire, fireproofing must be applied to maintain circuit integrity in a manner to comply with product's certification listing. The nature and thickness of any passive fire protection materials used in conjunction with wiring and raceways has a quantifiable impact upon the ampacity derating.

Cable trays are used in industrial areas where many insulated cables are run together. Individual cables can exit the tray at any point, simplifying the wiring installation and reducing the labour cost for installing new cables. Power cables may have fittings in the tray to maintain clearance between the conductors, but small control wiring is often installed without any intentional spacing between cables. Since wires run in conduits or underground cannot dissipate heat as easily as in open air, and adjacent circuits contribute induced currents, wiring regulations give rules to establish the current capacity (ampacity). Special fittings are used for wiring in potentially explosive atmospheres.

Power Engineering

Power engineering, also called "power systems engineering," is a subfield of engineering that deals with power systems, specifically electric power generation, electric power transmission and electric power distribution, power conversion, and electromechanical devices. Out of necessity, power engineers also rely heavily on the theory of control systems.

A power engineer supervises, operates, and maintains machinery and boilers that provide heat, power, refrigeration, and other utility services to heavy industry and large building complexes. Also it deals with the conception of new power sources. Power Engineering deals with the generation, transmission and distribution of electricity as well as the design of a range of related devices. These include transformers, electric generators, electric motors and power electronics.

In many regions of the world, governments maintain an electrical network that connects a variety electric generators together with users of their power. This network is called a power grid. Users purchase electricity from the grid avoiding the costly exercise of having to generate their own. Power engineers may work on the design and maintenance of the power grid as well as the power systems that connect to it. Such systems are called on-grid power systems and may supply the grid with additional power, draw power from the grid or do both.

Power engineers may also work on systems that do not connect to the grid. These systems are called off-grid power systems and may be used in preference to on-grid systems for a variety of reasons. For example, in remote locations it may be cheaper for a mine to generate its own power rather than pay for connection to the grid and in most mobile applications connection to the grid is simply not practical. Today, most grids adopt three-phase electric power with an alternating current. This choice can be partly attributed to the ease with which this type of power can be generated, transformed and used.

Often, the power is split before it reaches residential customers whose low-power appliances rely upon single-phase electric power. However, many larger industries and organisations still prefer to receive the three-phase power directly because it can be used to drive highly efficient electric motors such as three-phase induction motors.

Transformers play an important role in power transmission because they allow power to be converted to and from higher voltages. This is important because higher voltages suffer less power loss during transmission. This is because higher voltages allow for lower current to deliver the same amount of power as power is the product of the two. Thus, as the voltage steps up, the current steps down. It is the current flowing through the components that result in both the losses and the subsequent heating. These losses, appearing in the form of heat, are equal to the current squared times the electrical resistance through which the current flows.

For these reasons, electrical substations exist throughout power grids to convert power to higher voltages before transmission and to lower voltages suitable for appliances after transmission.

Types of Electrical Connector

An electrical connector is a conductive device for joining electrical circuits together. The connection may be temporary, as for portable equipment, or may require a tool for assembly and removal, or may be a permanent electrical joint between two wires or devices. There are hundreds of types of electrical connectors. In computing, an electrical connector can also be known as a physical interface. Connectors form 2 or more circuits, unlike Terminals, which form a single circuit.

A terminal is a simple type of electrical connector that connects two or more wires to a single connection point. Wire nuts are another type of single point connector.

Terminal Blocks (boards): Terminal blocks provide a convenient means of connecting individual electrical wires. They are usually used to connect wiring among various items of equipment within an enclosure or to make connections among individually enclosed items. Since terminal blocks are readily available for a wide range of wire sizes and terminal quantity, they are one of the most flexible types of electrical connector available. Some disadvantages are that connecting wires is more difficult than simply plugging in a cable and the terminals are generally not very well protected from contact with persons or foreign conducting materials.

One type of terminal block accepts wires that are prepared only by removing (stripping) a short length of insulation from the end. Another type accepts wires that have ring or spade terminal lugs crimped onto the wires. Printed circuit board (PCB) mounted terminal blocks allow individual wires to be connected to the circuit board. PCB mounted terminal blocks are soldered to the board, but they are available in a pull-apart version that allows the wire-connecting half of the block to be unplugged from the part that is soldered to the PCB.

Crimp-on Terminals: Most types of crimp-on terminals (or lugs) are attached to wires to allow the wires to be easily connected to screw terminals and fast-on or quick-disconnect terminals. There are also crimp-on terminals for connecting two wires together either permanently or with disconnect capability. Crimp-on terminals are attached by inserting the stripped end of a stranded wire into the tubular portion of the terminal. The tubular portion of the terminal is then compressed tightly around the wire or crimped by squeezing it with a special crimping pliers.

Insulation Displacement Connectors: Since stripping the insulation from wires is time-consuming, many connectors intended for rapid assembly use insulation-displacement connectors so that insulation need not be removed from the wire. These generally take the form of a fork-shaped opening in the terminal, into which the insulated wire is pressed and which cut through the insulation to contact the conductor within. To make these connections reliably on a production line, special tools are used which accurately control the forces applied during assembly. If properly assembled, the resulting terminations are gas-tight and will last the life of the product.

A common example is the multi-conductor flat ribbon cable used in computer disk drives; to terminate each of the many (approximately 40) wires individually would be slow and error-prone, but an insulation displacement connector can terminate all the wires in (literally) one stroke. Another very common use is so-called "punch down" blocks used for terminating telephone wiring. Insulation displacement connectors are usually used with small conductors for signal purposes and at low voltage. Power conductors carrying more than a few amperes are more reliably terminated with other means, though "hot tap" press-on connectors find some use in automotive applications for additions to existing wiring.

Plug and Socket Connectors: Plug and socket connectors are usually made up of a male plug and a female socket, although hermaphroditic connectors exist, such as the original IBM token ring LAN connector. Plugs generally have one or more pins or prongs that are inserted into openings in the mating socket. The connection between the mating metal parts must be sufficiently tight to make a good electrical connection and complete the circuit. When working with multi-pin connectors, it is helpful to have a pinout diagram to identify the wire or circuit node connected to each pin.

Component and device connectors: Electrical and electronic components and devices sometimes have plug and socket connectors or terminal blocks, but individual screw terminals and fast-on or quick-disconnect terminals are more common. Small components have bare lead wires for soldering. They are manufactured using casting

Common Connectors

8P8C

8P8C is short for "eight positions, eight conductors", and so an 8P8C modular connector (plug or jack) is a modular connector with eight positions, all containing conductors. The 8P8C modular plugs and jacks look very similar to the plugs and jacks used for FCC's registered jack RJ45 variants, although the true and extremely uncommon RJ45 is not really compatible with 8P8C modular connectors. It neither uses all eight conductors nor does it fit into 8P8C because the true RJ45 is "keyed". The connector is probably most famous for its use in Ethernet and widely used on CAT5 cables.

DE-9

The DE-9 (9-pin D-shell connector) is a type of D-subminiature electrical connector most commonly used for the RS 232 serial port on the IBM AT and compatible computers. DB-9 is a common misnomer for the DE-9. The DE-9 connector is used in many different applications, for computers, telecommunications, and test and measurement instruments. A few examples are older monitors (MGA, CGA, EGA), the Commodore 64, MSX, Apple II, Amiga and Atari joysticks and mouses, and game consoles such as Atari, Sega and Amiga.

USB connectors

The Universal Serial Bus is a serial bus standard to interface devices, founded in 1996. It is currently widely used among PCs, Apple Macintosh and many other devices. There are several types of USB connectors, and some have been added as the specification has progressed. The most commonly used is the (male) series "A" plug on peripherals, when the cable is fixed to the peripheral. If there is no cable fixed to the peripheral, the peripheral always needs to have a USB "B" socket.

In this case a USB "A" plug to a USB "B" plug cable would be needed. USB "A" sockets are always used on the host PC and the USB "B" sockets on the peripherals. It is a 4-pin connector, surrounded by a shield. There are several other connectors in use, the mini-A, mini- B and mini-AB plug and socket.

Safety Switches

Arc-fault Circuit Interrupter (AFCI)

An arc fault circuit interrupter (AFCI) is a circuit breaker designed to prevent fires by detecting non-working electrical arcs and disconnect power before the arc starts a fire. The AFCI should distinguish between a working arc that may occur in the brushes of a vacuum sweeper, light switch, or other household devices and a non-working arc that can occur, for instance, in a lamp cord that has a broken conductor in the cord from overuse. Arc faults in a home is one of the leading causes for household fires.

AFCIs resemble a GFCI/RCD in that they both have a test button, though it is important to distinguish between the two. GFCIs are designed to protect against electrical shock, while AFCIs are primarily designed to protect against fire.

Starting with the 1999 version of the National Electrical Code in the United States and the 2002 version of the Canadian Electrical Code in Canada, AFCI are now required in all circuits that feed receptacles in bedrooms of dwelling units. The National Electrical Code is an industry consensus document adopted by many U.S. municipalities. This requirement of the NEC is typically accomplished by using a kind of circuit-breaker in the breaker panel that provides combined arc-fault, ground-fault, and over-current protection.

The AFCI is intended to prevent fire from arcs to ground and works at a higher threshold (30 mA) than the GFCI/RCD (Ground-Fault Circuit Interrupt/Residual-Current Device) implementations protecting against the safety hazard of electric shock (which operate at 6 mA). However, advanced electronics inside an AFCI breaker detect sudden bursts of electrical current in milliseconds, long before they would trip a regular overcurrent circuit breaker or fuse. Combined devices are available which trip at the lower, 6 mA threshold of a true GFCI/RCD.

In 2002, the NEC removed the word "receptacle" leaving "outlets", in effect adding lights within dwelling bedrooms to the requirement [debated interpretation]. The 2005 code made it more clear that all outlets must be protected, despite code making panel discussion about excluding bedroom smoke detectors from the requirement. Beginning Jan 2008, only "combination type" AFCI's will meet the NEC requirement. These can protect cords as well as wiring.

Even AFCIs, however, do not provide protection against all of the possible circuit faults that could ignite a fire. In particular, they provide no special protection against so-called "glow faults" where a relatively low-resistance short circuit draws a modest amount of current but heats the localised area of the fault to red heat. Glow faults also can occur where a connection in series with a load suddenly develops a high resistance; this might be the result of a now-defective switch, socket, plug, or wire connection. No practical circuit breaker could detect either such fault as there is no measurable characteristic that any circuit breaker could employ to distinguish a glow fault from the normal operation of a branch circuit.

Autorecloser

An autorecloser is a circuit breaker equipped with a mechanism that can automatically close the breaker after it has been opened due to a fault.

They are used in coordinated protection schemes for overhead line power distribution circuits. These circuits are prone to transitory faults such as nearby lightning strikes, wind-borne debris, squirrels climbing insulators, and the like. With a conventional circuit breaker or fuse, a transient fault would open the breaker or blow the fuse, disabling the line until a technician could manually reclose the circuit breaker or replace the blown fuse. But an autorecloser will make several pre-programmed attempts to re-energise the line.

If the transient fault has cleared, the autorecloser's circuit breaker will remain closed and normal operation of the power line will resume. If the fault is some sort of a permanent fault the autorecloser will exhaust its pre-programmed attempts to re-energise the line and remain tripped off until manually commanded to try again. 90% of faults on overhead power lines are transient and can be cured by autoreclosing. The result is increased reliability of supply.

Autoreclosers are made in single-phase and three-phase versions, and use either oil or vacuum interrupters.

Controls for the reclosers range from the original electromechanical systems to digital electronics with metering and SCADA functions. The ratings of reclosers run from 2400V - 38kV for load currents from 10A - 1200A and fault currents from 1000A - 16kA.

Circuit Breaker

A circuit breaker is an automatically-operated electrical switch designed to protect an electrical circuit from damage caused by overload or short circuit. Unlike a fuse, which operates once and then has to be replaced, a circuit breaker can be reset to resume normal operation. Circuit breakers are made in varying sizes, from small devices that protect an individual household appliance up to large switchgear designed to protect high voltage circuits feeding an entire city.

Magnetic circuit breakers are implemented using a solenoid whose pulling force increases with the current. The circuit breaker's contacts are held closed by a latch and, as the current in the solenoid increases beyond the rating of the circuit breaker, the solenoid's pull releases the latch which then allows the contacts to open by spring action. Some types of magnetic breakers incorporate a hydraulic time delay feature wherein the solenoid core is located in a tube containing a viscous fluid. The core is restrained by a spring until the current exceeds the breaker rating.

During an overload, the solenoid pulls the core through the fluid to close the magnetic circuit, which then provides sufficient force to release the latch. The delay permits brief current surges beyond normal running current for motor starting, energizing equipment, etc. Short circuit currents provide sufficient solenoid force to release the latch regardless of core position thus bypassing the delay feature. Ambient temperature affects the time delay but does not affect the current rating of a magnetic breaker.

Thermal breakers use a bimetallic strip, which heats and bends with increased current, and is similarly arranged to release the latch. This type is commonly used with motor control circuits. Thermal breakers often have a compensation element to reduce the effect of ambient temperature on the device rating. Thermomagnetic circuit breakers, which are the type found in most distribution boards, incorporate both techniques with the electromagnet responding instantaneously to large surges in current (short circuits) and the bimetallic strip responding to less extreme but longer-term overcurrent conditions.

Circuit breakers for larger currents are usually arranged with pilot devices to sense a fault current and to operate the trip opening mechanism. Under short-circuit conditions, a current many times greater than normal can flow. When electrical contacts open to interrupt a large current, there is a tendency for an arc to form between the opened contacts, which would allow the flow of current to continue. Therefore, circuit breakers must incorporate various features to divide and extinguish the arc.

In air-insulated and miniature breakers an arc chute structure consisting (often) of metal plates or ceramic ridges cools the arc, and blowout coils deflect the arc into the arc chute. Larger circuit breakers such as those used in electrical power distribution may use vacuum, an inert gas such as sulphur hexafluoride or have contacts immersed in oil to suppress the arc. The maximum short-circuit current that a breaker can interrupt is determined by testing.

Application of a breaker in a circuit with a prospective short-circuit current higher than the breaker's interrupting capacity rating may result in failure of the breaker to safely interrupt a fault. In a worst-case scenario the breaker may successfully interrupt the fault, only to explode when reset, injuring the technician. Small circuit breakers are either installed directly in equipment, or are arranged in a breaker panel. Power circuit breakers are built into switchgear cabinets. High-voltage breakers may be free-standing outdoor equipment or a component of a gas-insulated switchgear line-up.

When supplying a branch circuit with more than one live conductor, each live conductor must be protected by a breaker pole. To ensure that all live conductors are interrupted when any pole trips, a "common trip" breaker must be used. These may either contain two or three tripping mechanisms within one case, or for small breakers, may externally tie the poles together via their operating handles. Two pole common trip breakers are common on 120/240 volt systems where 240 volt loads span the two live wires. Three pole common trip breakers are typically used to supply three phase power to large motors or further distribution boards.

There are many different technologies used in circuit breakers and they do not always fall into distinct categories. Types that are common in domestic, commercial and light industrial applications at low voltage (less than 1000 V) include:

— MCB (Miniature Circuit Breaker)—rated current not more than 100 A. Trip characteristics normally not adjustable. Thermal or thermal-magnetic operation. Breakers illustrated above are in this category.

— MCCB (Moulded Case Circuit Breaker)—rated current up to 1000 A. Thermal or thermal-magnetic operation. Trip current may be adjustable.

Electric power systems require the breaking of higher currents at higher voltages. Examples of high-voltage AC circuit breakers are:

— Vacuum circuit breaker—With rated current up to 3000 A, these breakers interrupt the current by creating and extinguishing the arc in a vacuum container.

These can only be practically applied for voltages up to about 35,000 V, which corresponds roughly to the medium-voltage range of power systems. Vacuum circuit breakers tend to have longer life expectancies between overhaul than do air circuit breakers.

— Air circuit breaker—Rated current up to 10,000 A. Trip characteristics are often fully adjustable including configurable trip thresholds and delays. Usually electronically controlled, though some models are microprocessor controlled via an integral electronic trip unit. Often used for main power distribution in large industrial plant, where the breakers are arranged in draw-out enclosures for ease of maintenance.

High-voltage breakers

Electrical power transmission networks are protected and controlled by high-voltage breakers. The definition of "high voltage" varies but in power transmission work is usually thought to be 72,500 V or higher, according to a recent definition by the International Electrotechnical Commission (IEC). High-voltage breakers are nearly always solenoid-operated, with current sensing protective relays operated through current transformers. In substations the protection relay scheme can be complex, protecting equipment and busses from various types of overload or ground/earth fault.

High-voltage breakers are broadly classified by the medium used to extinguish the arc.

— Oil-filled (dead tank and live tank)

— Oil-filled, minimum oil volume

— Air blast

— Sulphur hexafluoride or SF6

High voltage breakers are routinely available up to 765 kV AC. Live tank circuit breakers are where the enclosure that contains the breaking mechanism is at line potential, that is, "Live". Dead tank circuit breaker enclosures are at earth potential.

Interrupting principles for high-voltage circuit-breakers: High-voltage circuit-breakers have greatly changed since they were first introduced about 40 years ago, and several interrupting principles have been developed that have contributed successively to a large reduction of the operating energy. Current interruption in a high-voltage circuit-breaker is obtained by separating two contacts in a medium, such as sulphur hexafluoride (SF_6), having excellent dielectrical and arc quenching properties. After contact separation, current is carried through an arc and is interrupted when this arc is cooled by a gas blast of sufficient intensity.

Gas blast applied on the arc must be able to cool it rapidly so that gas temperature between the contacts is reduced from 20,000 K to less than 2000 K in a few hundred microseconds, so that it is able to withstand the transient recovery voltage that is applied across the contacts after current interruption. Sulphur hexafluoride is generally used in present high-voltage circuit-breakers. In the 1980s and 1990s, the pressure necessary to blast the arc was generated mostly by gas heating using arc energy. It is now possible to use low energy spring-loaded mechanisms to drive high-voltage circuit-breakers up to 800 kV.

Dead Man's Switch

A dead man's switch, as its name suggests, is a device intended to stop a machine in case the human operator becomes incapacitated, and is a form of fail-safe. They are commonly used in train locomotives, freight elevators, lawn mowers, tractors, jet skis, outboard motors, snowblowers and snowmobiles. Interest in dead-man's controls increased with the introduction of electric streetcars and especially electrified rapid transit trains, though dead-man equipment was quite rare on US streetcars until comparatively recently.

In conventional steam railroad trains, there was always a second person with the engineer, the fireman, who could bring the train to a stop if necessary. For many decades this practice continued on electric & diesel locomotives, even though a single person could theoretically operate them. With modern urban and suburban railway systems, the driver was typically alone in an enclosed cab. Though automatic devices were already beginning to be deployed on newer installations of the New York City Subway system in the early 20th century, it took the disastrous Malbone Street Wreck on the Brooklyn Rapid Transit system in 1918 to point out the need for universal deployment of such devices to halt trains in the event of an operator's disability.

Types of dead man's switch

Handle: Pneumatically or electrically linked dead-man's controls, still used today, involve relatively simple modifications of the controller handle, the device that regulates traction power. The main requirement is that the train's emergency brakes are applied if pressure is not maintained on the controller.

Typically, the controller handle is a horizontal bar, rotated to apply the required power for the train. Attached to the bottom of the handle is a rod which, when pushed down, contacts a solenoid or switch inside the control housing. The handle springs up if pressure is removed, releasing the rod's contact with the internal switch, instantly cutting power and applying the brakes. Though there are ways that this type of dead-man's control could conceivably fail, they have proven highly reliable.

On some earlier equipment, pressure was not maintained on the entire controller, but on a large button protruding from the controller handle. This button also had to be pressed continuously, typically with the palm of the hand so that the button was flush with the top of the handle. Another method used, particularly with some lever-type controllers, which are pushed or pulled rather than rotated, requires that the handle on the lever be turned through 90 degrees and held in that position while the train is in operation.

Some dead-man's controls require the motorman to hold it in the mid-position rather than apply full pressure. In many modern New York Subway trains, for example, the dead man's switch is incorporated into the train's speed control. On the R142A the train operator must continually hold the lever in place. This was depicted in the movie and book The Taking of Pelham 123, in which a group of men hijack a New York City subway train for ransom, but because of the Dead-man's feature, cannot escape while the train is moving. Every lawn mower sold in the US since 1982 has an "operator-presence" device, which by law must stop the blades within 3 seconds after the user lets go of the controls.

Touch Sensor: On the Nottingham Express Transit vehicles, the tram's speed controller is fitted with a capacitive touch sensor to detect the driver's hand. If the hand is removed for more than a short period of time, the track brakes are activated. Gloves, if worn, have to be finger-less for the touch sensor to operate. A back up Dead-man's switch button is provided on the side of the controller for use in the case of a failed touch sensor or if it is too cold to remove gloves.

Pedal: A pedal can be used instead of a handle. In the Waterfall train disaster, it appears that the driver, who was overweight, slumped on his seat, keeping the pedal pressed when he died.

Seat Switches: On tractors, the switch is beneath the seat, and will cut the engine if the operator gets off the tractor while the transmission is engaged or the power take-off is spinning.

Key Switches: On recreational water vehicles, such as jet skis and wave runners, the user has the ignition key attached to his wrist or waist by a leash. The key will be removed from the ignition switch if the rider falls into the water, thus turning off the engine.

Dead-man's Vigilance Device

The main safety failing with the basic dead man's system is the possibility of the operating device being held permanently in position, either deliberately or accidentally. Vigilance control was developed to detect this condition by requiring that the dead man's device be released momentarily and re-applied at timed intervals.

Something that could be considered an early vigilance control device is the one-legged stool issued to watchmen: If the watchman were to fall asleep on his stool, he would fall over and be woken. There has also been a proposal to introduce a similar system to automotive cruise controls. A hybrid between a dead man's switch and a vigilance control device is a dead-man's vigilance device.

Software versions of dead man's switches are generally only used by people with technical expertise, and can serve several purposes; such as sending a notification to friends or deleting and encrypting data. The "non-event" triggering these can be almost anything, such as failing to log in consecutively for a week, not responding to an automated e-mail ping, a GPS-enabled telephone not moving for a period of time, or merely failing to type a code within a few minutes of a computer's boot.

Motivations vary, depending on the individual's needs. For example, somebody in a police state may be concerned about the security of their data (or deleting it), while others may just wish to alert friends or the authorities by e-mail that something undesirable might be going on.

Inertial Switch

An inertial switch is a switch, firmly mounted upon a vehicle or other mobile device, that senses shock or vibration. It is a part of electrical circuits that may either enable or disable some function.

The switch shown to the right is intended to disable an electric fuel pump in automotive applications. This functionality is required in some vehicle racing applications, since an electric fuel pump may otherwise continue operating after a collision or rollover. If the fuel line is broken or the vehicle is inverted, fuel may be spilled, creating a fire hazard. A small loose weight (called a proof mass) is trapped within a spring loaded cage. A shock in any direction will cause relative movement of the mass relative to the cage, and if sufficiently shocked the cage will spring open, actuating an associated switch.

The switch is reset by pressing the cage closed through the flexible (red) top cover, retrapping the mass. These switches are also used to open a contactor (a large relay) to disable the high power circuit of a battery electric vehicle upon collision. A normally open switch is used to activate passenger safety equipment early in a collision, typically to pre-tension seat belts and/or to activate air-bags to protect the occupant(s) from collision with the vehicle interior or the steering wheel.

Isolator Switch

An isolator switch is part of an electrical circuit and is most often found in industrial applications, however they are commonly fitted to domestic extractor fans when used in bathrooms in the UK. The switch does exactly what its name suggests in that it electrically isolates the circuit or circuits that are connected to it. Such a switch is not used normally as an instrument to turn on/off the circuit in the way that a light switch does. Either the switch isolates circuits that are continually powered or is a key element which enables an electrical engineer to safely work on the protected circuit.

Isolator switches may be fitted with the ability for the switch to padlock such that inadvertent operation is not possible. In some designs the isolator switch has the additional ability to earth the isolated circuit thereby providing additional safety. Such an arrangement would apply to circuits which inter-connect power distribution systems where both end of the circuit need to be isolated.

Major difference between isolator and circuit breaker is that isolator is an off-load device, whereas circuit breaker is an on-load device.

Kill Switch (e-stop)

A kill switch is a security measure used to shut off a device in an emergency situation in which it cannot be shut down in the usual manner. Unlike a normal shut down, which shuts down all systems naturally and turns the machine off without damaging it, a kill switch is designed to completely abort the operation at all costs. Often times, they are used to protect people from sustaining an injury or being killed, in which case, damaging the machine is acceptable.

A similar system, usually called a dead man's switch is used to shut down vehicles and machinery if the operator loses control or is ejected. A common example of this would be the kill switches used by boaters wherein a cord connects the kill switch to the operator (usually by their life jackets), and if the operator is thrown overboard in an accident, the cord will pull the switch and immediately shut down the vessels' engine.

NASCAR requires all their stock cars to be equipped with a steering wheel-mounted kill switch, in case the accelerator pedal sticks and the driver needs to shut down the engine. A kill switch is also used for gasoline pumps or any other device that pumps large amounts of explosive or flammable chemicals. There is commonly a single kill switch for all pumps at a pumping station. Kill switches are also used on land vehicles as an anti-theft device and as an emergency power off.

Also, an electronic musical instrument, such as a guitar or bass guitar, may have a kill switch. It is used infrequently but most commonly in heavy metal music. Contrary to popular belief, a kill switch doesn't break the circuit but works by switching between the hot signal from a pick-up and the ground signal.

A typical way of achieving this is by turning down the volume on one of the pick-ups then alternating the pick-up selector switch between that pick-up and one with the volume turned all the way up. They are sometimes used when a singer doubles as a guitar player and isn't playing or sometimes used as an effect during a song. Tom Morello of Rage Against the Machine and Audioslave, and Buckethead are well known for their use of the kill switch.

Knife Switch

A knife switch is a type of switch used to control the flow of electricity in a circuit. It is comprised of a hinge which allows a metal lever, or knife, to be lifted from or inserted into a slot or jaw. The hinge and jaw are both fixed to an insulated base, and the knife has an insulated handle to grip at one end. Current flows through the switch when the knife is pushed into the jaw.

Knife switches can take several forms, including single throw, in which the "knife" engages with only a single slot, and double throw, in which the knife hinge is placed between two slots and can engage with either one. Also, multiple knives may be attached to a single handle and can be used to activate more than one circuit simultaneously.

Though once common in the early days of electricity, knife switches are now rare, finding use largely in science experiments where the position of the switch may be plainly seen in demonstration. The knife switch is extremely simple in construction and use, but its exposed metal parts present a great risk of electrocution, and the switch is subject to arcing when opened at higher voltages, which poses a further risk of shock or burns to the operator and can cause fires or explosions under certain conditions.

Open knife switches were supplanted by safety switches with current carrying contacts inside a metal enclosure which can only be opened by switching off the power. In modern applications, automatic switches, and manual switches such as circuit breakers are used. These devices use a snap action mechanism which opens the switch contacts rapidly, and feature an arc chute where the arc caused by opening the switch is quenched. These devices also prevent injury due to accidental contact, as all of the current carrying metal parts of the switch are hidden within or surrounded with insulated guards.

Earthing System

It is well known that most electricity systems need to be earthed and this practice probably started in the very first days of electrical experiments. Then, as now, static was discharged by connection to a plate which was in contact with the general mass of earth. The practice has continued and been progressively developed, such that connections to earth occur at almost every point in the electricity system. This includes the generating station, the lines and cables which distribute electricity and the premises at which it is used.

The need for such a connection is sometimes enshrined in legislation. For example in the UK, the Electricity Supply Regulations 1988, clause 5(1), require all systems to be earthed at one point. This does not actually extend to the installation within premises and whilst it is still the most common arrangement to earth such installations, the standards allow for certain unearthed arrangements.

Whilst earthing forms an intrinsic part of the electricity system, it still remains in general a misunderstood subject and is often referred to as a "black art" - even sometimes by well qualified engineers. In recent years there have been rapid developments in the modelling of earthing systems at power frequencies and higher, mainly facilitated by computer hardware and software. This has increased our understanding of the subject at the same time that the design task has become significantly more difficult and emerging standards are requiring a more detailed, safer design. There is thus an opportunity to explain earthing concepts more clearly and a need for this to be conveyed to earthing system designers and installers so that a greater understanding may be gained.

Earthing of electrical installations is primarily concerned with ensuring safety. The earthing system is normally designed to provide two safety functions. The first is termed bonding. Any exposed conductive metalwork which can be touched is connected together via bonding conductors. Most electrical equipment is housed inside metal enclosures and if a live conductor comes into contact with this, the enclosure will temporarily also become live. Bonding is to ensure that, should such a fault develop, then the potential on all exposed conductive metalwork is virtually the same. In other words, the bonds equalise potential within the site so that the resulting potential differences are minimal. An equipotential 'platform' is thus created.

If a person is in contact simultaneously with two different pieces of exposed metalwork, a bonding conductor should ensure that the person does not receive a shock, as the potential difference between equipment should be insufficient for this to occur. The same principle applies within large electricity substations, factories and houses. In factories, bonding of exposed metalwork would normally ensure that an electrical fault to the frame of one machine did not create a potential difference between that and earthed metalwork on an adjacent machine. In the home, bonding ensures that, should a fault to the frame of a washing machine or cooker develop, someone simultaneously touching either of these and the metal sink would not experience an electric shock.

The second function of the earthing system is to ensure that, in the event of an earth fault, any fault current which does result can return to source in a controlled manner. By a controlled manner, we mean that the return path is predetermined such that damage to equipment or injury to individuals does not occur. The earth connection is not of infinite capacity and zero impedance. However, the impedance of the earthing system should be low enough that sufficient earth fault current can flow to operate protective devices correctly, which will in turn initiate the operation of circuit breakers or fuses to interrupt the flow of current.

The required impedance value is normally calculated by the protection designer via fault analysis programmes and this would be provided to those responsible for the design of the earthing system. In addition, the rise in potential which the earthing system will experience whilst fault current is flowing, should also be limited to a pre-determined value. These are the functions that the earthing system must provide, but they are required to meet a wide range of different problems. The first is a conventional fault, e.g. that arising from damage to a cable or breakdown of the phase to earth insulation in a piece of equipment. The equipment can be in a substation, a factory or the home. We term these "power frequency" faults, since most of the energy dissipated in the fault will be at mains frequency (50 Hz).

In some locations, such as radio or television transmitters, sites where large amounts of power are rectified or capacitor banks are switched, then energy will be available at higher frequencies than normal. The earthing system must be specially designed to provide a low impedance at these frequencies. Many electrical installations are prone to the risk of damage as a result of a lightning strike and special arrangements are necessary to reduce the risks involved. An adequate earthing system is a fundamental part of this arrangement. Because a lightning impulse is steep fronted and a source of high frequency currents, special earthing system designs are again necessary.

For example, bends in above ground conductors will form a small inductance which will be insignificant at power frequency, but may create a high impedance to lightning current. This may be sufficient for there to be a 'flashover' whereby the current flows through other routes to ground in preference to the designed route - possibly causing significant damage in the process. The earthing system is also used as a means of achieving safe working conditions during some types of maintenance or construction. Plant which was previously energised has to be switched off and its previously live components are connected to earth before any work can commence. This allows any stored energy to be discharged safely to ground and helps prevent dangerous voltages arising on the equipment being worked on.

In some industrial premises the earthing system is required to continuously discharge the build up of static, and thus prevent a fire or explosion risk. Examples include paper manufacturing plants or when explosives or volatile chemicals are present. A popular misconception is that the earthing system is only required during fault conditions. In fact it also serves a number of vital roles during routine operation. For example, many power supplies now include a connection to earth, through which residual and harmonic currents are dispersed to ground. The previously held belief that these currents could be 'dumped' to earth with no adverse consequences is now known to be false.

Currents which flow to ground, in this way must return to source, forming a loop. These loops will create potential differences which, although small, cause 'noise', 'hum' and possible damage to electronic equipment. This process, together with the increasing amount of harmonic current being injected into the public supply network, is a growing cause of significant power quality problems. Some equipment contains earthed screens, which operate continuously to reduce the field produced outside the case or reduce the impact of external fields on the equipment performance.

In recent years, a number of factors have drawn attention to earthing systems. One is the increased use of plastic sheathed underground cables, another the use of plastic water pipes. Plastic water pipes have had a particular impact on domestic properties, which used to place great reliance on the earthing facility provided by the older metal pipes. Plastic sheathed cables are now used instead of the previous types which had a lead sheath and steel armouring in direct contact with the soil. This has had a detrimental effect on the overall efficiency of earthing systems and placed more reliance on the remaining components of the earthing system, including the earth electrodes installed at all electricity substations. It is now more important than before to ensure that the earth electrode systems are correctly designed, installed and maintained.

Clearly, the earthing system performs a wide range of similar functions throughout all the stages of providing electricity, i.e. at the generating station, the electricity company substations through to the electrical installations in homes, offices and factories. Copper is the most widely used material for these earthing systems. Its well tried and tested properties of relatively low electrical resistance, malleability and good corrosion resistance have ensured that it has been the preferred material for very many years.

Electrical Safety Basics

There are three basic electrical hazards that cause injury and death: shock, arc-flash, and arc-blast.

Shock: Current can pass through the human body's nervous or vascular systems, and across the surface of the body. The current required to light a 71/2 W, 120 V lamp, passing through the chest, can cause death. Of those killed while working on voltages below 600 V, half were intentionally working on "hot" energised equipment. Most electrocutions can be avoided with proper training, planning, job preparation, procedures, and equipment.

Arc-flash: As many as 80 percent of all electrical injuries are burns resulting from an arc-flash contact and ignition of flammable clothing. Arc temperatures can reach 35,000 F four times hotter than the sun's surface. Arc-flash can cause second and third degree burns.

Arc-blast: An arc-blast may result in a violent explosion of circuit components and thrown shrapnel. The blast can destroy structures, and knock workers from ladders or across a room. The blast can rupture eardrums and collapse lungs.

Electrical Safety

Training: An important aspect of electrical safety is training. To be qualified, workers need training on the tasks and procedures that are essential to conducting their work in a safe manner.

Planning: Take the time to prepare a work plan that considers all possible eventualities. Before starting the job, think about each step and try to visualise the potential for hazards. Anticipate unexpected results. When thinking about a job, break each task into small steps. Understand that plans can change, so be ready to modify the plan. Make sure that everyone involved in the job is working according to the same plan. Whenever work is required near an electrical hazard, a written plan is needed to outline the scope of the job.

Procedures

Identify the hazard: After your work plan is complete, review each step. Consider that the equipment might be perfectly safe under normal conditions and very unsafe when systems are not working properly. Also consider potential hazards that may be unrelated to electrical energy.

Assess people's abilities: Any person assigned to tasks associated with electrical energy must be qualified and trained for thc job at hand. He or she must be able to identify electrical hazards, avoid exposure to those hazards, and understand the potential results of all action taken.

Electrically safe work condition

Use the right tool for the job: Use the appropriate tools for the job at hand, keep them accessible and in good working condition. Using a screwdriver for a job that requires a fuse puller is an invitation to an accident.

Isolate the equipment: The best way to avoid an accident is to reduce exposure to the hazards present. Keep doors closed. Keep barricades in place. Install temporary voltage-rated blankets covering exposed live parts. Put the equipment in a safe working condition prior to performing maintenance. Lock out the disconnect.

Protect the person: Use the proper personal protection equipment for the job. This may include safety glasses or goggles, head protection, voltage-rated gloves, safety belts and harnesses, or flame-resistant clothing.

Minimize the hazard: If it is impossible to establish an electrically safe work environment, be sure to shut down every possible energy source. Understand that sometimes a de-energised circuit can become re-energised and do something to lessen the risk.

Tagout Standard

The Lockout/Tagout Standard was created to help reduce the death and injury rate caused by the unexpected energisation or start-up of machines or the release of stored energy. Normal production operations, cords and plugs under exclusive control, and hot tap operations are not covered. This standard applies to energy sources such as electrical, mechanical, hydraulic, chemical, nuclear, and thermal.

Procedures for applying the lock/tag:

— Before the shutdown, know the unit and power sources

— Power down the equipment

— Isolate the power source(s)

— Apply the lock and/or tag

— Use proper techniques, personal protective equipment, and test measuring devices to verify that the electrical circuit is de-energised

— Release residual energy

— Try to power up

Procedure for removing the lock/tag:

— Inspect machine and/or equipment

— Give notification to personnel

— Remove the lockout/tagout device

4

Refrigeration and Air Conditioning

Air conditioning is the process of treating and distributing air to control temperature, humidity, and air quality in selected areas. For temperature and humidity control, air is moved over chilled or heated coils and/or a spray of water at a controlled temperature. Direct water sprays also remove dust and odors. Other air cleaning systems may include mechanical separation, adhesion, screening, filtration, or static attraction, depending on the type of air contaminants encountered and the required air quality.

Refrigeration is the process of lowering the temperature of a substance below that of its surroundings and includes production of chilled water for air conditioning or process applications. Chilled water for use in processes such as injection molding may be in the same temperature range as chilled water used for air conditioning. Refrigeration systems are also used to provide chilled antifreeze solutions (brines) at temperatures below the freezing point of water. Brines are used in icemaking and cold storage, in addition to a variety of chemical process applications.

Chilled water may be used in air washers, either in closed coils or as spray water. Chilled water may also be used for closed systems and for individual spray water systems. Many methods are used to produce and distribute chilled air. In central air conditioning systems, air is passed over coils chilled by water, by brine, or by direct expansion of a volatile refrigerant. The chilled air is then distributed through ductwork.

The water systems associated with air conditioning can be classified into three general categories: open recirculating cooling, air washers, and closed or open chilled water systems. In water treatment applications, open recirculating cooling systems are similar to open chilled water systems. The basic mechanical components of an air conditioning system are the air and water distribution systems, a refrigeration machine, and a heat rejection system. Refrigeration for air conditioning is usually provided by either absorption or compression cycles.

Absorption refrigeration uses low-pressure steam or high-temperature hot water as the energy source, water as the refrigerant, and lithium bromide or lithium chloride as the absorbent. Compression refrigeration systems generally utilise a halocarbon compound or ammonia as the refrigerant. An internal combustion engine, turbine, or electric motor supplies the power to drive a centrifugal or positive displacement compressor.

Refrigeration, or cooling, occurs when the liquid refrigerant absorbs heat by evaporation, generally at low temperature and pressure. When the refrigerant condenses, it releases heat to any available cooling medium, usually water or air.

Refrigeration Cycle

The basic refrigeration cycle used for single-stage vapour compression has four components in the system. They are the compressor, condenser, metering device, and evaporator. Low-pressure liquid refrigerant in an evaporator extracts heat from the fluid being cooled and evaporates. The low-pressure vapour is then compressed to a pressure at which the refrigerant vapour can be condensed by the cooling media available. The vapour then flows to the condenser, where it is cooled and condensed.

The liquid refrigerant flows from the condenser to a metering device, where its pressure is reduced to that of the evaporator. The cycle is thus completed. In industrial or commercial air conditioning systems, the heat is usually rejected to water. Once-through cooling may be used, but municipal restrictions and water costs generally dictate recirculation and evaporative cooling processes.

Evaporative condensers or cooling towers are normally used for evaporative cooling. A spray pond may be used as an alternative. Recirculation of the water in a cooling system reduces the makeup water requirement to less than 3% of the water that would be needed for once-through cooling. Cooling capacity is measured in tons of refrigeration. A ton of refrigeration is defined as the capacity to remove heat at a rate of 12,000 Btu/hr at the evaporator or chiller.

An absorption refrigeration system that removes 12,000 Btu/hr requires heat energy input of approximately 18,000 Btu/hr to drive the absorption process. This means that the heat rejection at the cooling tower approximates 30,000 Btu/hr per ton of refrigeration. With a 15°F (8°C) temperature drop across the tower, the heat rejection of an absorption system requires circulation of approximately 4 gpm of water per ton of air conditioning. Evaporation of the recirculating water occurs at a rate of approximately 3.7 gph per ton.

Other than the solution and refrigerant pumps, there are no moving parts in an absorption system. Although this is an economical design advantage, the cost of producing the necessary low-pressure steam or high-temperature hot water (HTHW) must also be considered.

Compression systems also impose an additional heat load. This is due to the energy required to compress low-pressure, low-temperature refrigerant gas from the evaporator and deliver it to the condenser at a higher pressure.

The compressor energy input is approximately 3,000 Btu/hr per ton of refrigeration. Accordingly, normal heat rejection in a compression system approximates 15,000 Btu/hr per ton of refrigeration, requiring evaporation of about 2 gal/hr of cooling water. Compression refrigeration systems require a cooling water circulation rate of approximately 3 gpm per ton of refrigeration, with a 10°F temperature drop across the cooling tower.

The major energy consumer in a compression refrigeration system is the compressor, which is designed to operate at a certain head pressure for a given load. This pressure equals the refrigerant pressure in the condenser. The term "high head pressure" refers to condenser pressure that is higher than it should be at a specific load condition. High head pressure can be costly in two ways. First, it presents the danger of a system shutdown; a safety control will stop the compressor motor when the safe maximum head pressure is exceeded in the compressor. Second, an increase in power consumption results when a compressor operates at greater than design head pressure.

Fouled condenser tubes are a common cause of high head pressures. Fouling increases the resistance to heat transfer from the refrigerant to the cooling water. In order to maintain the same heat transfer rate, the temperature of the refrigerant must be increased. The compressor fulfills this need by increasing the pressure at which the refrigerant is condensed. With a centrifugal chiller, a 1°F increase in condensing temperature increases compressor energy consumption by approximately 1.7%.

Fouling and the formation of scale in absorption systems also reduce operating efficiency. Because the highest water temperatures exist in the condenser, deposition first occurs in this unit. Under extreme conditions, scale formation can also occur in the absorber.

Deposition in the condenser imposes a higher back-pressure on the generator, so that increased steam or HTHW is required to liberate the refrigerant from the absorbent. The result is an increase in refrigerant vapour pressure and a greater temperature differential between the condensing water vapour and the cooling water. Although this compensates for the resistance to heat flow, more energy is required to provide the increased heat input.

If water conditions are severe enough to cause deposition in the absorber, less refrigerant is removed by the absorber, and cooling capacity is reduced. The reduction in refrigerant circulation diminishes the ability of the equipment to satisfy cooling requirements. If the absorption rate in the absorber is reduced while the absorbent is heated above the normal temperature in the generator, the danger of over-concentrating the brine solution also exists. This over-concentration can cause crystallisation of the brine, leading to a system shutdown.

Fouling and scale formation waste energy and can ultimately cause unscheduled system shutdown. Effective water treatment can minimise the possibility of high head pressure and excessive steam consumption caused by condenser deposition. Corrosion can cause problems in either the open recirculating or chilled water circuits. When corrosion is not properly controlled, the resulting corrosion products inhibit heat transfer, increasing energy consumption in the same manner as fouling and scale formation. Unchecked corrosion can cause heat exchanger leaks and catastrophic system failures.

In any cooling application, attention to cooling tower operation is important. Proper tower maintenance maximises cooling efficiency, or ability to reject heat. This is critical for continuously running refrigeration machinery at full load conditions. For best performance, the cooling tower fill should be kept clean and protected from deterioration. The water distribution system must provide uniform wetting of the fill for optimal air-water contact.

Other components, such as drift eliminators, fill supports, regulating valves, distribution decks, and tower fans, should be kept clean to maintain efficient heat rejection. Inefficient cooling or heat rejection increases the temperature of the water in the cooling tower sump and, consequently, that of the water sent to the condenser. This makes it necessary to condense the refrigerant at a higher temperature (absorption) or higher temperature and pressure (compression) to reject heat at the same rate into the warmer water. This increases the amount of energy required to operate the system.

Problems of Cooling Water

The water in open cooling systems is subject to problems of scale, corrosion, slime, and algae.

Scale

As water evaporates in a cooling tower or an evaporative condenser, pure vapour is lost and dissolved solids concentrate in the remaining water. If this concentration cycle is allowed to continue, the solubilities of various solids will eventually be exceeded. The solids will then deposit in the form of scale on hotter surfaces, such as condenser tubes. The deposit is usually calcium carbonate. Calcium sulphate, silica, and iron deposition may also occur, depending on the minerals contained in the water.

Deposition inhibits heat transfer and reduces energy efficiency.

Deposition is prevented by threshold inhibitors that increase the apparent solubility of the dissolved minerals. Therefore, they do not precipitate and are removed by blowdown. Blowdown is automatically replaced by fresh water. The ratio of dissolved solids in the circulating water to that in the makeup water is called "cycles of concentration." With correct treatment, cycles of concentration can be increased so that less makeup water and consequently less chemicals are required.

The cooling capacity of a tower is affected by how finely the water is atomised into droplets. Smaller droplets lose more heat to the atmosphere; however, more of the smaller droplets are carried away by the air drawn through the tower. This "windage loss," or "drift loss," becomes part of the total blowdown from the system. Windage loss is approximately 0.1 to 0.3% of the water circulation rate.

Windage can have undesirable effects, such as the staining of buildings and the spotting and deterioration of car finishes. These problems are caused by the dissolved solids in the circulating water, which evaporate to dryness as water droplets fall on surfaces. Because water treatment chemicals produce only a slight increase in the dissolved solids content of the water, they usually do not contribute significantly to spotting problems.

Continuous blowdown, or bleed-off, is adequate for scale control in some cooling systems. The importance of continuous blowdown, as opposed to periodic complete draining, cannot be overemphasised. The volume of water in most cooling systems is small compared to the amount of water evaporated. Therefore, excess solids concentrations can develop in a short period of time. Continuous blowdown prevents excessive solids concentrations from developing in the tower water. In order to maintain solids in solution, water that is high in alkalinity and hardness may require the feed of sulphuric acid or an acid salt in addition to blowdown.

Acid feed requires careful handling and control and should only be used where the blowdown rate would otherwise be excessive. Sodium zeolite softening of the makeup water is also an effective way to control scale. However, this process does not decrease the alkalinity of the tower water. Because the resulting low-hardness, high-alkalinity, high-pH water is particularly aggressive to copper alloys, it may necessitate acid feed in addition to softening. Also, carbon steel corrosion control is more difficult with softened water than with hard water.

Polyphosphates are of some value for scale control but must be applied cautiously, because hydrolysis of the polyphosphate results in the formation of orthophosphate ions. If this process is not properly controlled, calcium phosphate deposits may result. Chemicals are now available that inhibit scale formation without this undesirable side effect. Therefore, polyphosphates are now used primarily for corrosion inhibition. A treatment which controls calcium carbonate particle growth and prevents deposition can permit a reasonable blowdown rate and eliminate the need for pH depression with acid.

Phosphonates are particularly useful as threshold inhibitors of scale formation and as iron oxide dispersants. Certain low-molecular-weight polymers also have the ability to control calcium carbonate scale formation. Suspended solids contribute to general fouling and can aggravate scale formation. The deposits may also cause localised under-deposit corrosion. Fouling of heat transfer surfaces has an insulating effect that reduces the energy efficiency of the process. Failure to control scale formation also reduces the rate of heat transfer. Accordingly, a properly designed treatment program must include polymeric dispersants and scale control agents to minimise general fouling and inhibit scale formation.

Corrosion

Water in an open recirculating cooling system is corrosive because it is saturated with oxygen. Systems in urban areas often pick up acidic gases from the air that can be beneficial in scale reduction. However, excessive gas absorption can result in severely corrosive water. Chromate-based corrosion inhibitors are very effective, but their use is now prohibited in comfort cooling towers. The most commonly used corrosion inhibitors are phosphate, molybdate, zinc, polyphosphate, silicate, and organic-based treatments. These inhibitors can be applied in low or alkaline pH treatment ranges.

At low pH, a high phosphate level is used to promote the passivation of steel. At high pH, a combination of various corrosion inhibitors and deposit control agents is used. These programs use organic inhibitors in combination with zinc, phosphate, or molybdate. Where these are environmentally unacceptable, silicates may be used at an alkaline pH. This type of inhibitor program also includes deposit control agents. However, silica concentration must be controlled to prevent deposition of silicate, which forms a hard and persistent scale.

Azoles, functioning as copper corrosion inhibitors, are used in most programs to improve the corrosion protection of copper and to minimise pitting of ferrous metals. Because the heat load on many cooling tower systems varies with changing weather conditions, water evaporation rates tend to be irregular. As a result, cooling system protection can be less than desired or expected under conditions of wide load fluctuation. Automated water treatment control equipment substantially improves treatment results in systems that operate under these conditions.

Slime and Algae

Many types of antimicrobials are available for control of algae and biological slime in open cooling systems. Nonoxidizing organic materials are frequently used. Some antimicrobials can be detoxified before discharge into the environment. Microbiological programs often employ a combination of nonoxidizing and oxidizing chemicals. Oxidizing chemicals include chlorine, hypochlorites, organic chlorine donors, and bromine compounds.

Chlorine gas requires chlorination equipment and controls, which are not practical for most air conditioning systems. Chlorine and hypochlorites must be applied carefully, because excessive chlorine will increase corrosion and may contribute to deterioration of cooling tower wood and reduction of heat transfer efficiency.

Air Washers

Air washers are spray chambers in which air is conditioned by direct contact with water. The chilled water is contained in an open system, or circulated from a closed system. Air washers remove dust, smoke, and odors from the air. Additionally, the return air from a manufacturing process may contain unique contaminants that must be removed. Process contaminants include fiber and oil in textile plants, tobacco dust in tobacco plants, and sizing material in cloth weaving plants.

Filters remove particulate matter from the air before it passes through the spray section. Eliminator blades prevent mist or water droplets from leaving the unit with the air. In addition to cleaning, air washers usually perform other functions. Air temperature and humidity can be controlled through adjustment of the spray water temperature.

When air must be humidified in winter, some water is evaporated. This increases the solids concentration in the remaining liquid. Generally, scale does not form, because the temperature of the water is relatively low. If the spray water temperature is below the dew point of the entering air, the air is dehumidified. In summer, dehumidification involves condensing water vapour from the air, diluting the solids in the recirculating water, and causing water to overflow from the bottom sump or pan of the air washer.

Corrosion can develop in air washers as it does in recirculating cooling water systems. The spray water is saturated with atmospheric oxygen and, when present, acidic airborne contaminants lowei the pH and contribute to its corrosivity. Accordingly, the use of a corrosion inhibitor is important in air washer treatment. Cleanliness of the air washer helps to prevent objectionable odors in the air. The volume of air in relation to the water circulation rate in air washers is much greater than it is in cooling towers. Therefore, the tendency to accumulate sludge is much greater.

Sludge can cause localised corrosion or promote biological activity that produces odors. Therefore, dispersants and/or surfactants are an integral part of a water treatment program for air washers. The air being washed also contains numerous microorganisms and materials that will feed bacteria. Therefore, biological slime is a significant problem in air washers.

Nonoxidizing chemicals are used for microbiological control. However, undesirable odors may result from this treatment. If the air washer must be sterilised, the air flow is stopped and a solution of oxidizing or nonoxidizing antimicrobial is circulated through the washer. The unit must then be hosed until the material loosened by the treatment is thoroughly flushed from the bottom of the air washer.

Closed Systems

Closed systems are not subject to scale formation except when hard makeup water must be used. Many closed systems use zeolite-softened water or condensate as makeup to prevent scale problems. In closed systems, the oxygen concentration is lower than that of aerated systems. Therefore, the potential for corrosion is much lower. However, some corrosion exists, and loose corrosion products can cause fouling of piping, automatic valves, and vents.

Theoretically, closed water systems should not require corrosion inhibitors. Any oxygen introduced with the initial makeup water should soon be depleted by oxidation of system metals, after which corrosion should no longer occur. However, closed systems usually lose enough water and leak enough air to require corrosion protection.

The inhibitors most commonly used are molybdate, silicate, or nitrite based. The use of chromates may be restricted because of regulations that classify them as carcinogens. The amount of inhibitor needed depends on the system water temperature and its metallurgy. Closed systems usually require little additional treatment after the initial charge. Therefore, relatively high treatment levels can be used to provide a greater margin of safety at relatively low cost.

Sulphite-based programs are also used to control corrosion. Unlike the other inhibitors, a corrosion inhibitor film is not established; the sulphite prevents oxygen corrosion by reacting with and removing dissolved oxygen. An alkaline pH is maintained to prevent acidic corrosion.

In the case of air leaks, sulphite requirements are not proportional to water loss and can be very high. High sulphite consumption adds to the dissolved solids content of the circulating water and increases the cost of treatment.

Therefore, air in-leakage should be minimised. Insulating couplings are used in closed systems to control galvanic corrosion. These couplings are mostly phenolic resins, which may be attacked at high pH.

Water Treatment Program

Weather changes cause solids concentration changes in open cooling water systems and particularly in air washers. Air conditioning system design does not always properly address water treatment needs.

Often, water pump volumes are reduced in cooling tower designs to minimise system weight. This results in a lower ratio between volume and circulation rate, which causes a more rapid change in water solids concentration with variations in load. Also, low-capacity water pans are used in evaporative condensers and air washers in order to reduce space and weight.

A water treatment program can be complicated by any of the following factors:

— cooling towers near smokestacks can pick up airborne dirt and acidic gases
— cooling towers are often installed and operated in such a way that considerable water overflows from the system on shutdown
— additional makeup water may be required during hot weather to reduce water temperature

For open systems, an effective and efficient treatment program includes continuous blowdown, continuous feed of corrosion inhibitor and dispersant, and daily water testing. Systems should not be treated and controlled solely on the basis of weekly tests. Additional chemical treatment may be needed to ensure adequate protection.

Refrigerators

A refrigerator is a cooling appliance comprising a thermally insulated compartment and a mechanism to transfer heat from it to the external environment, cooling the contents to a temperature below ambient. Refrigerators are extensively used to store foods which deteriorate at ambient temperatures; spoilage from bacterial growth and other processes is much slower at low temperatures.

A device described as a "refrigerator" maintains a temperature a few degrees above the freezing point of water; a similar device which maintains a temperature below the freezing point of water is called a "freezer". The refrigerator is a relatively modern invention amongst kitchen appliances. It replaced the common icebox which had been placed outside for almost a century and a half prior, and is sometimes still called by the original name "icebox".

Freezers keep their contents, usually foods, frozen. They are used both in households and for commercial use. Most freezers operate at around -18 °C (0 °F). Domestic freezers can be included as a compartment in a refrigerator, sharing the same mechanism or with a separate mechanism, or can be standalone units. Domestic freezers are generally upright units, resembling refrigerators, or chests, resembling upright units laid on their backs. Many modern freezers come with an icemaker.

Commercial fridge and freezer units, which go by many other names, were in use for almost 40 years prior to the common home models. They used toxic ammonia gas systems, making them unsafe for home use. Practical household refrigerators were introduced in the 1915 and gained wider acceptance in the United States in the 1930s as prices fell and non-toxic, non-flammable synthetic refrigerants such as Freon or R-12 were introduced. It is notable that while 60% of households in the US owned a refrigerator by the 1930s, it was not until 40 years later, in the 1970s, that the refrigerator achieved a similar level of penetration in the United Kingdom.

Before the invention of the refrigerator, icehouses were used to provide cool storage for most of the year. These structures were mainly built and used in ancient Persia (Iran). Placed near freshwater lakes or packed with snow and ice during the winter, they were once very common. Using the environment to cool foodstuffs is still common today. On mountainsides run off from melting snow higher up is a convenient way to cool drinks, and during the winter months simply placing one's milk outside one's window is sufficient to greatly extend its useful life.

The first known artificial refrigeration was demonstrated by William Cullen at the University of Glasgow in 1748, and relied on the vapour-compression refrigeration process explained by Michael Faraday. Between 1805, when Oliver Evans designed the first refrigeration machine that used vapour instead of liquid, and 1902 when Willis Haviland Carrier demonstrated the first air conditioner, scores of inventors contributed many small advances in cooling machinery. In 1850 or 1851, Dr. John Gorrie demonstrated an ice maker.

In 1857, Australian James Harrison introduced vapour-compression refrigeration to the brewing and meat packing industries. The absorption refrigerator was invented by Baltzar von Platen and Carl Munters in 1922, while they were still students at the Royal Institute of Technology in Stockholm, Sweden. It became a worldwide success and was commercialised by Electrolux. Other pioneers included Charles Tellier, David Boyle, and Raoul Pictet.

At the start of the 20th Century, about half of households in the United States relied on melting ice (and an icebox) to keep food cold, while the remaining half had no cooled storage at all. The ice used for household storage was expensive because ice had to be cut from winter ponds (or mechanically produced), stored centrally until needed, and delivered regularly. In a few exceptional cases, mechanical refrigeration systems had been adapted by the start of the 20th century for use in the homes of the very wealthy, and might be used for cooling both living and food storage areas. One early system was installed at the mansion of Walter Pierce, an oil company executive.

Marcel Audiffren of France championed the idea of a refrigerating machine for cooling and preserving foods at home. His U.S. patents, issued in 1895 and 1908, were purchased by the American Audiffren Refrigerating Machine Company. Machines based on Audiffren's sulphur dioxide process were manufactured by General Electric in Fort Wayne, Indiana and marketed by the Johns-Manville company. The first unit was sold in 1911. Audiffren machines were expensive, selling for about $1,000 — about twice as much as an automobile cost at the time.

General Electric sought to develop refrigerators of its own, and in 1915 the first Guardian unit was assembled in a back yard wash house as a predecessor to the Frigidaire. In 1916 Kelvinator and Servel came out with two units among a field of competing models. This number increased to 200 by 1920.

In 1918, Kelvinator had a model with automatic controls. These home units usually required the installation of the mechanical parts, motor and compressor, in the basement or an adjacent room while the cold box was located in the kitchen. There was a 1922 model that consisted of a wooden cold box, water-cooled compressor, an ice cube tray and a 9 cubic foot compartment for $714.

In 1923 Frigidaire introduced the first self-contained unit. About this same time porcelain covered metal cabinets began to appear. Ice cube trays were introduced more and more during the 1920s; up to this time freezing was not a function of the modern refrigerator. The first refrigerator to see widespread use was the General Electric "Monitor-Top" refrigerator introduced in 1927. The compressor assembly, which emitted a substantial amount of heat, was placed above the cabinet, and surrounded with a decorative ring. Over 1,000,000 units were produced. This refrigerator used sulphur dioxide refrigerant. Many units are still functional today.

The introduction of freon expanded the refrigerator market during the 1930s, and freezer units became a little more common and requested during the 1940s. Home units did not go into mass production until after WWII. The 1950s and 60s saw technical advances like automatic defrosting and automatic ice making. Developments of the 1970s and 80s brought about more efficient refrigerators, and environmental issues banned the use of CFC (freon) refrigerants used in sealed systems.

Refrigerators used to consume more energy than any other home appliance, but in the last twenty years, great strides have been made to make refrigerators more energy efficient. Current models that are Energy Star qualified use 50 percent less energy than models made before 1993. Early refrigerator models (1916 and on) featured a cold compartment for ice cube trays. Successful processing of fresh vegetables through freezing began in the late 1920s by the Postum Company which had acquired the technology when it bought the rights to Clarence Birdseye's successful fresh freezing methods.

Working of a Refrigerator

Refrigerators work by the use of heat pumps operating in

a refrigeration cycle. An industrial refrigerator is simply a refrigerator used in an industrial setting, usually in a restaurant or supermarket. They may consist of either a cooling compartment only or a freezing compartment only or contain both. The industry has nicknames for these units as well sometimes referring to them as a "cold box" or a "walk-in." The dual compartment was introduced commercially by General Electric in 1939.

The vapour compression cycle is used in most household refrigerators. In this cycle, a circulating refrigerant such as freon enters the compressor as a vapour at its boiling point. The vapour is compressed and exits the compressor as a superheated vapour. The superheated vapour travels through part of the condenser which removes the superheat by cooling the vapour. The vapour travels through the remainder of the condenser and is condensed into a liquid at its boiling point.

The saturated liquid refrigerant passes through the expansion valve where its pressure abruptly decreases. The decrease in pressure results in the flash evaporation and auto-refrigeration of a portion of the liquid. The cold and partially vaporized refrigerant travels through the coil or tubes in the evaporator. There a fan circulates room air across the coil or tubes, and the refrigerant is totally vaporized, extracting heat from the air which is then returned to the food compartment. The refrigerant vapour returns to the compressor inlet to complete the thermodynamic cycle.

An absorption refrigerator works differently from a compressor refrigerator, using a source of heat, and typically runs more quietly. The Peltier effect uses electricity directly to pump heat; refrigerators using this effect are sometimes used for camping, or where noise is not acceptable. They are totally silent, but less energy-efficient than other methods. Other alternatives to the vapour-compression cycle but not in current use include thermionic, vortex tube, air cycle, magnetic cooling, Stirling cycle, Malone refrigeration, acoustic cooling, pulse tube and water cycle systems.

Domestic Refrigerators

Domestic refrigerators and freezers for food storage are made in a range of sizes. Amongst the smallest is a 4 L Peltier fridge advertised as being able to hold 6 cans of beer. A large domestic fridge stands as tall as a person and may be about 1 m wide with a capacity of 600 L. Some models for small households fit under kitchen work surfaces, usually about 86 cm high. Fridges may be combined with freezers, either stacked with fridge or freezer above, below, or side by side. A fridge without a true freezer may have a small compartment to make ice. Freezers may have drawers to store food in, or they may have no divisions.

Compressor refrigerators are by far the most common type; they make a noticeable noise. Absorption or Peltier units are used where quiet running is required; Peltier coolers are used in the smallest refrigerators as they have no bulky mechanism. Compressor and Peltier refrigerators are invariably powered by electricity; absorption units can in principle be designed to be powered by any heat source. Gas-only and dual power gas/electricity units are available. Refrigeration units for commercial and for non-food use are made in a huge range of sizes and styles.

Virtually all homes in the developed world have a refrigerator of one kind or another. The invention of the refrigerator has allowed the modern family to purchase, store, freeze, prepare and preserve food products in a fresh state for much longer periods of time than was previously possible. For the majority of families without a sizeable garden in which to grow vegetables and raise livestock, the advent of the refrigerator along with the modern supermarket led to a vastly more varied diet and improved health resulting from improved nutrition. Dairy products, meats, fish, poultry and vegetables can all be kept refrigerated in the same space within the kitchen.

The refrigerator allows families to consume more salads, fresh fruits and vegetables during meals without having to own a garden or an orchard. Exotic foodstuffs from far-off countries that have been imported by means of refrigeration can be enjoyed in the home because of the availability of domestic refrigeration. The luxury of freezing allows households to purchase more foods in bulk that can be eaten at leisure while the bulk purchase provides cost savings.

Ice cream, a popular commodity of the 20th century, was previously only available by travelling long distances to where the product was made fresh and had to be eaten on the spot. Now it is a practically ubiquitous food item. Ice on-demand not only adds to the enjoyment of cold drinks, but is useful in first-aid applications, not to mention cold packs that can be kept frozen for picnics or in case of emergency.

An increasingly important environmental concern is the disposal of old refrigerators - initially because of the freon coolant damaging the ozone layer, but as the older generation of refrigerators disappears it is the destruction of CFC-bearing insulation which causes concern. Modern refrigerators usually use a refrigerant called HFC-134a (1,2,2,2-tetrafluoroethane) instead of freon, which has no ozone layer depleting properties.

Disposal of discarded refrigerators is regulated, often mandating the removal of doors: children playing hide-and-seek have been asphyxiated while hiding inside a discarded refrigerator. This was particularly true for the older models that had latching doors. More modern units use a magnetic door gasket to hold the door sealed but can actually be pushed open from the inside. However, children can be unwittingly harmed by hiding inside any discarded refrigerator.

Absorption Refrigerator

The absorption refrigerator is a refrigerator that utilizes a heat source to provide the energy needed to drive the cooling system rather than being dependent on electricity to run a compressor. These refrigerators are popular where electricity is unreliable, costly, or unavailable, where noise from the compressor is problematic, or where surplus heat is available, e.g., from turbine exhausts or industrial processes.

An absorption refrigerator is similar to a regular compressor refrigerator in that the refrigeration takes place by evaporating a liquid with a very low (sub-zero) boiling point. In both cases, when a liquid evaporates or boils, it takes some heat away with it, and can continue to do so either until the liquid is all boiled, or until everything has become so cold that the sub-zero boiling point has been reached.

The difference between the two is how the gas is changed back into a liquid so that it may be used again. A regular refrigerator uses a compressor to increase the pressure on the gas, and then condenses the higher pressure gas back to a liquid by heat exchange with a coolant (usually air). An absorption refrigerator uses a different method that requires no moving parts and is powered only by heat.

Absorptive refrigeration uses a source of heat to provide the energy needed to drive the cooling process. The most common use is in commercial climate control and cooling of machinery. Absorptive refrigeration is also used to air-condition buildings using the waste heat from a gas turbine or water heater.

The process is very efficient, since the gas turbine produces electricity, hot water and air-conditioning. The basic thermodynamic process is not a conventional thermodynamic cooling process based on Charles Law. Instead, it is based on evaporation, carrying heat, in the form of fast-moving (hot) molecules from one material to another material that preferentially absorbs hot molecules.

The most familiar example is human sweating. The water from sweat evaporates and is "absorbed" into cool dry air, carrying away heat in fast-moving water molecules. However, absorptive refrigerators differ in that they regenerate their coolants in a closed cycle, while people drink water recycled outside their bodies.

The classic gas absorption refrigerator cools by evaporating liquid ammonia in a hydrogen environment. The now-gaseous ammonia is then absorbed into water, and then later separated by a small source of heat. This drives off the dissolved ammonia gas which is then condensed into a liquid. The liquid ammonia then enters the hydrogen-charged evaporator to repeat the cycle. A similar system, common in large commercial plants, uses a solution of lithium bromide salt and water.

Water is evaporated under low pressure from the coils that are being chilled. The water is absorbed by a lithium bromide/water solution. The water is driven off the lithium bromide solution using heat. Another variant uses air, water, and a salt solution. Warm air is passed through a sprayed solution of salt water. The spray absorbs humidity from the air. The air is then passed through an evaporative cooler. Humidity is removed from the cooled air with another spray of salt solution. The salt solution is regenerated by heating it under low pressure, causing water to evaporate. The water evaporated from the salt solution is recondensed, and rerouted back to the evaporative cooler.

Process

A single-pressure absorption refrigerator uses three substances: ammonia, hydrogen gas, and water, whereas large industrial units generally use only two, a refrigerant such as ammonia, and an absorbent such as water. Normally, ammonia is a gas at room temperature (with a boiling point of -33 °C), but the system is pressurized to the point that the ammonia is a liquid at room temperature.

The cooling cycle starts at the evaporator, where liquefied anhydrous ammonia enters. The "evaporator" contains another gas (in this case, hydrogen), whose presence lowers the partial pressure of the ammonia in that part of the system. The total pressure in the system is still the same, but now not all of the pressure is being exerted by ammonia, as much of it is due to the pressure of the hydrogen. Ammonia doesn't react with hydrogen - the hydrogen is there solely to take up space - creating a void that still has the same pressure as the rest of the system, but not in the form of ammonia.

Per Dalton's law, the ammonia behaves only in response to the proportion of the pressure represented by the ammonia, as if there was a vacuum and the hydrogen wasn't there. Because a substance's boiling point changes with pressure, the lowered partial pressure of ammonia changes the ammonia's boiling point, bringing it low enough that it can now boil below room temperature, as though it wasn't under the pressure of the system in the first place. When it boils, it takes some heat away with it from the evaporator - which produces the "cold" desired in the refrigerator.

The next step is getting the liquid ammonia back, as now it's a gas and mixed with hydrogen. Getting the hydrogen away is simple, and this is where the "absorber" comes in. Ammonia readily mixes with water, and hydrogen does not. The absorber is simply a downhill flow of tubes in which the mixture of gases flows in contact with water being dripped from above. Once the water reaches the bottom, it's thoroughly mixed with the ammonia, and the hydrogen stays still.

At this point, the ammonia is a liquid mixed with water and still not usable for refrigeration, as the mixture won't boil at a low enough temperature to be a worthwhile refrigerant. It's now necessary to separate the ammonia from the water. This is where the heat from the flame comes in. When the right amount of heat is applied to the mixture, the ammonia bubbles out. This phase is called the "generator".

The ammonia isn't quite dry yet - the bubbles contain gas but they're made of water, so the pipe twists and turns and contains a few minor obstacles that pop the bubbles so the gas can move on. The water that results from the bubbles isn't bad - it takes care of another need, and that is the circulation of water through the previous absorption step. Because that water has risen a bit while it was bubbling upwards, the flow of that water falling back down due to gravity can be used for this purpose. The maze that makes the ammonia gas go one way and the bubble water go the other is called the "separator".

The next step is the condenser. The condenser is a sort of heat sink or heat exchanger that cools the hot ammonia gas back down to room temperature. Because of the pressure and the purity of the gas (there is no hydrogen here), the ammonia condenses back into a liquid, and at that point, it's suitable as a refrigerant and the cycle starts over again.

Air Conditioners

An air conditioner is an appliance, system, or mechanism designed to extract heat from an area using a refrigeration cycle. In construction, a complete system of heating, ventilation, and air conditioning is referred to as HVAC. Its purpose, in the home or in the car, is to provide comfort during hot days and nights.

Basics and Theories

Refrigeration cycle

In the refrigeration cycle, a heat pump transfers heat from a lower temperature heat source into a higher temperature heat sink. Heat would naturally flow in the opposite direction. This is the most common type of air conditioning. A refrigerator works in much the same way, as it pumps the heat out of the interior into the room in which it stands.

This cycle takes advantage of the universal gas law PV = nRT, where P is pressure, V is volume, R is the universal gas constant, T is temperature, and n is the number of moles of gas (1 mole = 6.022×10^{23} molecules).

The most common refrigeration cycle uses an electric motor to drive a compressor. In an automobile the compressor is driven by a pulley on the engine's crankshaft, with both using electric motors for air circulation. Since evaporation occurs when heat is absorbed, and condensation occurs when heat is released, air conditioners are designed to use a compressor to cause pressure changes between two compartments, and actively pump a refrigerant around.

A refrigerant is pumped into the cooled compartment, where the low pressure and low temperature cause the refrigerant to evaporate into a vapour, taking heat with it. In the other compartment, the refrigerant vapour is compressed and forced through another heat exchange coil, condensing into a liquid, rejecting the heat previously absorbed from the cooled space.

Humidity of the air

Refrigeration air conditioning equipment usually reduces the humidity of the air processed by the system. The relatively cold evaporator coil condenses water vapour from the processed air, (much like an ice cold drink will condense water on the outside of a glass), sending the water to a drain and removing water vapour from the cooled space and lowering the relative humidity. Since humans perspire to provide natural cooling by the evaporation of perspiration from the skin, drier air (up to a point) improves the comfort provided.

The comfort air conditioner is designed to create a 40% to 60% relative humidity in the occupied space. In food retailing establishments large open chiller cabinets act as highly effective air dehumidifying units. Some air conditioning units dry the air without cooling it. They work like a normal air conditioner, except that a heat exchanger is placed between the intake and exhaust. In combination with convection fans they achieve a similar level of comfort as an air cooler in humid tropical climates, but only consume about 1/3 of the electricity. They are also preferred by those who find the draft created by air coolers uncomfortable.

Refrigerants

"Freon" is a trade name for a family of haloalkane refrigerants manufactured by DuPont and other companies. These refrigerants were commonly used due to their superior stability and safety properties. Unfortunately, evidence has accumulated that these chlorine bearing refrigerants reach the upper atmosphere when they escape. The chemistry is poorly understood but general consensus seems to be that CFCs break up in the stratosphere due to UV-radiation, releasing their chlorine atoms. These chlorine atoms act as catalysts in the breakdown of ozone, which does severe damage to the ozone layer that shields the Earth's surface from the strong UV radiation.

The chlorine will remain active as a catalyst until and unless it binds with another particle forming a stable molecule. CFC refrigerants in common but receding usage include R-11 and R-12. Newer and more environmentally-safe refrigerants include HCFCs (R-22, used in most homes today) and HFCs (R-134a, used in most cars) have replaced most CFC use. HCFCs in turn are being phased out under the Montreal Protocol and replaced by hydrofluorocarbons (HFCs), such as R-410A, which lack chlorine.

Evaporation (Swamp) Coolers

In very dry climates, so-called "swamp coolers" are popular for improving comfort during hot weather. This type of cooler is the dominant cooler used in Iran which has the largest number of units than anywhere else in the world, hence some referring to "swamp coolers" as Persian coolers. An evaporative cooler is a device that draws outside air through a wet pad, such as a large sponge soaked with water. The sensible heat of the incoming air, as measured by a dry bulb thermometer, is reduced.

The total heat (sensible heat plus latent heat) of the entering air is unchanged. Some of the sensible heat of the entering air is converted to latent heat by the evaporation of water in the wet cooler pads. If the entering air is dry enough, the results can be quite comfortable. These coolers cost less and are mechanically simple to understand and maintain.

Absorptive Chillers

Some buildings use gas turbines to generate electricity. The exhausts of these are hot enough to drive an absorptive chiller that produces cold water. The cold water is then run through radiators in air ducts for hydronic cooling. The dual use of the energy, both to generate electricity and cooling, makes this technology attractive when regional utility and fuel prices are right. Producing heat, power, and cooling in one system is known as trigeneration.

Central Air Conditioning

Central air conditioning is an air conditioning system which uses ducts to distribute cooled and/or dehumidified air to more than one room, or uses pipes to distribute chilled water to heat exchangers in more than one room, and which is not plugged into a standard electrical outlet.

With a typical split system, the condenser and compressor are located in an outdoor unit; the evaporator is mounted in the air handling unit. With a package system, all components are located in a single outdoor unit that may be located on the ground or roof.

Central air conditioning performs like a regular air conditioner but has several added benefits:

— When the air handling unit turns on, room air is drawn in from various parts of the house through return-air ducts. This air is pulled through a filter where airborne particles such as dust and lint are removed. Sophisticated filters may remove microscopic pollutants as well. The filtered air is routed to air supply ductwork that carries it back to rooms. Whenever the air conditioner is running, this cycle repeats continually.

— Because the central air conditioning unit is located outside the home, it offers a lower level of noise indoors than a free-standing air conditioning unit.

Thermostat

Thermostats control the operation of HVAC systems, turning on the heating or cooling systems to bring the building to the set temperature. Typically the heating and cooling systems have separate control systems so that the temperature is only controlled "one-way". That is, in winter, a building that is too hot will not be cooled by the thermostat.

Thermostats may also be incorporated into facility energy management systems in which the power utility customer may control the overall energy expenditure. In addition, a growing number of power utilities have made available a device which, when professionally installed, will control or limit the power to an HVAC system during peak use times in order to avoid necessitating the use of rolling blackouts. The customer is given a credit of some sort in exchange.

Equipment Capacity

Air conditioner equipment power in the U.S. is often described in terms of "tons of refrigeration". A "ton of refrigeration" is defined as the cooling power of one short ton (2000 pounds or 907 kilograms) of ice melting in a 24-hour period. This is equal to 12,000 BTU per hour, or 3517 watts. Residential "central air" systems are usually from 1 to 5 tons (3 to 20 kW) in capacity.

The use of electric/compressive air conditioning puts a major demand on the nation's electrical power grid in warm weather, when most units are operating under heavy load. In the aftermath of the 2003 North America blackout locals were asked to keep their air conditioning off. During peak demand, additional power plants must often be brought online, usually natural gas fired plants because of their rapid startup.

A 1995 study of various utility studies of residential air conditioning concluded that the average air conditioner wasted 40% of the input energy. This energy is lost in the form of heat, which must be pumped out. There is a huge opportunity to reduce the need for new power plants and to conserve energy. In an automobile the A/C system will use around 5 hp (4 kW) of the engine's power.

The Association of Home Appliance Manufacturers (AHAM) offers a worksheet that can help you estimate how powerful an air conditioner you need. The worksheet guides you through the measurements needed to calculate the size of the air conditioner, and then it automatically calculates the final answer for you.

Insulation

Insulation reduces the required power of the air conditioning system. Thick walls, reflective roofing material, curtains, and trees next to buildings also cut down on system and energy requirements.

Home Air Conditioning Systems

Domestic air conditioning is most prevalent and ubiquitous in developed Asian nations such as Japan, Taiwan, South Korea, Singapore and Hong Kong, especially in the latter two due to most of the population living in small high-rise flats. In this area, with soaring summer temperatures and a high standard of living, air conditioning is considered a necessity and not a luxury.

Japanese-made domestic air conditioners are usually window or split types, the latter being more modern and expensive. It is also increasing in popularity with the rising standard of living in tropical Asian nations such as India, Malaysia and the Philippines. In the United States, home air conditioning is more prevalent in the South and on the East Coast, in most parts of which it has reached the ubiquity it enjoys in East Asia. Central air systems are most common in the United States, and are virtually standard in all new dwellings in most states.

In Europe, home air conditioning is less common in part due to higher energy costs and more moderate summer temperatures. The lack of air conditioning in homes, in residential care homes and in medical facilities was identified as a contributing factor to the estimated 35,000 deaths left in the wake of the 2003 heat wave.

Maintenance of Refrigerators

Keep the refrigerator clean: The refrigerator has to be kept clean. It is a good to clean the refrigerator atleast once a month with a vacuum or cleaning cloth. The products in the refrigerator need to be removed so that a thorough cleaning is done. The crispers where the meat and vegetables are stored need to be removed and emptied every month. They need to be washed with soap and water. Most modern refrigerators use ducts and small fans to force the cooled air to circulate inside. It stands to reason that the ducts are not blocked and you leave adequate space around food contents for the air circulation.

In the event of poor circulation of air, or if the fans fail, you will have hot regions across the refrigerator. This will keep the compressor running always which requires professional attention. Do not attempt to open the inside. You will end up damaging the internal insulation which will cause corrosion on the metal body or cause the live wire which feeds the fans or the light to come in contact with the metal body resulting in a shock or electrocution hazard. There are no user serviceable parts in a refrigerator. Call qualified service technicians.

Thermostat setting: It is advisable to keep the thermostat between 37 to 42 degrees F in the refrigerator and at 0 degrees F in the freezer. A thermometer can be used to determine the temperature if the temperature dial in the refrigerator has only numbers. The refrigerator should not be placed under direct sunlight or near any heat source such as an oven.

The cooler the surrounding temperature, it is easier for the refrigerator to maintain a cold temperature inside. It is recommended not to open the door of the refrigerator very often as it only wastes energy. The interior temperature of the unit can shoot up to 10-20 degrees F each time the door gets opened. Ensure that the door of the refrigerator is tightly closed every time you open it.

Leak check: Over time and usage, the rubber seals on the refrigerator doors tend to become harder or twisted. This gasket has to be checked periodically to ensure that leaking does not occur. It is advised to use an automotive polish wax on the exterior of the refrigerator on the exterior cabinet and doors so that it is protected from rust. This is particularly recommended for people living near the beach or coastal areas.

Trouble shooting guidelines: If only the light works and the refrigerator does not run, then temperature setting should be checked. Always ensure that there is at least three inch space between the refrigerator and the wall. Clean the condenser coils; sometimes unplugging the refrigerator for two hours and then replugging could also help if the problem is caused by compressor overheat.

In case water gets splashed accidentally on to the back of the unit and it trips your mains power supply, simply unplug the refrigerator and leave it to dry on its own. The compressor is a hermetically sealed unit and only its contacts must have been affected by the water. A slight leakage to the ground can trip the ground fault circuit interrupters (RCD/GFCI). Re plug after sometime and check if it trips again. It is a good idea to call the technician to check the insulation of the cable. If the problem persists, call the technician before connecting the unit to the mains.

A common complaint is that the refrigerator / freezer is not cold enough. In this case, check the temperature setting and ensure that there is enough airflow in refrigerator/freezer. Check for airflow restrictions in vents, temperature control, condenser coils, door seals, defrost heater, defrost timer, evaporator fan and clog in the drain tube. Alternatively if the refrigerator and freezer is too cold then check temperature settings and temperature control. If the refrigerator is noisy then check the drain pain, condenser fan, evaporator fan and inspect the compressor mounts. Hissing and popping noise is normal in frost-free refrigerator as it is the defrost heater making such noises.

Maintenance of Air Conditioner

For your home central air conditioning system to last as long as possible, proper maintenance is a must. By caring for your unit properly, you will extend its life, keep energy costs down, and will keep your system running at peak performance.

To keep your central air conditioner system in top-performing condition, follow these tips:

— Check all of the hoses for leaks at least twice a year. The best times to do this are before you turn on your unit for the summer season, and just before you turn it off for the winter. Make sure the condensate tube is draining freely. By checking this you will be able to catch onto any problems before they get to be too serious for repair.

— Keep the outside compressor as clean as possible. Keep it clear of tall grass and shrubs. Plantings should be at least one foot away from the entire unit for adequate airflow.

— Change the air filter monthly, particularly during the summer when dust and allergens circulate.

— Vacuum registers and air vents regularly.

— Sealing ducts will save energy and money all year round. Use mastic tape or sealer rather than plain duct tape, which will dry out and peel off over time.

— Have the ductwork professionally cleaned every few of years. This maintenance can extend the life of your air conditioner.

— During the winter months, keep the compressor covered. This you protect it from cold weather as well as harsh conditions such as snow and sleet.

— Be sure to keep furniture and drapes away from the registers.

— Raise your thermostat. Each degree of temperature can represent up to 9% savings in cooling costs.

— Keep the unit fan on "AUTO." It's not necessary to run the fan constantly when the air conditioner is not operating.

— When working around your air conditioner, be sure to shut the power off before you start.

It's also important to have your entire air conditioning system inspected by a professional service technician. A professional can measure the refrigerant to see if it needs recharging and measure the airflow over the air conditioner's cooling coils. They will also clean and inspect the motor, compressor, air handler, ducts, coils and air filter. An annual tune-up can reduce your cooling costs by five percent.

5

Hotel Communication Systems

The components of a communications system serve a common purpose, are technically compatible, use common procedures, respond to controls, and operate in unison.

Benefits of Internal Communication System

The technology age has provided the means for sharing knowledge and providing regular up-to-date information 'in-house'. During the 1990's, the intranet alongside the email, was proven to be a powerful communication tool. However, whilst many industries are enjoying the benefits of the intranet as an internal communication system, hospitality companies are still questioning some of it's uses.

The benefits of the intranet are simple: information, knowledge, experience and events can be shared. The intranet enables individual hotels and staff to access beneficial information, learn form one another, display collected data and tap into centralised activities, regardless of geographic location.

Some market leaders in the hotel industry have their finger on the pulse. When drafting strategies to encourage and enable knowledge exchange, the intranet (an internal online publishing tool) enables inter-department, inter-hotel and inter-group information to be displayed. Group training programmes are stored and down loaded. Administration forms are held and easily accessed, group maps, staff job descriptions and job openings, news on developments, business reports, movements, vital staff information, feedback forums, customer feedback, socialising events and outings are all accessible. There is no room for the hording of information or people not being in the 'know'.

A prime advantage of an intranet site is the speed in which information can be updated. In the past, a small change to a method, procedure or policy would means mass reprintings. The paper printed documents would then be sent to sites and offices in thousands of locations worldwide. With the intranet site, the original documents are changed, and can then be downloaded on the centralisied site by staff. The outline of changes can then be emailed in bite size pieces and sent out in mass to draw attention to the specific changes. Staff can then implement the work methods accordingly. Both time and money is saved when the intranet is used as a central library and reference source for company information.

A further reason for using the intranet are the results; intranet sites have a powerful impact on staff. Evidence so far has noted a positive increase in staff motivation. Being connected gives a greater sense of belonging, and being part of a team larger than the immediate. This provides a sense of belonging to a group and a reason to work for the good of the 'Group'. Installing an internal communication systems has become part of reinforcing and creating a company culture and brand standards.

Another intangible but measurable advantage is the increased sense of 'Trust'. Colleagues and management become more open as a company fosters knowledge and information sharing. Openness increases levels of trust. Generally communication on the intranet is relaxed and ideas and job related topics can be talked about by a wider circle of professionals in the same position or with similar interests.

Difficulties with the Intranet

There are of course obstacles, as with any new initiative. Sharing and discussion rely on personal participation which takes both time and skill, as well as willingness. A simple example of a declining discussion forum is one when exchanging 'case studies' has become an anecdote chat or even a further decline into an exchange of 'Gossip' stories. There is a need to still operate within a frame work to keep the focus on themes and trends, rather than one of incidences.

Many employees leave because the managers didn't communicate well. Some personalities manage with a style of openness well. For others their competitiveness makes sharing difficult and for others again, hierarchy represents restrictiveness and limitations. Some managers doubt whether sharing information has an impact on long term success. Whilst it is interesting to transfer knowledge, how it is used by one hotel differs to another, as one individual differs with another. There still needs to be the assumption that it is essential to make unique decisions.

It is also thought that too much transparency without contextual explanation can prohibit the jobs in hand. Misinterpretation can reign. Overtime, selective sharing becomes more commonplace as there is doubt as to how this knowledge can be used. It then becomes inappropriate to share certain knowledge with all members of staff.

Whether using the intranet or not, communication gurus are in agreement that communicating face to face and in writing enables great concepts to become action plans. Everyone needs to know what is expected of them. If employees can't understand what you expect, then they can't feel the rush of excitement of a job well done. Frequent communication and follow up are crucial so you know that others understand your expectations. Managers must communicate their expectations to staff, Groups their changes and developments, and individual staff, their findings.

Role of Intercom System

An intercom (intercommunication device) is an electronic communications system within a building or group of buildings. Intercoms are generally composed of fixed microphone/speaker units which connect to a central control panel. A small home intercom might connect a few rooms in a house. Larger systems might connect all of the rooms in a school or hospital to a central office. Intercoms in larger buildings often function as public address systems, capable of broadcasting announcements.

In many schools, tones signalling the change of classes are sounded over the intercom, taking the place of the electromechanical bells used in older schools. Additionaly many schools now use audio / video intercoms to identify visitors trying to gain access to a locked school building. Many intercom systems can be interfaced with the buildings access control system. Intercom systems can also be found on passenger and rapid transit trains and aboard ships and aircraft.

Wiring Intercoms

While every system is different, most systems have much in common. The following is based on wiring for the LEF system from Aiphone, which is a popular brand in the United States for residential use. These must be connected to a 12v DC power supply:

— + Positive

— - Negative

Other wires include:

— E, or common wire

— C, or unit identifier / call terminal.

— R, or occupied terminal.

— number terminals (1 to 10) depending on master unit.

If one connects a wire colour to the C screw terminal in a unit (called the 1 screw terminal in door stations), energising that wire (by pressing the button associated with the screw terminal the wire is connected to) will initialise a call. In other words, if one attaches the pink wire to the LEF5C in the hallway, and attach the pink wire to screw terminal 4 in the LEF5C in the study, pressing button 4 in the study will energise the pink wire and the common (E) wire. This will initiate a call between the study and the hallway units, with the study unit monitoring the hallway unit.

Two-Wire Broadcast Intercom System

Intercom systems are widely used in TV stations and outside broadcast vehicles such as those seen at sporting events or entertainment venues. There are essentially two different types of intercoms used in the television world: two-wire party line or four-wire matrix systems. In the beginning, TV stations would simply build their own communication systems using old phone equipment. However, today there are several manufacturers offering off-the-shelf systems. From the late 70's until the mid 90's the two-wire party line type systems were the most popular, primarily due to the technology that was available at the time.

The two channel variety used a 32 Volt impedance generating central power supply to drive external stations or belt packs. This type of format allowed the two channels to operate in standard microphone cable, a feature highly desired by the broadcasters. These systems were very robust and simple to design, maintain and operate but had limited capacity and flexibility as they were usually hardwired. A typical user on the system could not choose who to talk to. He would communicate with the same person or group of people until the system was manually reconfigured to allow communication with a different group of people.

Two-wire routers or source assignment panels were then implemented to allow quick re-routing of a two-wire circuit. This reconfiguration was usually handled at a central location, but because voltage is used on the circuit to power the external user stations as well as communicate, there would usually be a pop when the channels were switched. So while one could change the system on-the-fly, it was usually not desirable to do so in the middle of a production, as the popping noise would distract to the rest of the production crew.

Four-wire Broadcast Intercoms

In the mid-90's four-wire technology started gaining more prominence due to the technology getting cheaper and smaller. Four-wire circuit technology had been around for quite some time but was very expensive to implement. It usually required a large footprint in the physical TV Plant, thus was only used at very large stations or TV networks. Also, the large physical size made it virtually impossible to use on a mobile platform such as an outside broadcast vehicle. The term four-wire comes from the fact that the system uses a transmit pair and a receive pair for the audio to and from the intercom, i.e. four wires. That said, in a modern four-wire system there are actually six to eight wires: two (or four) for data and the remaining four for audio. There are also a few manufacturers that use digital audio techniques in the form of fiber or coax cable. Nevertheless, the four wire phrase has stuck, and it is the accepted term for this kind of system today.

One major advantage of four-wire vs. the two-wire systems is the ability to perform point to point communication at will. Point to point communication allows a user to speak directly to another user similar to how someone would call another person directly using a phone. This ability is extremely useful in today's complex production environments. The difference between a phone system, however, and a four-wire intercom is the ability to not only perform point to point but also point to multi-point, party-lines, interrupt fold back (IFB) and many other configurations, which are useful to the production environment. It should be noted that four-wire systems are essentially audio routers. This makes them very useful not only for the communications aspect of a production, but also routing of audio for confidence monitoring or actual on-air use.

In the past, forms of communications such as IFB, audio monitoring and, point to point all had to be separate systems. In the modern four-wire intercom system, these forms of communications are typically all in one compact package. Today the tables have turned, making a four-wire system cheaper and easier to implement than a two-wire system.

Wireless Intercoms

For installations where it is not desired to run wires to support an intercom system, there are also wireless intercom systems available. There are two major benefits of a wireless intercom system over the traditional wired intercom. The first is that installation is much easier since no wires have to be run between intercom units. The second is that you can easily move the units at any time. But with that ease of installation and convenience there is risk of interference from other wireless and electrical devices.

Other wireless devices near the intercom such as cordless telephones, wireless data networks, and remote audio speakers can interfere. Electrical devices such as motors can also cause noise. There may also be less privacy since conversations may be picked up on a scanner, baby monitor, cordless phone, or a similar device on the same frequency. However, there are wireless intercoms that reduce or eliminate both of these risks. Wireless Systems in the United States and Canada have several frequency ranges for wireless intercom systems and other wireless products. They are 49MHz, FM band (200KH - 270KHz), 900MHz, 2.4GHz, 5.8GHz, and MURS (150 MHz). There are also Power Line Carrier units that communicate over house wiring that are referred to as wireless intercoms.

Closed-Circuit Television System (CCTV)

Closed Circuit Television (CCTV) is the use of video cameras to transmit signal to a specific, limited set of monitors. It differs from broadcast television in that the signal is not openly transmitted, though it may employ point to point wireless links. CCTV is often used for surveillance in areas which need monitoring, such as banks, casinos, airports, military installations and convenience stores. Increasing use of CCTV in public places has caused debate over public surveillance versus privacy. In industrial plants, CCTV equipment may be used to observe parts of a process that are remote from a control room, or where the environment is not comfortable for humans. CCTV systems may operate continuously or only as required to monitor a particular event.

The first CCTV system was installed by Siemens AG at Test Stand VII in Peenemunde Germany in 1942, for observing the launch of V2-rockets. The noted German engineer Walter Bruch was responsible for the design and installation of the system. CCTV recording systems are often used at launch sites to record the flight of the rockets, in order to find the possible causes of malfunctions. Film cameras are also used for this purpose. Larger rockets are often fitted with CCTV allowing pictures of stage separation to be transmitted back to earth by radio link. CCTV is also used to observe the launch pad before the launch, especially when no person may be there because of safety reasons.

Industrial processes which take place under conditions dangerous for humans are today often supervised by CCTV. These are mainly processes in the chemical industry, the interior of reactors or facilities for manufacture of nuclear fuel. Use of thermographic cameras allow operators to measure the temperature of the processes. The usage of CCTV in such processes is sometimes required by law.

CCTV for use outside government special facilities was developed as a means of increasing security in banks. Today it has developed to the point where it is simple and inexpensive enough to be used in home security systems, and for surveillance. Surveillance of public areas in the United Kingdom by CCTV was developed partly in response to IRA bombings. Experiments in the UK during the 1970s and 1980s (including outdoor CCTV in Bournemouth in 1985), led to several larger trial programmes in the early 1990s. These were deemed successful in the government report "CCTV: Looking Out For You", issued by the Home Office in 1994, and paved the way for a massive increase in the number of CCTV systems installed.

Today, systems cover most town and city centres, and many stations, car-parks and estates. The exact number of CCTV cameras in the UK is not known but a 2002 working paper by Michael McCahill and Clive Norris of UrbanEye, based on a small sample in Putney High Street, estimated the number of surveillance cameras in private premises in London is around 500,000 and the total number of cameras in the UK is around 4,200,000. The UK has one camera for every 14 people.

Claims that they reduce or deter crime have not been clearly borne out by independent studies, though the government claims that when properly used they do result in deterrence, rather than displacement. One clear effect that has been noted is a reduction of car crime when used in car parks. Cameras have also been installed in taxis to deter violence against drivers, and also in mobile police surveillance vans. In some cases CCTV cameras have become a target of attacks themselves. Middlesbrough council have recently installed "Talking CCTV" cameras in their busy town-centre. It is a system pioneered in Wiltshire which allows CCTV operators to communicate directly with the offenders they spot. This idea is first known to have appeared in George Orwell's famous cautionary tale Nineteen Eighty-Four.

The use of CCTV in the United States is less common, though increasing, and generally meets stronger opposition. In 1998 3,000 CCTV systems were found in New York City. There are 2,200 CCTV systems in Chicago. The most measurable effect of CCTV is not on crime prevention, but on detection and prosecution. Several notable murder cases have been solved with the use of CCTV evidence, notably the Jamie Bulger case, and catching David Copeland, the Soho nail bomber. The use of CCTV to track the movements of missing children is now routine.

After the bombings of London on 7 July 2005, CCTV footage was used to identify the bombers. The media was surprised that few tube trains actually had CCTV cameras, and there were some calls for this to be increased. On July 22, 2005, Jean Charles de Menezes was shot dead by police at Stockwell tube station. CCTV footage has debunked some police claims. Because of the bombing attempts the previous day, some of the tapes had been supposedly removed from CCTV cameras for study, and they were not functional. The use of DVR technology may solve this problem.

A CCTV system may be installed where an operator of a machine cannot directly observe people who may be injured by unexpected machine operation. For example, on a subway train, CCTV cameras may allow the operator to confirm that people are clear of doors before closing them and starting the train. Operators of an amusement park ride may use a CCTV system to observe that people are not endangered by starting the ride. A CCTV camera and dashboard monitor can make reversing a vehicle safer, if it allows the driver to observe objects or people not otherwise visible.

Closed Circuit Digital Photography (CCDP)

A development in the world of CCTV (October 2005) is in the use of megapixel digital still cameras that can take 1600 x 1200 pixel resolution images of the camera scene either on a time lapse or motion detection basis. Images taken with a digital still camera have higher resolution than those taken with a typical video camera. Relatively low-cost digital still cameras can be used for CCTV purposes, using CCDP software that controls the camera from the PC. Images of the camera scene are transferred automatically to a computer every few seconds. Images may be monitored remotely if the computer is connected to a network.

Closed Circuit Digital Photography (CCDP) is more suited for capturing and saving recorded photographs, whereas Closed Circuit Television (CCTV) is more suitable for live monitoring purposes.

Traffic monitoring system

Many cities and motorway networks have extensive traffic-monitoring systems, using closed-circuit television to detect congestion and notice accidents. Many of these cameras however, are owned by private companies and transmit data to drivers GPS systems. The London congestion charge is enforced by cameras positioned at the boundaries of and inside the congestion charge zone, which automatically read the registration plates of cars. If the driver does not pay the charge then a fine will be imposed. Similar systems are being developed as a means of locating cars reported stolen.

Opponents of CCTV point out the loss of privacy of the people under surveillance, and the negative impact of surveillance on civil liberties. Furthermore, they argue that CCTV displaces crime, rather than reducing it. Critics often dub CCTV as "Big Brother surveillance", a reference to George Orwell's novel Nineteen Eighty-Four, which featured a two-way telescreen in every home through which The Party would monitor the populace. The recent growth of CCTV in housing areas also raises serious issues about the extent to which CCTV is being used as a social control measure rather than simply a deterrent to crime.

Quite apart from government-permitted use (or abuse), questions are also raised about illegal access to CCTV recordings. The Data Protection Act 1998 in the United Kingdom led to legal restrictions on the uses of CCTV recordings, and also mandated their registration with the Data Protection Agency. The successor to the DPA, the Information Commissioner in 2004 clarified that this required registration of all CCTV systems with the Commissioner, and prompt deletion of archived recordings. However subsequent case law (Durant vs. FSA) has limited the scope of the protection provided by this law, and not all CCTV systems are currently regulated.

A 2007 report by the UK's Information Commissioner's Office, highlighted the need for the public to be made more aware of the "creeping encroachment" into their civil liberties created by the growing use of surveillance apparatus. A year prior to the report Richard Thomas, the Information Commissioner, warned that Britain was "sleepwalking into a surveillance society".

In 2007, the UK watchdog CameraWatch claimed that the majority of CCTV cameras in the UK are operated illegally or are in breach of privacy guidelines. In response, the Information Office denied the claim adding that any reported abuses of the Data Protection Act are swiftly investigated. In the United States there are no such data protection mechanisms. It has been questioned whether CCTV evidence is allowable under the Fourth Amendment which prohibits "unreasonable searches and seizures". The courts have generally not taken this view.

In Canada the use of video surveillance has grown exponentially. In Ontario, both the Municipal and Provincial versions of the Freedom of Information and Protection of Privacy Act outline very specific guidlines that control how Images and Information can be gathered by this method and/or released.

Recent developments

The first CCTV cameras used in public spaces were crude, conspicuous, low definition black and white systems without the ability to zoom or pan. Modern CCTV cameras use small high definition colour cameras that can not only focus to resolve minute detail, but by linking the control of the cameras to a computer, objects can be tracked semi-automatically. For example, they can track movement across a scene where there should be no movement, or they can lock onto a single object in a busy environment and follow it. Being computerised, this tracking process can also work between cameras.

The implementation of automatic number plate recognition produces a potential source of information on the location of persons or groups. There is no technological limitation preventing a network of such cameras from tracking the movement of individuals. Reports have also been made of plate recognition misreading numbers leading to the billing of the entirely wrong people.

CCTV critics see the most disturbing extension to this technology as the recognition of faces from high-definition CCTV images. This could determine a persons identity without alerting him that his identity is being checked and logged. The systems can check many thousands of faces in a database in under a second. The combination of CCTV and facial recognition has been tried as a form of mass surveillance, but has been ineffective because of the low discriminating power of facial recognition technology and the very high number of false positives generated. This type of system has been proposed to compare faces at airports and seaports with those of suspected terrorists or other undesirable entrants.

Computerised monitoring of CCTV images is under development, so that a human CCTV operator does not have to endlessly look at all the screens, allowing an operator to observe many more CCTV cameras. These systems do not observe people directly. Instead they track their behaviour by looking for particular types of body movement behaviour, or particular types of clothing or baggage. The theory behind this is that in public spaces people behave in predictable ways. People who are not part of the 'crowd', for example car thieves, do not behave in the same way. The computer can identify their movements, and alert the operator that they are acting out of the ordinary.

Recently in the latter part of 2006, news reports on UK television brought to light new technology developed which uses microphones in conjunction with CCTV. If a person is observed to be shouting in an aggressive manner (i.e., provoking a fight), the camera can automatically zoom in and pinpoint the individual and alert a camera operator. Of course this then lead to the discussion that the technology can also be used to eavesdrop and record private conversations from a reasonable distance (e.g., 100 metres or about 330 feet).

The same type of system can track an identified individual as they move through the area covered by CCTV. This is being developed in the USA as part of the project co-funded by the US Defense Advanced Research Projects Agency. With software tools, the system will be able to develop three-dimensional models of an area and track/monitor the movement of objects within it.

To many, the development of CCTV in public areas, linked to computer databases of people's pictures and identity, presents a serious breach of civil liberties. Critics fear the possibility that one would not be able to meet anonymously in a public place or drive and walk anonymously around a city. Demonstrations or assemblies in public places could be affected as the state would be able to collate lists of those leading them, taking part, or even just talking with protesters in the street.

Storage and Preservation

The long-term storage and archiving of CCTV recordings is an issue of concern in the implementation of a CCTV system. Re-usable media such as tape may be cycled through the recording process at regular intervals. There also may be statutory limits on retention of data under some sort of Data Protection Act. However, individual recordings may be retained for indefinite periods for use in investigations or as evidence in legal proceedings.

Recordings are kept for several purposes. Firstly, the primary purpose for which they were created (e.g., to monitor a facility). Secondly, they need to be preserved for a reasonable amount of time to recover any evidence of other important activity they might document (e.g., a group of people passing a facility the night a crime was committed). Finally, the recordings may be evaluated for historical, research or other long-term information of value they may contain (e.g., samples kept to help understand trends for a business or community).

CCTV countermeasures

Unless physically protected, CCTV cameras have been found to be vulnerable against a variety of tactics.

— Some will deliberately destroy cameras.

— Simply spraying certain substances over the lens will make the image too blurry to be read.

— Laser pointers will temporarily blind some cameras, and higher powered lasers can damage them. However, since lasers are monochromatic, colour filters can reduce the effect of laser pointers.

— For wireless networks, broadcasting a signal at the same frequency of the CCTV network is reported to be able to jam it.

— Some will shoot at the cameras. Some outdoor cameras, such as those employed by the Chicago Police Department, have bullet-resistant housing.

— Some will find where the CCTV's feed is recorded (such as at a VCR) and take or destroy the recording device or media. This can be countered using decoy recording devices while the real recording device is in a less obvious place.

PUBLIC-ACCESS TELEVISION SYSTEM

Public access television is a form of Citizen media, similar to Canada's Community channel, Australia's Community television and other models of media created by private citizens. In its conception, Public access television pertained only to the cable television technology of the times, but many Public access organisations now include television, radio and the internet within the spectrum of communications. Public access television is one type of PEG access, short for Public, Educational, and Governmental, the three traditional structures of access within a municipality.

Public access is a result of the cable television industry. There was concern within communities as cities began contracting for cable TV service that companies were using public by-ways (such as roads and sidewalks to run cable wires) to make a profit and many advocates believed some form of 'rent' should be paid for their use. Cable companies at the time were greater in number and smaller in size and negotiating this arrangement was eventually confirmed by the FCC and US cable companies were then required to provide a percentage of revenue from the cable TV subscription fees to provide Public access to the cable systems.

PEG access is a government mandate that provides television production equipment, training and airtime on a local cable system so members of the public, educational system, and the government can produce their own shows and televise them to a mass audience.

Municipalities must take initiative and petition the cable operator to provide the funding for PEG access as laid out by law, but municipalities may also choose to take no action and will instead keep the franchise fees in a general fund. A municipality may also choose to allow Governmental access but not Public access or may replace it with Governmental access or may take away Public access altogether, depending on the disposition of the local government or its voters.

Municipalities have a broad spectrum of franchise agreements (a government-granted monopoly) with cable television service providers. Depending on the size of the community and their contractual agreement the PEG and LO channels may take many forms. Large communities often have a separate organisation for each PEG type, smaller communities may have a single organisation that manages all three. Because each organisation will develop its own policies and procedures, constituent services differ greatly between communities.

Public access television channels may be run by public grassroots groups or individuals, private non-profits or city organisations and policies and regulations are subject to their own ordinances and community standards.

Services available at Public access organisations are often low cost or free of charge, with an inclusive, content neutral, first-come, first-served, free speech ideology. Monies from cable franchise fees are hopefully used to operate the facilities, employ staff and trainers, develop curriculum, operate training workshops, schedule and maintain equipment, produce programming (live or pre-recorded), manage the cablecast of shows and publish promotion materials to build audiences. Funding and operating budgets vary significantly with the municipality's base cable subscriber volume so that organisations in densely populated areas may be able to offer different services than sparsely populated areas.

Users of Public access stations may participate at most levels of this structure to make content that is meaningful and reflective of their experience within their communities. Any member of a community may take advantage of public access. Users are not restricted to cable subscribers only. Many Public access channels carry primarily locally produced programmes while others also carry regionally or nationally distributed programming. Public access centers are not necessarily bound to traditional one and one half hour block schedules, programmes may be about 30 or 60 minutes but may also be of any length, depending on local organisational policies. In the event that a public access channel becomes filled up with programming a franchise may state that more channels may be added to suffice the demand.

Public access centers often allow members to sponsor programming that was produced outside of the municipality. A show that originates outside the municipality is often referred to as "bicycled" programming. Public access centers also may solicit programming that may be valuable to the community despite its origination point.

Educational Access Television

Educational access is the institution set aside for fulfilling the needs of the educational departments and organisations within the municipality. Educational access channels may be associated with a specific school, school district(s) or even private organisations that are contracted to operate the access station for the city.

Educational access centers usually operate a cable channel on the local cable system and often include elements and principle that echo Public access in terms of training and resources. Many school media and video training programmes are based in the Educational Access centers. Programming distributed by these centers ranges from student or parent produced media to coverage of local school functions and bodies (such as the School Council or Committee). There are a number of notable Educational access organisations that produce programming for a national audience and experiences a very broad distribution.

Government access television is a resource of the city to address local municipal programming needs. Often the city or town may use the G channel to cablecast city council meetings, election programming, local emergency announcements and other events and programmes as valued by the local government.

Local Origination

Local origination is typically local programming produced by a cable operator. In contrast with Public access, which is government mandated access for programming, Local origination programming is usually programming of local interest produced by cable company employees or contractors for the cable company. A local high school graduation ceremony produced by cable studio employees and aired on a local cable channel is one such example.

PEG Technologies

Equipment available for public access broadcasting is evolving quickly. At its birth, the state-of-the-art PEG facilities were composed of racks full of analog tape decks and an automated video switching system. Recently, the low cost of digital production and distribution equipment, such as cameras, non-linear editing systems, digital video playback servers and new internet technologies have made digital content production the norm. The dropping cost of digital production and distribution gear has changed the way many PEG facilities operate.

There are companies, like TVTN, that partner with municipalities to help provide hometown news, weather, traffic, and emergency information in a format that looks like other cable networks. This is one option for some PEG channels to improve the look and feel of their channels

PEG centers have come under fire from many angles including local governments and officials, local producers and viewers and even corporate litigations from potential copyright infringements. Special interest groups have also frequently applied pressure on local PEG operations.

PEG often struggles to balance freedom of speech with free, open access to the cable systems and as a result cable operators or PEG organisations have occasionally rightfully or wrongfully banned producers based on the impact of a specific programme, or have removed programming from the schedule because it pushed the legal boundaries of pornography, sedition or slander.

Local governments are required to contract PEG work to city organisations or private non-profits and funding for these groups are often managed through the municipality. Franchise fees ultimately come from the local cable subscribers, paid to the city by the cable operator, and paid then to the PEG centers. Centers have been known to experience interruptions in contract negotiations by the local governments, late payment of contracted operating monies, or obstructive or restricting behaviour from the municipalities in general.

PEG centers have also faced challenges from major marketshare cable giants who intend to squelch the single digit percentage of PEG funding that comes from their profit margins. As of 2006, Comcast, AT&T and Verizon are the largest marketshare companies in the United States and lobbied significant legislation through the US House of Representatives to reduce or end PEG funding.

The cable television cottage industry of the 1960's no longer exists. Since the mid 1980's, large marketshare cable television providers like Comcast, Verizon and AT&T collect billions of dollars across many states using public rights-of-way for cable, telephone and internet infrastructure each year. As cable television technology evolves and is replaced by digital media technology, and Congress and lobby groups struggle to redefine policy, public access organisations nationwide stand to lose massive percentages of operating budget. Public access television is dependent upon revenue from cable television services, should cable television disappear from the marketplace then one of the few institutions that supports Citizen media may vanish with it.

Public access organisations remain in service in their municipalities and continue to serve their missions of empowering communities and facilitating resident communication on a local level. In a changing technology industry, many PEG organisations began investing in training and technology to distribute media in new ways using the internet. In 2005, the consumer media market became flooded with blogs, vlogs, RSS syndication and aggregation, iPod and cell phone media, and countless new methods for distributing information and ideas. As cable television phases out in lieu of a new technology, many access centers adapted these new technologies in order to continue serving their missions and goals within their own constituency.

Many media reform and watchdog organisations have been formed to monitor and report on national and global media policy. Free Press, for example, is a "national, nonpartisan organisation working to reform the media." Free Press monitors PEG access legislation at Defend Local Access. Save Access, a watchdog organisation focused on PEG, is not associated with any specific non-profit organisation, nor does it receive any operating funds of any kind (either corporate, non-corporate or foundation related). Both organisations have been identified as respected sources.

The Public Broadcasting Service (PBS) is not Public access television and has no official connection with PEG. PBS is funded partly by government and tax resources, and partly by private grants and contributions. PEG is funded by cable television companies through subscription fees, and also by private grants and contributions. PBS does not regularly provide free use of facilities to produce programming.

Public Address System

A public address or "PA" system is an electronic amplification system with a mixer, amplifier and loudspeakers, used to reinforce a given sound (e.g.,a person making a speech, prerecorded music, or message) and distributing the 'sound' to the general public around a building. Simple PA systems are often used in small venues such as school auditoriums, churches, and small bars. PA systems with a larger number of speakers are widely used in institutional and commercial buildings, to read announcements or declare states of emergency. Intercom systems, which are often used in schools, also have microphones in each room so that the occupants can reply to the central office.

There is disagreement over when to call these audio systems Sound Reinforcement (SR) systems or PA systems. Some audio engineers distinguish between the two by technology and capability, while others distinguish by intended use (e.g., SR systems are for live music whereas PA systems are usually for reproduction of speech and recorded music in buildings and institutions). This distinction is important in some regions or markets, while in other regions or markets the terms are interchangeable.

Small PA systems

The simplest PA systems consist of a microphone, a modestly-powered mixer-amplifier (which incorporates a mixer and an amplifier in a single cabinet) and one or more loudspeakers. Simple PA systems of this type, often providing 50 to 200 watts of power, are often used in small venues such as school auditoriums, churches, and small bars.

In North America, PA systems are also sometimes referred to as "sound reinforcement systems" or simply "sound systems." In colloquial British English, a PA system installed for public address in a building is sometimes referred to as a "Tannoy" system after the company of that name.

Public Address systems typically consist of input sources, pre-amplifiers and/or signal routers, amplifiers, control and monitoring equipment, and loudspeakers. Input sources refer to the microphones and CD Players that provide a sound input for the system. These input sources are fed into the pre-amplifiers and signal routers that determine the zones that the 'audio signal' is fed to. The preamplified signals are then passed into the amplifiers. Depending on a countries' regulation these amplifiers will amplify the audio signals to 50V, 70V or 100V speaker line level. Control equipment monitors the amplifiers and speaker lines for faults before it reaches the loudspeakers.

Telephone Paging Systems

Most modern telephone systems, such as PBX and VOIP, use a paging system that acts as a liaison between the telephone and a PA amplifier. In key telephone systems such as those by Nortel, Toshiba or Avaya, paging equipment is usually built into the telephone system itself, and allows announcements to be paged over the phone speakers themselves, through external speakers or through both external and internal telephone speakers.

In PBX and larger VOIP telephone systems such as those by Nortel, Cisco, Avaya or Siemens, used for larger enterprise applications, paging equipment is not built into the telephone system. Instead the system provider must provide a separate paging controller connected to a trunk port on the actual telephone system. The paging controller is accessed as either an unused directory number or unused central office line. Access to the paging system is provided through a "trunk access" code or a preprogrammed feature button on the telephone set itself.

Many retailers and offices choose to use the telephone system as the sole access point for the paging system, because the equipment is already "paging system" ready. That is, the business does not have to buy a separate intercom or microphone. An additional advantage, is that each telephone can access the paging system, which makes initiating a page much more convenient than having just one microphone. Many schools and other larger institutions are no longer using the large bulky microphone PA systems and have switched to telephone system paging, as it can be accessed from many different points of the school in an emergency.

One disadvantage of telephone paging systems compared to microphone paging systems, is that the noise associated with hanging up the telephone can be heard over the speakers unless the user takes the initiative to press the "switchhook" on the telephone or if the phone is equipped, pressing the Release (RLS) button, which is most commonly found on Nortel telephone systems.

Large venue PA systems

For popular music concerts, a more powerful and more complicated PA System is used to provide live sound reproduction. In a concert setting, there are typically two complete PA systems: the "main" system and the "monitor" system. Each system consists of microphones, a mixing board, sound processing equipment, amplifiers, and speakers. There is disagreement over when to call these audio systems Sound Reinforcement (SR) systems or a Public Address (PA) systems. This distinction is important in some regions or markets, while in other regions or markets the terms are interchangeable.

The "main" system (also known as "Front of House", commonly abbreviated FOH), which provides the amplified sound for the audience, will typically use a number of powerful amplifiers driving a range of large, heavy-duty loudspeakers including low-frequency speaker cabinets called subwoofers, full-range speaker cabinets, and high-range horns. A large club may use amplifiers to provide 1000 to 2000 watts of power to the "main" speakers; an outdoor concert may use 10,000 or more watts.

The "monitor" system reproduces the sounds of the performance and directs them towards the onstage performers (typically using wedge-shaped monitor speaker cabinets), to help them to hear the instruments and vocals. In British English, the monitor system is referred to as the "fold back". The monitor system in a large club may use amplifiers to provide 500 to 1000 watts of power to the "monitor" speakers; at an outdoor concert, there may be several thousand watts of power going to the monitor system. At a concert in which live sound reproduction is being used, sound engineers and technicians control the mixing boards for the "main" and "monitor" systems, adjusting the tone, levels, and overall volume of the performance.

Acoustic Feedback

All PA systems have a potential for feedback, which occurs when sound from the speakers returns to the microphone and is then re-amplified and sent through the speakers again. This generally manifests itself as a sharp, sudden high-volume piercing sound which can damage the loudspeakers' high-frequency horns or tweeters - and audience members' hearing.

Sound engineers take several steps to prevent feedback, including ensuring that microphones are not pointed towards speakers, keeping the onstage volume levels down, and lowering frequency levels where the feedback is occurring, using a graphic equaliser, parametric equaliser a combination of both devices, or a notch filter.

PA Speakers

High-end PA speakers have been made lighter by using neodymium speaker magnets, and horns are often wired using protective circuitry such as light bulbs (which illuminate and absorb excess wattage) or polyswitches that protect the horn from damage in the event of feedback or a dropped microphone. These new approaches to speaker protection are more convenient than the formerly used approach of fuses, because the sound system needs to be turned off to change fuses.

Digital Signal Processors

Smasll PA systems for venues such as bars and clubs are now available with features that were formerly only available on professional-level equipment, such as digital reverb effects, graphic equalisers, and, in some models, feedback prevention circuits (which electronically sense and prevent feedback "howls" before they occur). These digital signal processing multi-effect devices offer sound engineers a huge range of sound processing options (reverb, delay, echo, compression, etc.) in a single unit. In previous decades, sound engineers typically had to transport a number of heavy "rack-mounted" cases of analog effect devices.

A number of PA companies are now making lightweight, portable speaker systems for small venues that route the low-frequency parts of the music (electric bass, bass drum, etc.) to a separately-powered subwoofer. Routing the low-frequency parts of the signal to a separate amplifier and low-frequency subwoofer can substantially improve the bass-response of the system. As well, the clarity of the overall sound reproduction can be enhanced, because low-frequency sounds take a great deal of power to amplify; with only a single amplifier for the entire sound spectrum, the power-hungry low-frequency sounds can take a disproportionate amount of the sound system's power.

6

Accidents and First Aids

The catering and hospitality industry covers a wide range of different businesses including hotels, pubs and restaurants, contract caterers in various industrial and commercial premises, fast food takeaways, cafes and bistros. This industry sector employs over 1.7 million people and is continuing to grow, therefore it is important that the causes of accidents and ill health are effectively controlled.

The main causes of injury continue to be:

— Slips, trips and falls on wet or contaminated floors
— Manual handling / musculoskeletal injuries
— Exposure to hot or harmful substances
— Struck by something (eg sharp knives or falling objects)

Treating Common Injuries

A guide to common injury and treatment. Information on diagnosis of severe as well as minor emergencies. As much as we'd like for it to be otherwise, injuries happen. Whether you suffer from a skinned knee or a broken arm, knowing how to treat common injuries (as well as knowing when to go to the doctor) is always useful.

What follows is a list of common injuries and some of the most common treatments for them. Should the injury have an odd look to it, excess pain or bleeding, or simply doesn't seem right, consult a doctor or local pharmacist. They may be able to offer better treatment options, or discover an underlying problem that could become severe if left untreated.

Bruises

Bruises are caused by hits or blunt objects breaking small blood vessels in the skin. The larger the area where the injury occurs is then the darker the bruise will be, since there will be more blood vessels broken and more blood will be in the skin. It is also possible to have sub-dermal bruises, or bruises beneath the skin, which are a result of a blow breaking blood vessels in bone or muscle tissue.

The best treatment for bruises is to simply apply heat and massage the area. There are also creams available to deaden any pain associated with the bruise and to speed the bruise in healing. Should the bruise be especially dark or continues to grow, don't hesitate to consult a doctor.

Abrasions

Scrapes, scuffs, and abrasions happen when the skin comes in contact with a rough material. Skinned knees or palms are the most common types of abrasions. Bleeding is usually minimal, and the pain often fades quickly. To treat an abrasion, clean the wounded area well with water and either soap or an alcohol pad. Apply antibacterial ointment, alcohol, or iodine and cover with clean gauze. Keep an eye on it until it is healed for any change in colour or puffiness that may indicate more serious conditions.

Cuts

Depending upon the source, cuts can come in a variety of types; deep or shallow, smooth or jagged, thin or wide. If the cut is a small one, or barely bleeding, clean the area and apply a bandage. If the cut is larger or bleeding heavily, apply pressure to the wound with a clean cloth and seek medical attention immediately. Cuts that bleed heavily or that are large or jagged may have damaged major veins or arteries, and even if they haven't may require stitches in order to heal correctly.

Sprains

A sprain is caused when a joint twists in a way that it shouldn't and damages the connective tissue, such as a sprained ankle or wrist. Swelling and pain accompany the injury, and use of the affected joint is extremely limited at best. The best treatment for a sprain is to keep pressure off of the injured area and to alternate heat and ice on the injury. Use of anti-inflammatory such as ibuprofen is also recommended. You may also wish to consult a doctor, as he can not only diagnose whether or not there is any further damage beyond just the sprain, but also may prescribe or recommend specific medicines for the pain and the swelling.

Degrees of Burns

How to treat a thermal burn by identifying First, Second and Third-degree burns and how to administer proper first aid until medical attention can be received. A thermal burn can be caused by fire, coming in contact with hot objects, flammable vapour that ignites causing an explosion, or contact to the skin by steam or other forms of hot liquid. In order to care for a burn properly until medical attention can be received, you must first determine the degree of the burn. First, second and third degree burns are different and need to be treated as such.

A first-degree burn is superficial, burning only the outer layer of the skin. Symptoms include redness, tenderness, pain and mild swelling. Healing usually occurs in a week without scarring. To care for a first-degree burn you may relieve pain by immersing the burned area in cold water or by applying a wet, cold cloth. Continue applying cold water, on and off, until the area is pain free. This process can take anywhere from 10 to 45 minutes. Cold water not only relieves pain, it will actually stop the progression of the burn into deeper areas of tissue.

Since moistening the skin helps to relieve itching and peeling, you may also apply an aloe vera gel or moisturiser to the skin. Aloe vera is an effective analgesic. A second-degree burn penetrates the entire outer layer of the skin into the inner skin layer. The characteristics of a second-degree burn are the forming of blisters, swelling and fluids beginning to seep from the burned area. Severe pain accompanies these symptoms, because the capillary blood vessels in the skin are damaged.

Do not open the blisters on the skin of a burned area. The blister is nature's way of providing a sterile, waterproof covering when a burn has damaged skin. Therefore, open blisters expose the burn victim to a much greater risk of infection. Again, immersing the burned area in cold water on and off for 10 to 45 minutes is recommended to relieve pain, as is the use of ibuprofen for pain and swelling.

Additionally, it is recommended to elevate a burned extremity to reduce gravity-induced swelling. Though applying a thin layer of antibiotic ointment to a burned area does not sterilise the area it may decrease the amount of bacteria that can enter an open burn. Other types of ointment, sprays or home remedies are not recommended for use on a Second-degree burn. Substances such as these are not sterile and can easily lead to infection.

Never place a wet dressing on a burn. A wet dressing can seal in heat causing even more tissue damage and will need to be removed by a physician by scraping the dressing away which will cause extra unnecessary pain to the burn victim.

The most severe burn is the third-degree burn. This type of burn penetrates all the skin layers deep down into the muscle and fat tissues. The appearance of the skin has a waxy or leathery look. It may look charred or gray as well. The victim of a third-degree burn feels no pain because the nerve endings have been damaged. Only pain from surrounding first and second-degree burns can be felt.

Respiratory damage may also occur with a victim of third-degree burn. Therefore, it is important to seek medical attention immediately. Until medical attention arrives you may cover the burn with a dry, non-sticking, sterile dressing or clean cloth only. Do not apply cold water or any type of ointment or spray on a third-degree burn. The victim of a third-degree burn may also be prone to shock. It is best to elevate the legs of the burn victim and keep them warm by covering them with a clean sheet or blanket until medical assistance arrives. In all cases of burn it is wise to have the burned area examined by a physician to protect the burn victim from the high risk of infection.

Treat Frostbite and Burns

Basic first aid treatments for 1st, 2nd, and 3rd degree burns, as well as how to treat frostbite and frostnip. These two conditions which both require first aid and often medical attention, are very opposite in the elements that cause them. However, knowledge of how to treat both of these is a basic part of essential first aid skills.

Starting with frostbite, it is, in simple terms, a freezing of the skin. If it is caught early enough and able to be reversed, it is referred to as frostnip. Often prone to frostnip are the nose, toes, and fingers. The skin will be red and later turn pale. There has been no permanent damage at this point. If frostnip is observed, it is vital to get those spots re-warmed right away so that it doesn't go further and become frostbite. Warm these spots by placing them against warmer skin elsewhere on the body.

When it has progressed to frostbite, the affected skin will be white. It is also very hard to the touch. First aid treatment is rapid re-warming in water. Slow re-warming when there is a danger of refreezing is not a recommended method. Transport the person suffering frostbite to a place where refreezing is not a possibility. DO NOT use water that is hotter than 106 degrees or you run the risk of a burn.

Do not rub or massage the skin as it is being warmed with water. The thawing in warm water will take about 40 minutes. This may be a painful process. When the skin has returned to red or pink and the skin is once again soft, the thawing is finished. A medication such as ibuprofen may be helpful, if the victim has no medical restrictions with taking it. Avoid alcohol and tobacco use during this period. Avoid using frostbitten feet or fingers when possible, or further damage may be done. Last step is to seek professional medical care.

The opposite side of the spectrum from treating frostbite is treating burns. Although there are three degrees of burns, all burns can become infected. The steps in general treatment are to remove the victim from the source that caused the burn, check breathing and begin CPR/ resuscitation if victim isn't breathing, and cover the burn with a wet and cool cloth. Do not break any blisters, as this may increase the risk of infection. Our skin serves as a barrier against infectious agents and loss of fluid, and the more intact, the better. Very important to remember is the fact that "home remedies" should not be used. Very dangerous among these is butter. DO NOT use butter on a burn.

It is said that 90% of the damage to the skin by burning begins within the first few seconds of contact with heat, and that even after removing the source of heat, the damage may continue to accumulate for up to a minute if the area is not cooled during that time period. Thus, there is benefit to removing the source of heat and cooling the area after a brief contact with heat, even if it already feels like the area has already been damaged or burned. If you can reach some cool liquid within several seconds, it sometimes turns out that what otherwise would be a first degree burn will not end up demonstrating any visible damage at all. The same applies for a more serious burn: what might end up a second degree burn may be lessened through prompt cooling of the area that has been burned, even if several seconds have elapsed without any intervention.

When the burn only involves the outer layer of skin, it is a first-degree burn. There will be redness, but no blistering. Cool the burn with a wet compress (NOT ice) and ibuprofen may help with the pain.

A second-degree burn is deeper with both red colouring and blisters. These burns are painful. Treat with cool water, cover with a dressing that will not stick to the burn, do not open blisters unless they are infected. If these second-degree burns involve more than 5% of the body, or are on the face, hands, genitals, or eyes, take the victim to a medical facility.

Third-degree burns are the most serious. They involve all layers of the skin including nerves, and often muscle.

Charring or blackness of the skin may be visible. Due to the nerve damage, there isn't always pain involved. Irrigate the area gently with saline or water, put on a dressing that will not stick to the burn, and these burns require medical attention by a physician.

Bone Fractures

A fracture consists of a break or crack in the bone. There are two types of fractures. The first is a "simple fracture." This term refers to a fracture in which the skin is intact and no wound is present anywhere near the fractured area.

The second type of fracture is known as a "compound fracture." This term is used when the underlying skin has been broken or damaged. This type of injury may result in the bone protruding through the victim's skin or as a result of a direct blow that cuts the skin at the time of impact. The bone itself may or may not be visible in the wounded area. It is not always possible to tell with the naked eye if a bone has been fractured.

In case of doubt, it is best to assume the victim has received a fracture and treat it accordingly. Here are a few signs and symptoms to assist you when you suspect a person has suffered a fracture and a few rules of administering the proper first aid to the victim until emergency medical assistance can be provided. Your first step in identifying a broken bone would be to check for deformity by comparing the injured counterpart on the opposite side of the victim's body. Second, look for an open wound, which may indicate an underlying fracture. Third, check for pain, which usually accompanies a fracture. The injured person will most likely be able to point to the area of pain. To assist in diagnosing a broken bone, gently feel along the bone. The victim will most certainly complain of tenderness or pain at the exact point of the fracture. Fourth, notice if the injured area is swollen.

Swelling in a fractured area happens rapidly, so look for this significant sign as well.

In some cases a victim of a fracture is able to move the fractured limb with little or no pain. In other cases, motion will produce pain and the victim will refuse to move the injured limb. Listen to the victim for additional clues by asking appropriate questions. An accident victim may have heard a bone snap at the time of injury. Taking a CPR and First Aid training course in your community is highly recommended to be properly prepared in this type of emergency situation. The best method of first aid to implement for a person with a suspected fracture is as follows:

— Though fractures are rarely life threatening it is recommended to check and monitor the victim's airway, breathing, circulation and to check for disabilities using your CPR and First Aid training skills.

— Treat the victim for shock if necessary.

— Ask questions to determine how the accident occurred and the location of the injury. This information will be valuable to trained medical personnel upon their arrival.

— Examine the injured area for swelling and/or deformities, lacerations and puncture wounds. Gently feel along the length of the bone for tenderness, swelling and deformities.

— Check the injured extremity for pulse. A pulseless arm or leg indicates an emergency requiring immediate surgical care. If this is the case, seek emergency medical help immediately.

— Lightly squeeze the victim's fingers or toes of the injured part (unless you suspect a fracture or other injury in these areas) asking the victim what they feel.

Loss of sensation is a sign of nerve or spinal damage. In this case, do not move the victim and call for immediate emergency medical assistance. Stay with the victim reassuring them and encouraging them not to attempt movement until medical emergency professionals arrive.

— You can also check for nerve damage by asking the victim to wiggle his or her fingers or toes connected to the injured extremity. Unless they are injured in these areas the victim should be able to produce some type of movement. Of course if the fingers or toes are injured, do not have the victim move them.

If you have not completed a First Aid and CPR training course, be sure to seek emergency medical attention for the injured person as not to mistreat them causing further damage. These basic courses mentioned are neither time consuming or costly. Local groups all across the country provide this type of training, in many cases at no charge. The training courses only require a few hours of your time. Trained medical professionals such as nurses and other emergency medical personnel normally teach these courses.

Receiving training in these areas of administering proper emergency procedures may very well provide the immediate care needed by a loved one in an emergency situation.

Bruise or Contusions

Bruises, or contusions, are those black, blue, purple or red marks that we get on a part of our body that has experienced recent trauma. For example, putting on a pair of ice skates for the first time and then falling on your butt may constitute trauma and cause a bruise to form.

In essence, bruises occur when our soft tissue is injured in some form, causing the tiny capillaries and veins that are located right beneath our skin to break. These broken veins and capillaries release red blood cells. It is these released red blood cells that collect under our skin causing a bruise to form.

Once our soft tissue is injured, the bruise seems to undergo some type of metamorphosis, in terms of colour. This process is called metabolising, which is a fancy way of saying that your body is attempting to heal itself. You may notice that when you first experience an injury, the area will be red and, oftentimes, a bump may form. A few days later, as the metabolising process starts churning, that bruise will begin turning a darker blue or black.

A week later, the bruise will begin to look yellow or green and then slowly taper off until it is completely gone. Of course, the time that it takes for a bruise to heal varies depending on the severity of the injury as well as the person. Also, depending on where the bruise is located, it may take longer. There have been studies which show that the lower the bruise is on your body (for example, your legs are lower than your arms), the longer it will take to heal. You will want to keep an eye on the bruise, however, as it should be gone within two to two and a half weeks. Any bruise that lingers for longer than that should be checked out by your primary care physician.

If you want to prevent easy bruising, you may want to incorporate more Vitamin C into your diet Of course, before making any change to your diet, it is best to always consult with your doctor. It has been said that those people with a Vitamin C deficiency are more prone to bruising due to weaker blood vessels. A simple way to incorporate more Vitamin C in your diet would be to eat more fruits and vegetables, including leafy greens like kale.

If you would like a bruise to heal quickly, the best thing you can do is after experiencing an injury or trauma, place an ice pack over the bruised area for at least ten minutes and up to thirty minutes, depending on the severity of the trauma. After that, there's not much you can do to help heal the bruise—just cover it up.

Preventing and Treating Insect Stings

The great outdoors offers a lot of activities: swimming, sports, gardening, barbequing just to name a few. The outdoors is also filled with creatures that bite and sting. This can often put a damper on activities. Take heart! There are ways to prevent these pesky creatures from invading your fun.

If you are going to be out, keep as much of your skin covered as you possibly can. Wear long pants and shirts. If you are gardening, you might want to wear gloves to protect your hands. Make sure you wear light coloured clothing. Dark colours and big patterns attract insects.

Spray your clothing or skin with bug spray. These products are available at most groceries and discount stores. If you don't like the smell of the spray, wipes are now available. You wipe them over the exposed skin, as well as the face. They are less odorous and you don't take the chance of the spray getting in your eyes. Avoid using strong scents. Use unscented deodorant. Don't use a lot of lotion or perfume when going outside. If at all possible, avoid using strong smelling shampoos, hair gels or hairspray. The strong scents will only attract the pesky creatures.

Standing water can stagnate and become a breeding ground for mosquitoes. After a hard rain, empty any containers with water standing in them to ward off swarms off mosquitoes. This is very important, especially since the West Nile Virus has begun to be so prevalent. Light citronella candles and torches when you are out at night. This will help to keep the bugs away. Depending on the activity, you may need several. Install bug zappers.

The bugs will be attracted to the light and will fly toward the zapper, thus being killed on impact.

Keep all doors and windows closed. If you have to have your windows and doors open, make sure they are protected by screens. Make sure that your screens are free of tears and holes. If you do suffer from insect stings and bites, there are ways to ease your suffering. These are very common treatments and include some items that we all keep in our homes.

When stung, the first thing to check for is the stinger. If the stinger is still present, remove it by scraping over it to work it out. If you try and pull it out, you risk the chance of pushing it further in and causing an infection. If the affected area starts to swell, place an ice pack on it to relieve the swelling.

There are many topical creams on the market today that help alleviate the itching that often accompanies stings and bites. Rubbing alcohol is also effective in helping to stop the itching. However, if you have been scratching the bite or sting, alcohol could burn when applied. Pouring bleach over fire ant bites often relieves the sting and itching immediately.

Back Injury Prevention

Many people with injured backs continue to perform activities which can cause even more damage. Here are actions to avoid or limit when your back is weak. Anatomically speaking, the human back is a very complex system. Large muscles remain in almost constant tension across the entire structure, supporting an ingenious set of interlocking bones called the spine. Our backs often bear the brunt of heavy loads and exercises intended for greater flexibility. With all of these systems working together constantly, it's no wonder that many of us suffer from one form of back injury or another.

Muscles may tear or strain from excessive work, or the cartilage between the vertebrae may slip out of place or become worn beyond repair. Some people develop a form of arthritis in their backs, or suffer from degenerative diseases such as osteoporosis or scoliosis. As a result, much of the population suffers from weakened backs.

The first thing to realise about having a weakened back is that you WILL have some problems performing activities you may believe are routine. Many injuries which aggravate weak backs are caused by people attempting too much too soon or not accepting their natural limitations. Before resuming any physical activity involving your back, try to accept the fact that you now have limitations. Through physical rehabilitation and pain management, you might be able to regain much of the back strength you lost after the accident or surgical procedure, but it would be unrealistic to expect 100% recovery. The best safety tip comes from within- understand what you can and cannot do safely with your particular back injury or condition. Few people can stop you from climbing a ladder or lifting a heavy box except you.

Specifically, there are some activities people with weakened back should avoid doing altogether. Other activities may need to be modified to prevent further injury. Here are some general types of activities people with back ailments should avoid or modify:

Heavy lifting: Most of us have heard the standard warning about lifting with our legs instead of our backs. This is great advice, but it needs to go farther when it comes to existing back injuries. Lifting a heavy box from the floor by bending at the knees will indeed prevent the back muscles from pulling the entire weight. But once the package has been lifted to the waist, the load has now been shifted primarily to the arms and shoulders, which are located at the top of the spinal structure. The spine is now compressed as the weight of the box pulls against the shoulder and upper vertebrae. Eventually the abdominal and lower back muscles will bear much of the dead weight. For people with weakened backs, this can cause further injury.

After lifting a heavy object with your legs, the next step for those with bad backs should be to find something which can hold the object for you. If you lift a large package from the ground, clear out a space on a work table or a wheeled cart. The less time you have to hold a large object at your waist, the better. You might also want to see if the object really needs to be lifted at all. A heavy box containing multiple parts might just as easily be opened on the floor and the individual parts transferred.

Overhead lifting: One of the least supported positions is an overhead lift. All of the weight and balance is placed on your arms, which must remain in tension until the object is released. The weight of that object is ultimately transferred to the spine, which is now in compression. If the object's center of gravity should shift, the arms and back must make major adjustments under strain. This is one of the worst maneuvers someone with a weak back can perform. Instead of lifting an object overhead, try to raise your body to the level of the task.

If a box must be placed in an overhead cabinet, try using a step ladder to bring your arms as level with the cabinet door as possible. If the box cannot rest on a shelf or table, have someone else hand you the box from below. You'll also want to align yourself so you won't have to twist as you lift.

Excessive bending at the waist: Many people are asked to perform tasks which appear very simple at first. Moving a couch from one end of the room to the other may sound easy, but for those with weakened backs it can be disastrous. Anytime you bend completely over at the waist, the back muscles must be involved. These muscles are designed to do one thing well- support the spinal column. Unlike the arm, abdominal or leg muscles, they are not especially good at handling dead weight lifts. Bending over to pick up the bottom of a couch will force the back muscles to assume a lot of weight while extended. Because they are not especially strong in contraction, back muscles are easily pulled or torn. The result can be the common injury known as a wrenched back. One sudden move can cause an injury which will last for days or aggravate existing back problems. Those with bad backs should automatically decline requests for furniture moving or other labour-intensive activities such as gardening.

Instead of risking a back injury, try using furniture moving disks or a hand truck. Inform those around you about your weakened back- trying to keep up with healthy furniture movers can only lead to trouble. If you still feel like assisting people, offer to perform other tasks which won't injure your back, such as packing and labelling boxes or driving the moving van.

Twisting motions: Twisting from side to side in a natural arc isn't a dangerous act in and of itself, but those with bad backs should avoid doing it with additional weight. Twisting puts a significant amount of tension on the back's support structure. Lifting a heavy object from one side and twisting your back to place it on the other can be a bad maneuver. Instead of twisting in place, those with bad backs may want to modify their action. Placing the heavy object on a cart and moving that cart to the unloading area will usually prevent unnatural twisting. People with weak backs may also try changing directions with their legs instead of their backs.

Care of Broken Arm

Taking care of a broken arm is not difficult. Use these tips to help someone recover as quickly and comfortably as possible. Broken bones, especially broken arms, are a very common occurrence especially among active children and teens. Fortunately, taking care of such a fracture is not as complicated as one might think. Simply having a few facts about the injury, first aid and treatment is all it takes to help someone recover as quickly as possible.

Usually, it is quite obvious that a bone has been broken, but if there is any uncertainty look for these signs:

— There is extreme pain in one area of the arm.
— The arm cannot be moved normally, or there is great pain with movement.
— Deformity or swelling is obvious when compared with the other arm.

Once a fracture is suspected, get the person to a physician quickly. You can also take these first aid steps to help ease the pain in the meantime:

— Try to keep the arm motionless using a home-made splint or sling if necessary. A sling is the easiest because all you need is a cloth wide enough to support the arm, with ends long enough to be tied comfortably around the neck.
— Keep the arm elevated above heart level to keep swelling to a minimum.

Also, even though it might seem to make sense, never try to put a fractured bone back into its normal position, even if it has torn through skin and is exposed. Instead, keep the injured area clean and covered and head for the emergency room.

There are two basic choices for treating a broken arm-internally or externally. External usually involves either a cast or splint and internal typically some type of surgery. One of the most important things you can do to aid the doctor in choosing the best treatment is to be able to provide detail about what caused the break. If the physician knows that it was caused by a fall or snap instead of crushing, it can help with proper diagnosis. This also means faster treatment. Besides inspecting the site of the break, the doctor may also take X-rays and reset the bone, both of which might require anesthetic. Because of this, it would also be a good idea to be able to explain any sensitivity or unusual reactions one may have to anesthetic.

Getting a Cast or Splint: Your physician may use one of many types of casts or splints depending on the amount of support needed during healing. Most are made of either a fiberglass material or plaster which wraps around a softer cloth layer that is closest to the skin. A patient may have a single cast or splint throughout the healing process or it may be altered gradually as swelling goes down. A cast or splint may also be applied after surgery to help support the mended bone.

Caring for a Cast or Splint: In order for a cast or splint to do its job, it must be cared for and used properly.

— In the first few days after application, continue to elevate the injured area to ease swelling and minimize pain just as was done when the injury first occurred. An ice pack can also be applied for a few minutes at a time throughout the day, as long as a thin barrier like a towel is between the pack and the cast.

— Keep all areas of a cast or splint dry at all times. Cover with a plastic bag while bathing and dry gently with a hair dryer if it becomes damp. Check for damaged or softened areas daily and report problems to your doctor.

— Never try to put powders or anti-itch treatments inside the cast. Never try to scratch inside.

— Be aware of any tingling, numbness, unusual swelling or skin irritations that are beyond what your physician has prepared you for. These symptoms may mean the fit needs to be adjusted. Contact your doctor.

Rehab and recovery

Recovery may take a few weeks or several months depending on the severity of the break. One of the earliest signs of healing is a decrease in pain. However, the arm will not be ready for normal activity just yet. Keep these tips in mind to make sure there is full recovery:

- Never remove a cast or other appliance by yourself unless instructed by your doctor.
- Do not expect to return to regular activity immediately after a cast is removed. Joints and muscles will be weak from non-use. Try easier tasks first.
- Follow prescribed physical therapy routines. You may be directed to see a professional, or your doctor may instruct you to do exercises to do at home. Both programmes are designed to bring your arm back to full function gradually.

Wound care bandages come in many types and forms these days. Do you know which type to buy for a skin injury that needs protection? It used to be that skin wounds were wrapped in strips of cotton or wool that had been salvaged from an old sheet or blanket. During the 20th century, however, medical treatment advances included the development of a new bandage form that padded cotton gauze with adhesive that would stick to the skin to protect the wound.

Originally there was one basic bandage style and size. Larger wounds might require the placement of several plastic bandages, while smaller ones had to make do with an oversized wrap or covering. Nowadays, however, all that has changed. Shop any pharmacy or supermarket and you will find multiple types of bandages to choose from.

How do you know which one to buy for a scrape or burn? Here are some of the more popular options:

— The traditional plastic bandage is about 4" long and 1" or 2" wide. The earliest products contained latex in the adhesive portion, which helped it stick to the skin and promote quicker healing. As more people developed latex allergies, however, it was replaced by plastic or vinyl. Many old-timers still use this bandage as the most recognisable and trustworthy design of its type.

— Plastic bandages now come in a variety of sizes and shapes. There are small round ones for blisters, and large square ones for larger burns. Kids' theme characters frequently provide colourful designs and patterns to encourage children to keep them in place. Clear bandages are another option if you don't care for the tan adhesive strips that hold the gauze to the skin.

— Water-resistant bandages became more common in recent years when it was observed that young children could lose wound coverings in the bathtub or swimming pool, or even when outside in the rain. These bandages cling tightly and can be stubborn to remove, but this helps to keep the wound securely covered to heal more quickly than if there were no bandage over it.

— Antibacterial ointment has been added to some brands of bandages. With this type you need not buy or add a separate medical treatment; just let the bandage do its work by staying in place until the wound begins to heal. Just check the wound every day while wearing these bandages to be sure no allergies have developed, as evidenced in a rash, redness, burning, or hives.

— For those who are allergic to any type of skin adhesive, you can always buy a separate roll of gauze to wrap around the wound and secure it with paper tape, which is hypo-allergenic. Potential problems include keeping the gauze pads and wrapping in place, since even with tape, they can slip away from the wound and expose it to more bacteria.

Whatever wound type you seek to protect, there is a bandage to cover it if you shop long enough. If you don't find one that you want, ask the pharmacist or supermarket health and beauty department manager to order the brand that will work best for you.

7

Fire Protection

Fire protection is the prevention and reduction of the hazards associated with fires. It involves the study of the behaviour, compartmentalisation, suppression and investigation of fire and its related emergencies as well as the research and development, production, testing and application of mitigating systems. In structures, be they land-based, offshore or even ships, the owners and operators are responsible to maintain their facilities in accordance with a design-basis that is rooted in laws, including the local building code and fire code, which are enforced by the Authority Having Jurisdiction.

Buildings must be constructed in accordance with the version of the building code that is in effect when an application for a building permit is made. Building inspectors check on compliance of a building under construction with the building code. Once construction is complete, a building must be maintained in accordance with the current fire code, which is enforced by the fire prevention officers of a local fire department. In the event of fire emergencies, Firefighters, fire investigators, and other fire prevention personnel called to mitigate, investigate and learn from the damage of a fire. Lessons learned from fires are applied to the authoring of both building codes and fire codes.

In the U.S.A., this term is used by engineers and code officials when referring only to fire sprinkler systems, not fire alarm or advance smoke detection. Often the American public will assume it is all-encompassing. How it is used, and by whom, will usually indicate how it is meant.

Fire protection has three major goals:

— Life safety (minimum standard in fire and building codes)

— Property protection (typically an insurance requirement, or a regulatory requirement where the protection of building components is necessary to enable life safety)

— Continuity of operations (typically an insurance requirement or an item of self-motivation for building owners - not a regulatory issue). Interruption of operations due to fire damage can be very costly. For instance, a nuclear reactor may cost about one million US dollars per day, if it is not making power that is being sold.

Types of Fires

When deciding on what fire protection is appropriate for any given situation, it is important to assess the types of fire hazard that may be faced. Some jursidictions operate systems of classifying fires using code letters. Whilst these may agree on some classifications, they also vary.

Components

Structural fire protection (in land-based buildings, offshore construction or onboard ships) is typically achieved via three means:

- Passive fire protection (use of integral, fire-resistance rated wall and floor assemblies that are used to form fire compartments intended to limit the spread of fire, or occupancy separations, or firewalls, to keep fires, high temperatures and flue gases within the fire compartment of origin, thus enabling firefighting and evacuation)
- Active fire protection (manual and automatic detection and suppression of fires, as in using and installing a Fire Sprinkler system or finding the fire (Fire alarm) and/or extinguishing it)
- Education (ensuring that building owners and operators have copies and a working understanding of the applicable building and fire codes, having a purpose-designed fire safety plan and ensuring that building occupants, operators and emergency personnel know the building, its means of Active fire protection and Passive fire protection, its weak spots and strengths to ensure the highest possible level of safety)

Balanced Approach of Fire

Passive fire protection (PFP) in the form of compartmentalisation was developed prior to the widespread use of active fire protection (AFP), mainly in the form of fire sprinklers. During this time, PFP was the dominant mode of protection provided in facility designs. With the widespread installation of fire sprinklers in the past 50 years, the reliance on PFP as the only approach was reduced. There is a perception by some fire protection engineers and some members of the fire protection construction industry that the model building codes have changed with too much reliance on AFP.

Lobby groups are typically divided into two camps favouring active or passive fire protection. Each camp tries to garner more business for itself through its influence in establishing or changing local and national building and fire codes. At present, the camp favouring AFP appears to be leading.

A balanced approach between all three parts, Education, AFP and PFP, is generally recognised to be the best overall approach, but there are disagreements in emphasis. This is to be expected, considering that many of the proponents of one camp or another have a vested interest in the outcome, as they are involved in the sales or construction of one of the systems. Many insider in the trade, who know how much field conditions can influence matters, conclude that no one side has all the answers.

The relatively recent inclusion of *performance based* or *objective based* codes tend to support AFP initiatives, and can lead to the justification for less substantial construction. Some proponents of PFP feel that this new approach is not properly balanced, as the use of automatic suppression with codes allowing *performance based* designs often favours the cost savings resulting from less solid structures. At times it works the other way around, as firewalls that protrude through the roof structure are used to "sub-divide" buildings such that the separated parts do not require sprinklers.

The decision to favour AFP versus PFP in the design of a new building may be affected by the lifecycle costs. Lifecycle costs can be shifted from capital to operational budgets and vice versa. AFP, may initially require less capital to install, but due to its nature requires significant operational resources to maintain. PFP on the other hand, may be more costly to install but less costly to maintain. Planners consider the expected life expectancy of a building to make the most beneficial long term decision.

CHECK COMMON ITEMS

If any one of the three components of Fire Protection fail, the fire safety plan can be immediately and severely compromised. For example, if the firestop systems in a structure were inoperable, a significant part of the fire safety plan would not work in the event of a fire. Since the overall plan depends on all pieces, it is important to see that each item is in fact functional. Likewise, if there were a sprinkler system or an alarm system, but it's down for lack of knowledgeable maintenance, or if building occupants prop open a fire door and then run a carpet through, the likelihood of damage and casualties is markedly increased. It is vital for everyone to realise that fire protection within a structure is a system that relies on all of its components.

There are many things that can and often do go wrong prior to and during the construction of a building. What happens afterwards, however, can also be substantially hazardous, to the point of entirely defeating the fire protection plan that was put in place during the design-phase of a building. Common operator errors include, but are not limited to, the following: failure to regularly clean grease ducts in commercial kitchens (usually every 3 - 6 months), re-entering firestops without proper repairs, damaging and removing spray fireproofing from structural steel elements, changing of the use or occupancy of parts of a building.

Any changes that affect the overall fire protection plan, however small they may appear to the layman, legally require the owner to either gain the approval of the fire prevention officer at the municipal fire department or to apply for a building permit with the local, municipal building department. The permit fee is intended to cover the time and expenses for the Authority

Having Jurisdiction to evaluate the contemplated change against applicable code requirements. Failure to obtain such approvals make the owner vulnerable to charges of negligence and culpability in a court of law.

Fire Alarm System

A fire alarm system is an active fire protection system that detects fire or the effects of fire, and as a result provides one or more of the following: notifies the occupants, notifies persons in the surrounding area, summons the fire service, and controls all the fire alarm components in a building. Fire alarm systems can include alarm initiating devices, alarm notification appliances, control units, fire safety control devices, annunciators, power supplies, and wiring.

The design of the overall goals, general system type, and integration into the other facility systems (active fire suppression, HVAC, lighting, electrical power, fire barriers, etc.) is performed by competent engineers with experience in fire protection, who are licensed within the geographical area of practice, such as a US State or a Canadian Province. This is done in conjunction with the architect's design team during the design phase of the building project. The detailed component selection and layout is provided by a technician as hired by the contractor during the construction phase. In the United states, that person is usually certified for fire alarm design by the National Institute for Certification of Engineering Technologies (NICET).

The design is typically provided in compliance with the model building codes having jurisdiction in that area. In the United States, NFPA 72, *The National Fire Alarm Code* is usually used for the installation methods, testing and maintenance. Property insurance company recommendations are also sometimes incorporated. Extensions of existing systems are done considering the originally installed fire alarm system, and more than likely will be proprietary to match the existing equipment.

A fire alarm system is composed of components which can be classified into the following categories.

— Initiating Devices - these devices either sense the effects of a fire, or are manually activated by personnel, resulting in a signal to the fire alarm panel. Examples are heat detectors, smoke detectors, manual pull stations or call points, and sprinkler pressure or flow switches.

— Main Fire alarm control (panel) - this is the central brain of the overall system, which coordinates the signals and resultant actions of the system.

Fire Alarm Control Unit (Panel) - any panel providing required functions, and has inputs and outputs. NAC Power booster panels are the most common example.

— Power supply - because one of the fire alarm system objectives is life safety, fire alarm system power supplies are redundant, and reliable when compared to electronic or electrical systems of similar complexities (e.g., HVAC control systems). Primary supply- Commercial light and power. Back-up/ secondary supply - Usually sealed, lead-acid batteries. NAC power supplies for additional notification appliances beyond the original capability of the FACP. Generators are permitted under strict rules.

— Notification appliances - these devices provide stimuli for initiating emergency action and provide information to users, emergency response personnel, and occupants. Examples are bell, siren, horn, speaker, light, or text display that provides audible, tactile, or visible outputs.

— Signaling line circuits (SLC) - the wiring which carries data information.

— Supervisory signals - detecting devices and signaling to indicate a condition in fire protection systems which is not normal and could prevent the fire protection system from functioning as intended in the event of a fire. An example is a closed valve which controls the water supply to a fire sprinkler system. This does not indicate the failure of a component or subsystem of the fire alarm system.

— Trouble signal - signaling to indicate a wiring fault. Sometimes specific components or features of the fire alarm system, of which could prevent the fire alarm or fire suppression system from functioning as intended. An example is a disconnected wire at a heat detector.

— Remote annunciation - A usually alpha-numeric display (may be graphic) that indicates where in the building the alarm originated. It may also indicate the type of device. Used by emergency personnel for locating the fire quickly. Sometimes these will contain some control functions such as alarm silence and alarm reset. Must be key or keypad controlled.

Fire alarm system devices

Fire alarm systems have devices connected to them to detect the fire/smoke or to alert the occupants of an emergency. Below is a list of common devices found on a fire alarm.

— Manual pull stations/manual call points - Devices to allow people to manually activate the fire alarm. Usually located near exits. Also called "manual pull boxes". Other countries have different devices as standard, for example the UK uses 'break-glass callpoints', when people break a small pane of glass to activate the alarm.

— Smoke detectors - Spot type: Photoelectric and Ionization; Line type: Projected Beam Smoke Detector; Air-Sampling type: Cloud Chamber

— Water Flow Switches - Detect when water is flowing through the fire sprinkler system

— Rate-of-Rise and Thermostat (heat) Detectors - Detect heat changes

— Valve Supervisory Switch - Indicates that a fire sprinkler system valve that is required to be open, is now closed (off-normal).

— Carbon Monoxide Detectors - Detects poisonous carbon monoxide gas and usually only connected to household fire alarm systems. Very rarely seen in commercial systems.

Appliances of fire alarm systems

— Notification Appliance: A fire alarm system component used to notify people of the need for action in connection with the activation of a fire alarm device. Notification appliances may employ audible, visible, tactile, textual or even olfactory stimuli to alert the occupants of a fire or other emergency. Audible or Visible signals are the most common and may utilize speakers to deliver live or pre-recorded instructions to the occupants. In the United States fire alarm evacuation signals are required to use a standardized interrupted four count temporal pattern to avoid confusion with other signals using similar sounding appliances.

— Magnetic Door Holders: Wall or floor mounted electromagnets controlled by a fire alarm system or directly connected smoke detectors that hold open spring-loaded self-closing smoke tight doors by magnetic attraction to a door mounted iron armature. When energized these magnets hold open the door to allow free movement in building corridor. Upon detection of smoke or other fire conditions power is removed from the electromagnet, and the spring-loaded door is allowed to return to its closed position thus limiting the transmission of smoke from one space to another through the door opening.

Emergency Voice Alarm Communications (EVAC)

An 'Emergency Voice Alarm Communication' system is part of a fire alarm system that uses high reliability speakers to notify the occupants of the need for action in connection with a fire or other emergency. These speakers are special types of fire alarm Notification Appliances. 'Emergency Voice Alarm Communication' systems are employed in large facilities where general undirected evacuation is considered impracticable or undesirable. The Audible Textual signals from the speakers are used to direct the occupant's response during a fire or other emergency.

The system may be controlled from one or more locations within the building known as Fire Wardens Stations, or from a single location designated as the building Fire Command Center. Speakers are automatically activated by the fire alarm system in a fire event, and following a pre-alert tone, selected groups of speakers may transmit one or more prerecorded messages directing the occupants to safety. These messages may be repeated in one or more languages. Trained personnel activating and speaking into a dedicated microphone can suppress the replay of automated messages in order to initiate or relay real time voice instructions.

Active Fire Protection (AFP)

Active fire protection (AFP) is an integral part of fire protection. AFP is characterised by items and/or systems, which require a certain amount of motion and response in order to work, contrary to passive fire protection.

AFP Falls into Two Categories

Fire suppression

The fire is extinguished by manual or automatic means, such as a fire extinguisher or a standpipe system or a fire sprinkler system, which automatically releases water, or a gaseous or foam based fire suppression system, to suppress a fire when a release mechanism is activated by heat.

Fire detection

The fire is detected either by locating the smoke or heat, and an alarm is sounded to enable emergency evacuation as well as to dispatch the local fire department.

Construction and Maintenance

All AFP systems are required to be installed and maintained in accordance with strict guidelines in order to maintain compliance with the local building code and the fire code. AFP works alongside modern architectural designs and construction materials and fire safety education to prevent, retard, and suppress structural fires.

Fire Extinguisher

A fire extinguisher is an active fire protection device used to extinguish or control small fires, often in emergency situations. Typically, a fire extinguisher consists of a handheld cylindrical pressure vessel containing an agent which can be discharged to extinguish a fire. The typical steps for operating a stored pressure fire extinguisher (described by the acronym "PASS") are the following:

- P - Pull the safety pin
- A - Aim the nozzle at the base of the fire, from a safe distance (about 1 to 3 meters (4 to 10 feet) away)
- S - Squeeze the handle
- S - Sweep the extinguisher from side to side while aiming at the base of the fire
- The approximate starting distance varies by the size and type of the extinguisher.
    - If using a cartridge operated extinguisher you must push down on the cartridge puncturing lever to pressurize the extinguisher after pulling the pin.
    - CO_2 fire extinguishers usually have a horn-shaped nozzle. Do not touch this horn (or the pipe linking it to the extinguisher) when attempting to put out a fire - your hand may freeze to the extinguisher, unless it is equipped with what is called a Frost Horn.

There are various types of extinguishers, which are used for different types of fires; using the wrong type can worsen the fire hazard, but using the right one can better the situation.

Installation Process

Fire extinguishers are typically fitted in buildings at an easily-accessible location, such as against a wall in a high-traffic area. They are also often fitted to motor vehicles, watercraft, and aircraft - this is required by law in many juristictions, for identified classes of vehicles. Under

NFPA 10 all commercial vehicles must carry at least one fire extinguisher (size/UL rating depending on type of vechical and cargo (ie. fuel tankers typically must have a 9.1 kg (20 lb). when most others can carry a 2.3 kg (5 lb).) The revised NFPA 10 created criteria on the placement of "Fast Flow Extinguishers" in locations such as those storing and transporting pressurized flammable liquids and pressurized flammable gas or areas with possiblity of three dimensional class B hazards are required to have "fast flow" extinguishers as required by NFPA 5.5.1.1.

Varying classes of competition vehicles require fire extinguishing systems, the simplest requirements being a 1A10BC handheld portable extinguisher mounted to the interior of the vehicle.

Kinds of Extinguishing Agents

Dry chemical

Powder based agent that extinguishes by cooling/steals energy because of a endothermic reaction and it to works like thermal ballast for the fire. More material to warm up. Powder isn´t toxic for humans. In nature it has a fertilizer effect.

— Ammonium phosphate, used on class A, B, and C fires. It receives its class A rating from the agents ability to melt and flow at 177 °C (350 °F) to smother the fire. More corrosive than other dry chemical agents. ABC Dry Chemical

— Sodium bicarbonate, used on class B and C fires. Interrupts the fire's chemical reaction.

— Potassium bicarbonate (aka Purple-K), used on class B and C fires. About two times as effective on class B fires as sodium bicarbonate. The preferred dry chemical agent of the oil and gas industry. The only dry chemical agent certified for use in AR-FF by the NFPA.

— Potassium bicarbonate & Urea Complex (aka Monnex), used on Class B and C fires. More effective than all other powders due to its ability to decrepitate (where the powder breaks up into smaller particles) in the flame zone creating a larger surface area for free radical inhibiton

Foams

Applied to fuel fires as either an aspirated (mixed & expanded with air in a branch pipe) or non aspirated form to form a frothy blanket or seal over the fuel, preventing oxygen reaching it. Unlike powder, foam can be used to progressively extinguish fires without flashback

— AFFF (aqueous film forming foam), used on A and B fires and for vapor suppression. The most common type in portable extinguishers. It contains flour tensides which can be accumulated in human body.

— AR-AFFF (Alcohol-resistant aqueous film forming foams), used on fuel fires containing alcohol. Forms a membrane between the fuel and the foam preventing the alcohol from breaking down the foam blanket.

— FFFP (film forming fluoroprotein) contains naturally occurring proteins from animal fats to create a foam blanket that is more heat resistant then the synthetic AFFF foams.

— CAFS (compressed air foam system) Any APW style extinguisher that is charged with a foam solution and pressurized with compressed air. Generally used to extend a water supply in wildland operations. Used on class A fires and with very dry foam on class B for vapor suppression.

— Arctic Fire is a liquid fire extinguishing agent that emulsifies and cools heated materials quicker than water or ordinary foam. It is used extensively in the steel industry. Effective on classes A, B, and D.

— FireAde, a foaming agent that emulsifies burning liquids and renders them non-flammable. It is able to cool heated material and surfaces similar to CAFS. Used on A and B (said to be effective on some class D hazards, although not recommended due to the fact that fireade still contains amounts of water which will react with some metal fires).

Water

Cools burning material

— APW (Air pressurized water) cools burning material by absorbing heat from burning material. Effective on only Class A fires, but has the advantage of being cheap, harmless, and relatively easy to clean up.

— Water Mist uses a fine misting nozzle to break up a stream of deionized water to the point of not conducting electricity back to the operator. Class A and C rated. Used widely in Hospitals.

Water Additivese

— Wet Chemical (potassium acetate) extinguishes the fire by forming a soapy foam blanket over the burning oil(saponification)and by cooling the oil below its ignition temperature. Generally class A and K (F in Europe) only.

— Wetting Agents Detergent based additives used to break the surface tension of water & improve penetration of Class A fires. Enables a 3 litre water extinguisher to achieve the fire fighting capacity of a 9 litre plain water type

Clean agents

Agent does not extinguish by smothering, but displaces oxygen, or inhibits chemical chain reaction. They are labeled clean agents because they do not leave any residue after discharge which is ideal for sensitive electronics and documents.

— Halon, a gaseous agent that inhibits the chemical reaction of the fire. Classes B:C for lower weight fire extinguishers (2.3 kg ; 5 lbs or less) and A:B:C for heavier weights (4.1-7.7 kg ; 9-17 lbs). Banned from new production, except for military use, as of January 1, 1994 as its properties contribute to ozone depletion and long atmospheric lifetime, usually 400 years. Halon was completely banned in Europe resulting in stockpiles being sent to the United States for reuse. Although production has been banned, the reuse is still permitted. Halon 1301 and 1211 are being replaced with new halons which have no ozone depletion properties and low atmospheric lifetimes, but are less effective.

— CO_2, a clean gaseous agent which displaces oxygen. Highest rating for 7.7 kg (20 pound) portable CO_2 extinguishers is 10B: C. Not intended for Class A fires.

— Mixtures of inert gases, including Inergen and Argonite.

Class D

Sodium Chloride/Bicarbonate Urea Graphite and Copper forms a crust over the burning metal and performs like a heat sink to draw heat away from the burning material, also smothers to a degree. Copper dry powder was developed by the U.S. Navy for lithium fires and will cling to vertical surfaces.

Fire Extinguisher Maintenance

Most countries in the world require regular fire extinguisher maintenance by a competent person to operate safely and effectively, as part of fire safety legislation. Lack of maintenance can lead to an extinguisher not discharging when required, or rupturing when pressurized. Deaths have occurred, even in recent times, from corroded extinguishers exploding.

There is no all-encompassing fire code in the United States. Generally, most municipalities (by adoption of the International Fire Code) require inspections every 30 days to ensure the unit is pressurized and unobstructed (done by an employee of the facility) and an annual inspection by a qualified technician. Hydrostatic pressure testing for all types of extinguishers is also required, generally every five years for water and CO2 models up to every 12 years for dry chemical models.

Recently the National Fire Protection Association and ICC voted to allow for the elimination of the 30 day inspection requirement so long as the fire extinguisher is monitored electronically. According to NFPA, the system must provide record keeping in the form of an electronic event log at the control panel. The system must also constantly monitor an extinguisher's physical presence, internal pressure and whether an obstruction exists that could prevent ready access. In the event that any of the above conditions are found, the system must send an alert to officials so they can immediately rectify the situation. Electronic monitoring can be wired or wireless.

In the UK, three types of maintenance are required:

— *Basic Service*: All types of extinguisher require a basic inspection annually to check weight, correct pressure (using a special tool, not just looking at the gauge) and for signs of damage or corrosion, cartridge extinguishers are opened up for internal inspection & check weighing of the cartridge, labels are checked for legibility, where possible dip tubes, hoses and mechanisms checked for clear free operation ;

— *Extended Service*: Water, Wet Chemical, Foam & Powder extinguishers require every five years a more detailed examination including a test discharge of the extinguisher and recharging- on stored pressure extinguishers this is the only opportunity to internally inspect for damage/corrosion. By recharging fresh agent is used as they all have a shelf life, even water goes foul inside an extinguisher; Note: extinguishers should be percentage tested according to total number of units in any given area. Some extinguishers contain pressure in excess of 1.38 MPa (200psi) and this internal pressure over periods of time affects each brand & make differently depending on their placement & location.

— *Overhaul*: CO2 extinguishers, due to their high operating pressure, are subject to pressure vessel safety legislation and must be hydraulic pressure tested, inspected internally & externally and date stamped every 10 years. As it cannot be pressure tested a new valve is also fitted. If replacing any part of the extinguisher (valve, horn etc) with a part from another manufacturer then the extinguisher will lose its fire rating. This may invalidate insurance, as would incorrect or inadequate servicing if it were to be found.

Fire Hydrant

A fire hydrant (also known colloquially as a fire plug in the United States or as a johnny pump in New York City), is an active fire protection measure, and a source of water provided in most urban, suburban and rural areas with municipal water service to enable firefighters to tap into the municipal water supply to assist in extinguishing a fire.

The concept of *fire plugs* dates to at least the 1600s. This was a time when firefighters responding to a call would dig down to the water mains and hastily bore a hole to secure water to fight fires via bucket brigades or, later, via *hand pumped* fire engines. The holes were then plugged with stoppers, which over time came to be known as *fire plugs*. This is the source of the colloquial term *fire plug* still used for fire hydrants today. After the Great Fire of London in 1666, the city installed water mains with holes drilled at intervals, equipped with risers, allowing an access point to the wooden fire plugs from street level.

It has been claimed that Birdsill Holly invented the fire hydrant, but his 1869 design was preceded by many other patents for fire hydrants, and a number of these earlier designs were produced and successfully marketed. Numerous wooden cased fire hydrant designs existed prior to the development of the familiar cast iron hydrant. Although the development of the first above ground hydrant in the USA traces back to Philadelphia in 1803, underground fire hydrants — common in parts of Europe and Asia — have existed since the 1700s.

A hose is attached to the fire hydrant, then the valve is opened to provide a powerful source of water, on the order of 350 kPa (50 lbf/in^2) (this pressure varies according to region and depends on various factors including the size and location of the attached water main). This hose can be further attached to a fire engine, which can then use a powerful pump to boost the water pressure and possibly split it into multiple streams. The hose may be connected with a threaded connection or a Storz connector. Care should be taken not to open or close a fire hydrant too quickly, as this can create a water hammer which can damage nearby pipes and equipment. The high water pressure inside the hose causes it to be very heavy, stiff, and unable to make a tight turn while pressurized. When a fire hydrant is unobstructed, this is not a problem, as there is enough room to adequately position the hose.

Most fire hydrant valves are not designed to throttle the water flow; they are designed to be operated full-on or full-off. The valving arrangement of most dry-barrel hydrants is for the drain valve to be open at anything other than full operation. Usage at partial-opening can consequently result in considerable flow directly into the soil surrounding the hydrant, which, over time, can cause severe scouring . A hose with a closed nozzle valve, or fire truck connection, or closed gate valve is always attached to the hydrant prior to opening the hydrant's main valve.

When a Firefighter is operating a hydrant, appropriate Personal protective equipment, such as gloves and a helmet with face shield, are typically worn. High pressure water coursing through a potentially aging and corroding hydrant could cause a failure, injuring the firefighter operating the hydrant or bystanders.

In most jurisdictions it is illegal to park a car within a certain distance of a fire hydrant. In North America the distances are commonly 3 to 5 m or 10 to 15 ft, often indicated by yellow or red paint on the curb. In the UK, yellow lines are used to keep cars from parking over underground hydrants. Parking restrictions are sometimes ignored (especially in cities where available street parking is scarce), however these laws are usually enforced. The rationale is that hydrants need to be visible and accessible in an emergency.

To prevent casual use or misuse, the hydrant requires special tools to be opened, usually a large wrench with a pentagon-shaped socket. Vandals sometimes cause monetary loss by wasting water when they open hydrants. Such vandalism can also reduce municipal water pressure and impair firefighters' efforts to extinguish fires. Sometimes those simply seeking to play in the water remove the caps and open the valve, providing residents a place to play and cool off in summer. However, this is usually discouraged as residents have been struck by passing automobiles while playing in the street in the water spray. In spite of this, some US communities provide low flow sprinkler heads to enable residents to use the hydrants to cool off during hot weather, while gaining some control on water usage.

In most US areas, contractors who need temporary water may purchase permits to use hydrants. The permit will generally require a Hydrant Meter, a gate valve and sometimes a clapper valve (if not designed into the hydrant already) to prevent back-flow into the hydrant. Additionally, residents who wish to use the hydrant to fill their in-ground swimming pool are commonly permitted to do so provided they pay for the water and agree to allow firefighters to draft from their pool in the case of an emergency.

Municipal services, such as street sweepers and tank trucks, may also be allowed to use hydrants to fill their water tanks. Often sewer maintenance trucks need water to flush out sewer lines, and fill their tanks on site from a hydrant. If necessary, the municipal workers will record the amount of water they used, or use a meter.

Construction of Fire Hydrant

In areas subject to freezing temperatures, only a portion

of the hydrant is above ground. The valve is located below the frost line and connected via a riser to the above-ground portion. A valve rod extends from the valve itself up through a seal at the top of the hydrant, where it can be operated with the proper wrench. This design is known as a "dry barrel" hydrant, in that the barrel, or vertical body of the hydrant, is normally dry. A drain valve underground opens when the water valve is completely closed; this allows all water to drain from the hydrant body to prevent the hydrant from freezing.

In warm areas, hydrants are used with one or more valves in the above-ground portion. Unlike cold-weather hydrants, it is possible to turn the water supply on and off to each port. This style is known as a "wet barrel" hydrant. Both wet- and dry- barrel hydrants typically have multiple outlets. Wet barrel hydrant outlets are typically individually controlled, while a single stem operates all the outlets of a dry barrel hydrant simultaneously. Thus, wet barrel hydrants allow single outlets to be opened, requiring somewhat more effort but simultaneously allowing more flexibility.

A typical U.S. dry-barrel hydrant has two smaller outlets and one larger outlet. The larger outlet is often a Storz connection if the local fire department has standardized on hose using Storz fittings for large diameter supply line. The larger outlet is known as a "steamer" connection, and a hydrant with such an outlet may be referred to as a "steamer hydrant" although this usage is becoming archaic. Likewise, an older hydrant without a steamer connection may be referred to as a "village hydrant."

Hydrant coloring may be due either to purely practical criteria or more artistic. In America, the AWWA and NFPA recommend hydrants be colored chrome yellow for rapid identification apart from the bonnet and nozzle caps which should be coded according to their available flow. Class AA hydrants (>1500gpm) should have their nozzle caps and bonnet colored light blue, Class A hydrants (1000-1499gpm), green, Class B hydrants (500-999gpm), orange, and Class C hydrants (0-499gpm), red. This aids arriving firefighters in determining how much water is available and whether to call for additional resources, or locate another hydrant.

Other codings can be and frequently are used, some of greater complexity, incorporating pressure information, others more simplistic. In Ottawa, hydrant colors communicate different messages to firefighters; for example, if the inside of the hydrant is corroded so much that the interior diameter is too narrow for good pressure, it will be painted in a specific scheme to indicate to firefighters to move on to the next one. In many localities, a white or purple top indicates that the hydrant provides non-potable water. Where artistic and/or aesthetic considerations are paramount, hydrants can be extremely varied, or more subdued. In both instances this is usually at the cost of reduced practicality.

Maintenance

In most areas fire hydrants require annual inspections and maintenance - they normally only have a one year warranty, but some have 5 year warranties. These inspections are generally performed by the local municipalities but they often do not inspect hydrants that are identified as private. Private hydrants are usually located on larger properties to adequately protect large buildings in case of a fire and in order to comply with the fire code. Some companies are contracted out to inspect private fire hydrants unless the municipality has undertaken that task.

Fire Hydrant manufacturers recommend lubricating the head mechanism and restoring the head gaskets and o-rings annually in order that the fire hydrant perform the service expected of them. Lubrication is generally done with a food grade non-petroleum lubricant to avoid contamination of the distribution system.

Occasionally a stone or foreign object will mar the seat gasket. In this case, most hydrants have a special seat wrench that allows removal of the seat to replace the gasket or other broken parts without removing the hydrant from the ground. Hydrants extensions are also available for raising a hydrant if the grade around the hydrant changes. Without extending the height, the wrenches to remove caps would not clear and the break flanges for traffic models would not be located correctly in case they were hit. Hydrant repair kits are also available to repair sacrificial parts designed to break when hit by a vehicle.

Many departments use the hydrants for flushing out water line sediments. When doing so, they often use a hydrant diffuser, which is a device that diffuses the water so that it doesn't damage property and is less dangerous to bystanders than a solid stream. Some diffusers also dechlorinate the water to avoid ground contamination. Hydrants are also sometimes used as entry or exit points for pipe cleaning pigs.

Fire Protection Engineering

Fire protection engineering (also known as fire engineering or fire safety engineering) is the application of science and engineering principles to protect people and their environments from the destructive effects of fire and smoke. The discipline of fire protection engineering includes, but is not exclusive to:

— Active fire protection - fire suppression systems, and fire alarm.
— Passive fire protection - fire and smoke barriers, space separation
— Smoke control and management
— Building design, layout, and space planning
— Fire prevention programs
— Fire dynamics and modeling
— Human behavior during fire events
— Risk analysis, including economic factors

In practice, fire protection engineers typically identify risks and design safeguards that aid in preventing, controlling, and mitigating the effects of fires. Fire protection engineers assist architects in evaluating buildings' life safety and property protection goals. FPEs are also employed as fire investigators, including such very large-scale cases as the analysis of the collapse of the World Trade Centers. NASA uses fire protection engineers in its space program to help improve safety.

Fire protection engineering (FPE) can lay a claim to roots dating as far back as Ancient Rome, when the Emperor Nero ordered the city to be rebuilt utilizing passive fire protection methods, such as space separation and non-combustible building materials, after a catastrophic fire. The discipline of fire protection engineering emerged in the early 20th century as a distinct discipline, separate from civil, mechanical and chemical engineering, in response to new fire problems posed by the Industrial Revolution. Fire protection engineers of this era concerned themselves with devising methods to protect large factories, particularly spinning mills and other manufacturing properties.

Another motivation to organize the discipline, define practices and conduct research to support innovations became clear in response to catasrophic conflagrations and mass urban fires that swept many major cities during the latter half of the 19th century. In 1903 the first degree program in fire protection engineering was initiated as the Armour Institute of Technology (later becoming part of the Illinois Institute of Technology).

As the 20th Century emerged, several catastrophic fires resulted in changes to buildings codes to better protect people and property from fire. It was only in the latter half of the 20th Century that fire protection engineering emerged as a unique engineering profession. The primary reason for this emergence was the development of the "body of knowledge," specific to the profession that occurred after 1950. Other factors contributing to the growth of the profession include the start of the Society of Fire Protection Engineers in 1950, the emergence of independent consulting fire protection engineers, and the promulgation of engineering standards for fire protection.

Fire protection engineers, like their counterparts in other engineering and scientific disciplines, undertake a formal course of education and continuing professional development to acquire and maintain their competence. This education typically includes foundation studies in mathematics, physics, chemistry, and technical writing. Professional engineering studies focus students on acquiring proficiency in material science, statics, dynamics, thermodynamics, fluid dynamics, heat transfer, engineering economics, ethics, Systems in engineering, reliability, and environmental psychology. Specialized studies in combustion, probabilistic risk assessment or risk management, the design of fire suppression systems, the application and interpretation of model building check the building increases the access control protection level. While the requirement that a person entering a restricted food storage area sign in and out, the addition of a time-lapse camera which records such entries obviously makes the access control stronger.

The protective features of having an electronic touch pad access to a severely restricted area can be further increased, for instance, by frequent and well-monitored changes to the access code. The example of the gender signs on restrooms is an excellent illustration of how specific access control techniques can overtly influence those whom we are trying to affect.

Access control attempts to limit, monitor, control and otherwise influence the movement onto, from and within a property of pedestrian and vehicular traffic. Many techniques and methods may be utilised successfully in this endeavour. Again, as is the case of all countermeasures, access control is property-specific and the methods and techniques utilised must be similarly individualised.

Access control of vehicular traffic begins at the entrance or entrances to the property. In the case of those properties which are located away from and out of sight of the main thoroughfares, access control sometimes begins off the property. In most instances, with the exception of exclusive resort properties, the entrances to the property are unmonitored. Signs are the most used access control devices at these points. Many properties post signs at the perimeter vehicular access points which enthusiastically welcome guests, and direct vendors. At the same time, these signs discourage unauthorised entrance.

Guests driving onto the property often require directions to the registration area. Clear, readable and attractive signs provide that needed service. Vendors and suppliers, likewise, require direction to their authorised destination. If the hours which property ca accommodate vendors and suppliers are restricted o limited, this information, too, will assist in the orderl conduct of business. Speed must be controlled, and th normal method of such control is speed limit signs Attention should be given to specific areas of greates concern—pedestrian crossings, playground areas an areas of possible traffic obstruction or danger. Particula attention should be given to the lighting or reflectiv quality of speed limit signs. Additional vehicular-contro limiting signs include signs which announce traffi direction limitation on turns and signs which announc destination limitations.

Motorists should be warned of possible dangers an situations which require their special attention. Sudde turns in the driveway, dangerous cross traffic, heav equipment or truck traffic and pedestrian crossings ar but a few of the examples which should be addressed Special attractions, times of operation and events ar often highlighted by the use of both permanent an temporary signs.

Designated parking, especially for employees, is major access control consideration. Developing, using an enforcing employee parking has several advantages: i maximises available designated space for guest parking, i allows for better attention to employee persona protection, it reduces the likelihood of employee thef and it allows for better control and safety of employe vehicles. Speeded bumps, when strategically placed carefully and prominently announced, are often ver effective in controlling speed in designated areas such a long, uninterrupted driveways or pedestrian crossings.

Devices designed to allow only one-way designate travel of vehicles are effective but should be use sparingly and carefully. Not only are the diagonally positioned teeth a hazard in and of themselves, bu inadvertent damage to tyres is not uncommon. Car access devices used most often for selected parking areas are less common in the lodging industry than in others. They are useful, however when circumstances dictate, but their expense should be considered.

The most common and useful technique of pedestrian access control is that of alarms and other electronic and mechanical deterrent devices. When such devices are used or considered, appropriate safeguards are essential. The maintenance department should assure appropriate factory mutual approval and proper code compliance. Perimeter and broad area protection devices, while common in many industry groups, are less so in the lodging industry. Some applications exist, however, including the alarming of perimeter gates, usually installed with a central station annunciating capacity. Application is also not uncommon in protecting pool areas during off-hours.

Point of entry devices are more commonly used in protecting window and door access points which cannot be otherwise monitored. Such devices are often hard wired to a central annunciation point and allow response when intrusion is attempted. In other circumstances, simple local alarm devices sound at the point of attempted intrusion. Several versions and approaches are possible depending on the circumstance—glass breakage devices; contact devices; heat sensor and movement devices are examples. The sophistication and capability of these devices increase consistent with their cost. Restricting exit pedestrian traffic at designated doors is another example of access control and provides an effective and relatively inexpensive way of restricting access to designated doors which cannot otherwise be monitored. Some are simple local alarms which annunciate when unauthorised access is attempted, but this approach is often inappropriate because of the effect which such noise has on guests.

Another softer approach, although more expensive, is hard wiring such alarms to a central annunciation point from which appropriate response can be dispatched. Obviously the decision regarding the type and placement of door alarms will be steeped in circumstances. Surveillance cameras are not an uncommon approach to access control. They can be useful but their use and appropriateness depends on the circumstance for which they were designed. For instance, surveillance cameras are not usually an effective access control tool when immediate response is required. There are several reasons for this limitation in effectiveness. Not only must a constant and alert capability be maintained at the monitoring point, but also situation diagnosis is often difficult to accomplish. Additionally, response capability and time are often inadequate. Better uses of surveillance cameras are in those instances when a recording backup exists and can later be appropriately viewed and diagnosed.

Vendor and contractor badging procedures either in conjunction with their sign-in/sign-out requirements or used independently are often appropriate. Not only do they provide a retainable documentation of visits, they act in and of themselves as a deterrent to unauthorised entry.

The decision to utilise employee badges is a major one. As a rule-of-thumb it is encouraged for several reasons. It provides a method for guests to easily identify employees. Badges can be used for time and attendance purposes as well as for identification. If badges are issued on a daily basis, the system provides for a quick check on attendance levels. Different coded or coloured badges are useful for department and/or area access authorisation. Badges provide ease of access control when a discharge or termination situation takes place. Badges are available in a great variety of designs, materials and uses. Management is well advised to plan carefully prior to codes, and the measurement and simulation of fire phenomena complete most curricula.

In the United States, the University of Maryland (UMd) offers an ABET-accredited bachelor of science degree program in fire protection engineering, as well as graduate degrees. Worcester Polytechnic Institute (WPI) offers a masters and a Ph.D. in fire protection engineering. Other institutions, such as Oklahoma State University, the University of Kansas, Illinois Institute of Technology, University of California, Berkeley, and University of Houston–Downtown have offered courses in fire protection engineering or technology.

Professional Registration of Fire Protection Engineering

Suitably qualified and experienced fire protection engineers may qualify for registration as a professional engineer. The recognition of fire protection engineering as a separate discipline varies from state to state in the United States. Few countries outside the United States regulate the professional practice of fire protection engineering as a discipline, although they may restrict the use of the title engineer in association with its practice.

The titles *fire engineer* and *fire safety engineer* tend to be preferred outside the United States, especially in the United Kingdom and Commonwealth countries influenced by the British fire service. Some proponents of the title *fire safety engineer* assert that the title *fire protection engineer* suggests a concern only with the design of active fire protection systems, such as automatic fire sprinklers, fire detection, fire alarm systems, smoke management systems, gaseous fire suppression and other special hazard systems.

The advocates of the title *fire safety engineer* suggest it more accurately indicates an interest in both preventive and protective measures. Those who prefer the title *fire engineer* suggest that it encompasses a broader range of professional activities associated with fire risk management, including the management of fire services. All titles are widely recognised. The Institution of Fire Engineers is one international organization that qualifies many aspects of the training and qualifications of fire engineers.

8

Water and Sanitation

Water is one of the most essential elements to good health—it is necessary for the digestion and absorbtion of food; helps maintain proper muscle tone; supplies oxygen and nutrients to the cells; rids the body of wastes; and serves as a natural air conditioning system. Health officials emphasise the importance of drinking at least eight glasses of clean water each and every day to maintain good health. Since water contains no calories and can serve as an appetite suppressant and helps the body metabolise stored fat, it may possibly be one of the most significant factors in losing weight.

Water is a key component in determining the quality of our lives. Today, people are concerned about the quality of the water they drink. Although water covers more than 70% of the Earth, only 1% of the Earth's water is available as a source of drinking. Yet, our society continues to contaminate this precious resource. Water is known as a natural solvent. Before it reaches the consumer's tap, it comes into contact with many different substances, including organic and inorganic matter, chemicals, and other contaminants.

Many public water systems treat water with chlorine to destroy disease-producing contaminants that may be present in the water. Although disinfection is an important step in the treatment of potable water, the taste and odour of chlorine is objectionable. And, the disinfectants that are used to prevent disease, can create byproducts which may pose significant health risks. Today, drinking water treatment at the point-of-use is no longer a luxury, it is a necessity! Consumers are taking matters into their own hands and are now determining the quality of the water they and their families will drink by installing a drinking water system that will give them clean, refreshing, and healthier water.

Properties: The freezing point of water is 0° C (32° F), and its boiling point is 100° C (212° F). Water reaches its maximum density at 4° C (39° F) and expands upon freezing. Water combines with salts to form hydrates and reacts with metal oxides to form acids.

Occurrence: Water is the only substance that occurs at ordinary temperatures in all three states of matter: solid, liquid, and gas. As a solid, ice, it forms glaciers, frozen lakes and rivers, snow, hail, and frost. It is liquid as rain and dew, and it covers three-quarters of the earth's surface in swamps, lakes, rivers, and oceans. Water also occurs in the soil and beneath the earth's surface as a vast groundwater reservoir. As gas, or water vapour, it occurs as fog, steam, and clouds.

Water in Life: Water makes up 50 to 90 percent of the weight of living things. Protoplasm is a solution of water and fats, carbohydrates, proteins, and salts. Water transports, combines, and chemically breaks down these substances. Water also aids the metabolic breakdown of proteins and carbohydrates.

Natural Water Cycle: The continuous movement of water between the earth and the atmosphere is the hydrological cycle. Water vapour from water and land surfaces and from living cells circulates through the atmosphere and falls as rain or snow. When it reaches the earth, water either flows into streams and then into oceans or lakes, or it enters, or infiltrates the soil. Some water becomes soil moisture, which may evaporate directly or move up through the roots of plants and be released by leaves. Some water percolates downward, accumulating in the so-called zone of saturation to form the groundwater reservoir, the upper surface of which is the water table. Under natural conditions, the water table rises in response to inflowing water and then declines as water drains into natural outlets such as wells and springs.

Composition: Because water dissolves numerous substances in large amounts, pure water rarely occurs in nature. Precipitation absorbs carbon dioxide and other gases, as well as traces of organic and inorganic material from the atmosphere. Because water reacts with minerals in the soil and rocks, surface and groundwater may contain many different dissolved substances. Surface waters may also contain domestic sewage and industrial wastes. Groundwater from shallow wells may contain nitrogen compounds and chlorides, but water from deep wells generally contains only dissolved minerals. Seawater contains many soluble compounds in addition to salt.

Water Purification: Impurities are removed from water by screening, sedimentation, filtration, chlorination, or irradiation. Aeration saturates water with air, usually by spraying fountains of water into the air. Aeration removes odors and tastes caused by decomposing organic matter, industrial wastes, and some gases. Various salts and metals cause hardness in water. Hardness may be removed by boiling, by adding sodium carbonate and lime, or by filtering through natural or artificial zeolites.

Water Desalinization: Three desalinisation processes, which involve evaporating salt water and then condensing the resulting steam, are known as multiple-effect evaporation, vapour-compression distillation, and flash evaporation. Freezing is another desalinization method, based on the different freezing points of fresh and salt water. Ice crystals are separated from the salt brine, washed, and melted into fresh water. In reverse osmosis, pressure forces fresh water through a membrane that does not allow minerals to pass. In electrodialysis, the positive and negative ions of the dissolved salt are removed from water by an electric current through special membranes.

Hard and Soft Water

Hard water is any water containing an appreciable quantity of dissolved minerals. Soft water is treated water in which the only cation is sodium. The minerals in water give it a characteristic taste. Some natural mineral waters are highly sought for their flavour and the health benefits they may confer. Soft water, on the other hand, may taste salty and may not be suitable for drinking.

When hard water is heated, the carbonates precipitate out of solution, forming scale in pipes and tea kettles. In addition to narrowing and potentially clogging the pipes, scale prevents efficient heat transfer, so a water heater with scale will have to use a lot of energy to give you hot water. Soap is less effective in hard water because its reacts to form the calcium or magnesium salt of the organic acid of the soap. These salts are insoluble and form grayish soap scum, but no cleansing lather. Detergents, on the other hand, lather in both hard and soft water. Calcium and magnesium salts of the detergent's organic acids form, but these salts are soluble in water.

Hard water can be softened by treating it with lime or by passing it over an ion exchange resin. The ion exchange resins are complex sodium salts. Water flows over the resin surface, dissolving the sodium. The calcium, magnesium, and other cations precipitate onto the resin surface. Sodium goes into the water, but the other cations stay with the resin. Very hard water will end up tasting saltier than water that had fewer dissolved minerals. Most of the ions have been removed in soft water, but sodium and various anions still remain. Water can be deionised by using a resin that replaces cations with hydrogen and anions with hydroxide. With this type of resin, the cations stick to the resin and the hydrogen and hydroxide that are released combine to form pure water.

Hard water

Hard water is water that has a high mineral content. Usually it consists of calcium (Ca^{2+}), magnesium (Mg^{2+}) ions, and possibly other dissolved metals such as bicarbonates and sulphates. Calcium usually enters the water as either calcium carbonate ($CaCO_3$), in the form of limestone and chalk, or calcium sulphate ($CaSO_4$), in the form of other mineral deposits. The predominant source of magnesium is dolomite ($CaMg(CO_3)_2$). Hard water is generally not harmful.

The simplest way to determine the hardness of water is the leather/froth test: soap or toothpaste, when agitated, lathers easily in soft water but not in hard water. More exact measurements of hardness can be obtained through a wet titration. The total water 'hardness' is read as parts per million or weight/volume (mg/L) of calcium carbonate ($CaCO_3$) in the water. Although water hardness usually only measures the total concentrations of calcium and magnesium, iron, aluminium, and manganese may also be present at elevated levels in some geographical locations.

Types of hard water

Hard water is categorised by the ions found in the water. A distinction is also made between 'temporary' and 'permanent' hard water.

Temporary hardness: Temporary hardness is caused by a combination of calcium ions and bicarbonate ions in the water. It can be removed by boiling the water or by the addition of lime. Boiling promotes the formation of carbonate from the bicarbonate and precipitates calcium carbonate out of solution, leaving water that is softer upon cooling.

The following is the equilibrium reaction when calcium carbonate ($CaCO_3$) is dissolved in water:

Upon heating, less CO_2 is able to dissolve into the water. Since there is not enough CO_2 around, the reaction cannot proceed from left to right, and therefore the $CaCO_3$ will not dissolve as rapidly. Instead, the reaction is forced to the left to reestablish equilibrium, and solid $CaCO_3$ is formed. Boiling the water will remove hardness as long as the solid $CaCO_3$ that precipitates out is removed. After cooling, if enough time passes the water will pick up CO_2 from the air and the reaction will again proceed from left to right, allowing the $CaCO_3$ to "re-dissolve" into the water.

Permanent hardness: Permanent hardness is hardness that cannot be removed by boiling. It is usually caused by the presence of calcium and magnesium sulphates and/or chlorides in the water, which become more soluble as the temperature rises. Despite the name, permanent hardness can be removed using a water softener or ion exchange column. Hard water causes scaling, which is the left over mineral deposits that are formed after the hard water had evaporated, this is also known as limescale. The scale can clog pipes, ruin water heaters, coat the insides of tea and coffee pots, and decrease the life of toilet flushing units.

Similarly, insoluble salt residues, that remain in hair after shampooing with hard water, tend to leave hair rougher and harder to untangle. In industrial settings, water hardness must be constantly monitored to avoid costly breakdowns in boilers, cooling towers, and other equipment that comes in contact with water. Hardness is controlled by the addition of chemicals and by large-scale softenings with zeolite and ion exchange resins.

Hard water softening

It is often desirable to soften hard water, as it does not readily form lather with soap. Soap is wasted when trying to form lather, and in the process, scum forms. Hard water may be treated to reduce the effects of scaling and to make it more suitable for laundry and bathing.

Process: A water softener works on the principle of cation or ion exchange in which ions of the hardness minerals are exchanged for sodium or potassium ions, effectively reducing the concentration of hardness minerals to tolerable levels.

The most economical way to soften household water is with an ion exchange water softener. This unit uses sodium chloride to recharge beads made of the ion exchange resins that exchange hardness mineral ions for sodium ions. Artificial or natural zeolites can also be used. As the hard water passes through and around the beads, the hardness mineral ions are preferentially absorbed, displacing the sodium ions. This process is called ion exchange. When the bead or sodium zeolite has a low concentration of sodium ions left, it is exhausted, and can no longer soften water.

The resin is recharged by flushing with saltwater. The high excess concentration of sodium ions alter the equilibrium between the ions in solution and the ions held on the surface of the resin, resulting in replacement of the hardness mineral ions on the resin or zeolite with sodium ions. The resulting saltwater and mineral ion solution is then rinsed away, and the resin is ready to start the process all over again. This cycle can be repeated many times.

Some softening processes in industry use the same method, but on a much larger scale. These methods create an enormous amount of salty water that is costly to treat and dispose of. Temporary hardness, caused by hydrogen carbonate (or bicarbonate) ions, can be removed by boiling. For example, calcium hydrogen carbonate, often present in temporary hard water, is boiled in a kettle to remove the hardness. In the process, a scale forms on the inside of the kettle in a process known as "furring of kettles". This scale is composed of calcium carbonate.

$$Ca(HCO_3)_2 \rightarrow CaCO_3 + CO_2 + H_2O$$

Hardness can also be reduced with a lime-soda ash treatment. This process, developed by Thomas Clark in 1841, involves the addition of slaked lime (calcium hydroxide—Ca(OH)2) to a hard water supply to convert the hydrogen carbonate hardness to carbonate, which precipitates and can be removed by filtration:

$$Ca(HCO_3)_2 + Ca(OH)_2 \rightarrow 2CaCO_3 + 2H_2O$$

The addition of sodium carbonate also softens permanently hard water containing calcium sulphate, as the calcium ions form calcium carbonate which precipitates out and sodium sulphate is formed which is soluble. The calcium carbonate that is formed sinks to the bottom. Sodium sulphate has no effect on the hardness of water.

$$Na_2CO_3 + CaSO_4 \rightarrow Na_2SO_4 + CaCO_3$$

Water Softener

A water softener reduces the calcium, magnesium, and to some degree manganese and ferrous iron ion concentration in hard water. These "hardness ions" cause three major kinds of problems. The metal ions react with soaps and calcium sensitive detergents, hindering their ability to lather properly and forming an unsightly precipitate- the familiar scum or "bathtub ring". Presence of "hardness ions" also inhibits the cleaning effect of detergent formulations. More seriously, calcium and magnesium carbonates tend to adhere to the surfaces of pipes and heat exchanger surfaces.

The resulting scale build-up can restrict water flow in pipes. In boilers, the deposits act as thermal insulation that impedes the flow of heat into the water; this not only reduces heating efficiency, but allows the metal to overheat which, in a pressurized system, can lead to failure." The presence of ions in an electrolyte can also lead to galvanic corrosion, in which one metal will preferentially corrode when in contact with another type of metal. The use of water softeners can aggravate this and cause sacrificial anodes in hot water heaters to corrode more quickly.

Conventional water-softening devices intended for household use depend on an ion-exchange resin in which "hardness" ions trade places with sodium ions that are electrostatically bound to the anionic functional groups of the polymeric resin. A class of minerals known as zeolites also exhibits ion-exchange properties; these minerals were widely used in earlier water softeners.

Working

The water to be treated passes through a bed of the resin. Negatively-charged resins absorb and bind metal ions, which are positively charged. The resins initially contain univalent hydrogen, sodium or potassium ions, which exchange with divalent calcium and magnesium ions in the water. This exchange eliminates precipitation and soap scum formation. As the water passes through both kinds of resin, the hardness ions replace the hydrogen, sodium or potassium ions which are released into the water. The "harder" the water, the more hydrogen, sodium or potassium ions are released from the resin and into the water.

Effects of sodium

For people on a low-sodium diet, the increase in sodium levels in the water can be significant, especially when treating very "hard" water. A paper by Kansas State University gives an example: "A person who drinks two liters (2L) of softened, extremely hard water (assume 30 gpg) will consume about 480 mg more sodium (2L x 30 gpg x 8 mg/L/gpg = 480 mg), than if unsoftened water is consumed." This is a significant amount, as they state:

"The American Heart Association (AHA) suggests that the 3 percent of the population who must follow a severe, salt-restricted diet should not consume more than 500 mg of sodium a day. AHA suggests that no more than 10 percent of this sodium intake should come from water. The EPA's draft guideline of 20 mg/L for water protects people who are most susceptible."

Most people who are concerned with the added sodium in the water generally have one faucet in the house that bypasses the softener, or have a reverse osmosis unit installed for the drinking water and cooking water, which was designed for desalinisation of sea water.

As these resins become loaded with hardness ions they gradually lose their effectiveness and must be regenerated by passing a concentrated brine or acid solution through them. Most of the salt used for regeneration gets flushed out of the system and may be released into the soil or sewer. The use of hydrochloric or sulphuric acid has been used as a regenerant. These processes can be damaging to the environment, especially in arid regions. Some jurisdictions prohibit such release and require users to dispose of the spent brine at an approved site or to use a commercial service company.

Most water softener manufacturers provide metered control valves to minimise the frequency of regeneration. It is also possible on most units to adjust the amount of salt used for each regeneration. Both of these steps are recommended to minimize the impact of water softeners on the environment and conserve on salt use. Using acid to regenerate lowers the pH of the regeneration waste.

In industrial scale water softening plants, the effluent flow from re-generation process can be very significant. Under certain conditions, such as when the effluent is discharged in admixture with domestic sewage, the calcium and magnesium salts may precipitate out as hardness scale on the inside of the discharge pipe. This can build up to such an extent so as to block the pipe as happened to a major chlor-alkali plant on the south Wales coast in the 1980s.

Water Quality

Water quality is the physical, chemical and biological characteristics of water, characterised through the methods of hydrometry. The primary bases for such characterisation are parameters which relate to drinking water, safety of human contact and for health of ecosystems. The vast majority of surface water on the planet is neither potable nor toxic. This remains true even if sea water in the oceans isn't counted. Another general perception of water quality is that of a simple property that tells whether water is polluted or not.

In fact, water quality is a very complex subject, in part because water is a complex medium intrinsically tied to the ecology of the Earth. Industrial pollution is a major cause of water pollution, as well as runoff from agricultural areas, urban stormwater runoff and discharge of untreated sewage (especially in developing countries).

Contaminants that may be in untreated water include microorganisms such as viruses and bacteria; inorganic contaminants such as salts and metals; pesticides and herbicides; organic chemical contaminants from industrial processes and petroleum use; and radioactive contaminants. Water quality depends on the local geology and ecosystem, as well as human uses such as sewage dispersion, industrial pollution, use of water bodies as a heat sink, and overuse.

The Environmental Protection Agency prescribes regulations that limit the amount of certain contaminants in the water provided by public water systems for tap water. Food and Drug Administration (FDA) regulations establish limits for contaminants in bottled water that must provide the same protection for public health. Drinking water, including bottled water, may reasonably be expected to contain at least small amounts of some contaminants. The presence of these contaminants does not necessarily indicate that the water poses a health risk.

Some people use water purification technology to remove contaminants from the municipal water supply they get in their homes, or from local pumps or bodies of water. For people who get water from a local stream, lake, or aquifer, their drinking water is not filtered by the local government. Toxic substances and high populations of certain microorganisms can present a health hazard for non-drinking purposes such as irrigation, swimming, fishing, rafting, boating, and industrial uses. These conditions may also impact wildlife which use the water for drinking or as a Habitat.

Measurement of Water Quality

The complexity of water quality as a subject is reflected

in the many types of measurements of water and Wastewater quality indicators. In England and Wales acceptable levels are listed in the Water Supply (Water Quality) Regulations 1989. These measurements include:

— Conductivity
— Dissolved Oxygen(DO)
— pH
— Colour of water
— Taste and odour (geosmin, 2-methylisoborneol (MIB), etc)
— Turbidity
— Total suspended solids (TSS)
— Dissolved metals and salts (sodium, chloride, potassium, calcium, manganese, magnesium)
— Chemical oxygen demand (COD)
— Biochemical oxygen demand (BOD)
— Microorganisms such as fecal coliform bacteria (Escherichia coli), Cryptosporidium, and Giardia lamblia
— Nutrients, such as nitrogen and phosphorus
— Dissolved metals and metalloids (lead, Mercury (element), arsenic, etc.)
— Dissolved organics: Coloured Dissolved Organic Matter (CDOM), Dissolved Organic Carbon (DOC)
— Temperature
— Pesticides
— Heavy Metals
— Pharmaceuticals
— Hormone analogs

More complex measurements that must be made in a lab setting require a water sample to be collected, preserved, and analysed at another location. Making these complex measurements can be expensive. Because direct measurements of water quality can be expensive, ongoing monitoring programs are typical conducted by government agencies. Individuals interested in monitoring water quality who cannot afford or manage lab scale analysis can also use biological indicators to get a general reading of water quality.

Biological monitoring metrics have been developed in many places, and one widely used measure is the presence and abundance of members of the insect orders Ephemeroptera, Plecoptera and Trichoptera (EPT). EPT indexes will naturally vary from region to region, but generally, within a region, the greater the number of taxa from these orders, the better the water quality. A number of websites originating in the United States offer guidance on developing a monitoring program and identifying members of these and other aquatic insect orders.

Water Treatment Process

Water treatment describes a process used to make water more acceptable for a desired end-use. These can include use as drinking water, industrial processes, medical and many other uses. The goal of all water treatment process is to remove existing components in the water, improving it for subsequent use. The goal may be to allow treated water to discharge into the natural environment without adverse ecological impact. These processes may be physical such as settling, chemical such as disinfection or coagulation, or biological such as lagooning, slow sand filtration or activated sludge.

Water purification is the removal of contaminants from untreated water to produce drinking water that is pure enough for its intended use, most commonly human consumption. Substances that are removed during the process of drinking water treatment include bacteria, algae, viruses, fungi, minerals such as iron and sulphur, and man-made chemical pollutants.

Sewage Treatment Process

Sewage treatment is the process that removes the majority of the contaminants from wastewater or sewage and produces both a liquid effluent suitable for disposal to the natural environment and a sludge. To be effective, sewage must be conveyed to a treatment plant by appropriate pipes and infrastructure and the process itself must be subject to regulation and controls.

Some wastewaters require different and sometimes specialised treatment methods. At the simplest level, treatment of sewage and most wastewaters is carried out through separation of solids from liquids, usually by settlement. By progressively converting dissolved material into solids, usually a biological floc which is then settled out, an effluent stream of increasing purity is produced.

Cooling towers can also scale up and corrode, but left untreated, the warm, dirty water they can contain will encourage bacteria to grow, and Legionnaires' Disease can be the fatal consequence. Domestic water can become unsafe to drink if proper hygiene measures are neglected.

Water Purification Process

Water purification is the process of removing contaminants from a raw water source. The goal is to produce water for a specific purpose with a treatment profile designed to limit the inclusion of specific materials; most water is purified for human consumption. Water purification may also be designed for a variety of other purposes, including to meet the requirements of medical, pharmacology, chemical and industrial applications. Methods include, but are not limited to: ultraviolet light, filtration, water softening, reverse osmosis, ultrafiltration, molecular stripping, deionisation, and carbon treatment.

Water purification may remove: particulate sand; suspended particles of organic material; parasites, Giardia; Cryptosporidium; bacteria; algae; virus; fungi; etc. Minerals calcium, silica, magnesium, etc. and toxic metals (lead, copper, chromium etc). Some purification may be elective in the purification process, including smell (hydrogen sulphide remediation), taste (mineral extraction), and appearance (iron incapsulation). Governments usually dictate the standards for drinking water quality. These standards will require minimum / maximum set points of contaminants and the inclusion of control elements that produce drinking water.

Quality standards in many countries require specific amounts of disinfectant (such as chlorine or ozone) in the water after it leaves the water treatment plant (WTP), to reduce the risk of re-contamination while the water is in the distribution system. Ground water (usually supplied as well water) is typically a more economical choice than surface water (from rivers, lakes and streams) as a source for drinking, as it is inherently pre-filtered by the aquifer from which it is extracted. Over large areas of the world, aquifers are recharged as part of the hydrologic cycle.

In more arid regions, water from an aquifer will have a limited output and can take thousands of years to recharge. Surface water is locally more abundant where subsurface formations do not function as aquifers; however, ground water is far more abundant than the more-visible surface water. Surface water is a typical raw water source used to make drinking water where it is abundant and where ground water is unavailable or of poor quality. However, it is much more exposed to human activity and its byproducts. As a water source it is carefully monitored for the presence of a variety of contaminants by the WTP operators.

It is not possible to tell whether water is safe to drink just by looking at it. Simple procedures such as boiling or the use of a household activated carbon filter are not sufficient for treating all the possible contaminants that may be present in water from an unknown source. Even natural spring water—considered safe for all practical purposes in the 1800s—must now be tested before determining what kind of treatment, if any, is needed. Chemical analysis, while expensive, is the only way to obtain the information necessary for deciding on method of purification.

Water Supply

The water emerging from some deep ground water may have fallen as rain many decades, hundreds, thousands or in some cases millions of years ago. Soil and rock layers naturally filter the ground water to a high degree of clarity before it is pumped to the treatment plant. Such water may emerge as springs, artesian springs, or may be extracted from boreholes or wells. Deep ground water is generally of very high bacteriological quality, but the water typically is rich in dissolved solids, especially carbonates and sulphates of calcium and magnesium.

Depending on the strata through which the water has flowed, other ions may also be present including chloride, and bicarbonate. There may be a requirement to reduce the iron or manganese content of this water to make it pleasant for drinking, cooking, and laundry use. Disinfection may also be required. Where groundwater recharge is practised, it is equivalent to lowland surface waters for treatment purposes.

Shallow groundwaters: Water emerging from shallow groundwaters is usually abstracted from wells or boreholes. The bacteriological quality can be variable depending on the nature of the catchment. A variety of soluble materials may be present including (rarely) potentially toxic metals such as zinc, copper or arsenic. Arsenic contamination of groundwater is a serious problem in some areas, notably from shallow wells in Bangladesh and West Bengal in the Ganges Delta.

Upland lakes and reservoirs: Typically located in the headwaters of river systems, upland reservoirs are usually sited above any human habitation and may be surrounded by a protective zone to restrict the opportunities for contamination. Bacteria and pathogen levels are usually low, but some bacteria, protozoa or algae will be present. Where uplands are forested or peaty, humic acids can colour the water. Many upland sources have low pH which require adjustment.

Rivers, canals and low land reservoirs: Low land surface waters will have a significant bacterial load and may also contain algae, suspended solids and a variety of dissolved constituents. Atmospheric water generation is a new technology that can provide high quality drinking water by extracting water from the air by cooling the air and thus condensing water vapour. Rainwater harvesting or fog collection which collect water from the atmosphere can be used especially in areas with significant dry seasons and in areas which experience fog even when there is little rain.

Pumping and containment: The majority of water must be pumped from its source or directed into pipes or holding tanks. To avoid adding contaminants to the water, this physical infrastructure must be made from appropriate materials and constructed so that accidental contamination does not occur.

Screening: The first step in purifying surface water is to remove large debris such as sticks, leaves, trash and other large particles which may interfere with subsequent purification steps. Most deep groundwater does not need screening before other purification steps.

Storage: Water from rivers may also be stored in bankside reservoirs for periods between a few days and many months to allow natural biological purification to take place. This is especially important if treatment is by slow sand filters. Storage reservoirs also provide a buffer against short periods of drought or to allow water supply to be maintained during transitory pollution incidents in the source river.

Pre-conditioning: Many waters rich in hardness salts are treated with soda-ash (Sodium carbonate) to precipitate calcium carbonate out utilising the common ion effect.

Pre-chlorination: In many plants the incoming water was chlorinated to minimise the growth of fouling organisms on the pipe-work and tanks. Because of the potential adverse quality effects, this has largely been discontinued.

Widely varied techniques are available to remove the fine solids, micro-organisms and some dissolved inorganic and organic materials. The choice of method will depend on the quality of the water being treated, the cost of the treatment process and the quality standards expected of the processed water.

pH Adjustment

Distilled water has an average pH of 7 (neither alkaline nor acidic) and sea water has an average pH of 8.3 (slightly alkaline). If the water is acidic (lower than 7), lime or soda ash is added to raise the pH. Lime is the more common of the two additives because it is cheap, but it also adds to the resulting water hardness. Making the water slightly alkaline ensures that coagulation and flocculation processes work effectively and also helps to minimise the risk of lead being dissolved from lead pipes and lead solder in pipe fittings.

Flocculation is a process which starts with clarifying the water. Clarifying means removing any turbidity or colour so that the water is clear and colourless. Clarification is done by causing a precipitate to form in the water. Initially the precipitate forms as very small particles but as the water is gently stirred, these particles stick together to form bigger particles—this process is sometimes called flocculation. Many of the small particles that were originally present in the raw water absorb onto the surface of these small precipitate particles and so get incorporated into the larger particles that coagulation produces.

In this way the coagulated precipitate takes most of the suspended matter out of the water and is then filtered off, generally by passing the mixture through a coarse sand filter or sometimes through a mixture of sand and granulated anthracite (high quality coal). Anthracite, with its high carbon content, is able to absorb much of the organic matter present in solution and this can remove odour and taste from the water.

A precipitate that is widely used to clarify water is iron (III) hydroxide. This is formed first by adjusting (if necessary) the pH of the incoming water to above 7 (by adding lime or sodium hydroxide), then by adding a solution of an iron (III) compound such as iron (III) chloride. Iron (III) hydroxide is extremely insoluble and forms even at a pH as low as 7. Aluminium hydroxide is also widely used as the flocculating precipitate.

Sedimentation

Water exiting the flocculation basin may enter the sedimentation basin, also called a clarifier or settling basin.

It is a large tank with slow flow, allowing floc to settle to the bottom. The sedimentation basin is best located close to the flocculation basin so the transit between does not permit settlement or floc break up. Sedimentation basins can be in the shape of a rectangle, where water flows from end to end, or circular where flow is from the center outward. Sedimentation basin outflow is typically over a weir so only a thin top layer-furthest from the sediment-exits.

The amount of floc that settles out of the water is dependent on the time the water spends in the basin and the depth of the basin. The retention time of the water must therefore be balanced against the cost of a larger basin. The minimum clarifier retention time is normally 4 hours. A deep basin will allow more floc to settle out than a shallow basin. This is because large particles settle faster than smaller ones, so large particles bump into and integrate smaller particles as they settle. In effect, large particles sweep vertically though the basin and clean out smaller particles on their way to the bottom.

As particles settle to the bottom of the basin a layer of sludge is formed on the floor of the tank. This layer of sludge must be removed and treated. The amount of sludge that is generated is significant, often 3%-5% of the total volume of water that is treated. The cost of treating and disposing of the sludge can be a significant part of the operating cost of a water treatment plant. The tank may be equipped with mechanical cleaning devices that continually clean the bottom of the tank or the tank can be taken out of service when the bottom needs to be cleaned.

Filtration of Water

After separating most floc, the water is filtered as the final step to remove remaining suspended particles and unsettled floc. The most common type of filter is a rapid sand filter. Water moves vertically through sand which often has a layer of activated carbon or anthracite coal above the sand. The top layer removes organic compounds, which contribute to taste and odour.

The space between sand particles is larger than the smallest suspended particles, so simple filtration is not enough. Most particles pass through surface layers but are trapped in pore spaces or adhere to sand particles. Effective filtration extends into the depth of the filter. This property of the filter is key to its operation: if the top layer of sand were to block all the particles, the filter would quickly clog.

To clean the filter, water is passed quickly upward through the filter, opposite the normal direction to remove embedded particles. Prior to this, compressed air may be blown up through the bottom of the filter to break up the compacted filter media to aid the backwashing process; this is known as air scouring. This contaminated water can be disposed of, along with the sludge from the sedimentation basin, or it can be recycled by mixing with the raw water entering the plant.

Advantages:

- Filters out much smaller particles than paper and sand filters can.
- Filters out virtually all particles larger than their specified pore sizes.
- They are quite thin and so liquids flow through them fairly rapidly.
- They are reasonably strong and so can withstand pressure differences across them of typically 2-5 atmospheres.
- They can be cleaned (back flushed) and reused.

Membrane filters are widely used for filtering both drinking water and sewage (for reuse). For drinking water, membrane filters can remove virtually all particles larger than 0.2 um-including Giardia and cryptosporidium. Membrane filters are an effective form of tertiary treatment when it is desired to reuse the water for industry, for limited domestic purposes, or before discharging the water into a river that is used by towns further downstream. They are widely used in industry, particularly for beverage preparation (including bottled water). However no filtration can remove substances that are actually dissolved in the water such as phosphorus, nitrates and heavy metal ions.

Slow sand filters

Slow sand filters may be used where there is sufficient land and space as the water must be passed very slowly through the filters. These filters rely on biological treatment processes for their action rather than physical filtration. The filters are carefully constructed using graded layers of sand with the coarsest at the top and finest at the base. Drains at the base convey treated water away for disinfection. Filtration depends on the development of a thin biological layer on the surface of the filter.

An effective slow sand filter may remain in service for many weeks or even months if the pre-treatment is well designed and produces water with a very low available nutrient level which physical methods of treatment rarely achieve. Very low nutrient levels allow water to be safely sent through distribution system with very low disinfectant levels thereby reducing consumer irritation over offensive levels of chlorine and chlorine by-products. Slow sand filters are not backwashed; they are maintained by having the top layer of sand scraped off when flow is eventually obstructed by biological growth.

Ultrafiltration

Ultrafiltration membranes are a relatively new development; they use polymer film with chemically formed microscopic pores that can be used in place of granular media to filter water effectively without coagulants. The type of membrane media determines how much pressure is needed to drive the water through and what sizes of micro-organisms can be filtered out.

Disinfection

Disinfection is accomplished both by filtering out harmful microbes and also by adding disinfectant chemicals in the last step in purifying drinking water. Water is disinfected to kill any pathogens which pass through the filters. Possible pathogens include viruses, bacteria, including Escherichia coli, Campylobacter and Shigella, and protozoans, including G. lamblia and other Cryptosporidia.

In most developed countries, public water supplies are required to maintain a residual disinfecting agent throughout the distribution system, in which water may remain for days before reaching the consumer. Following the introduction of any chemical disinfecting agent, the water is usually held in temporary storage—often called a contact tank or clear well to allow the disinfecting action to complete.

Chlorination: The most common disinfection method is some form of chlorine or its compounds such as chloramine or chlorine dioxide. Chlorine is a strong oxidant that rapidly kills many harmful micro-organisms. Because chlorine is a toxic gas, there is a danger of a release associated with its use. This problem is avoided by the use of sodium hypochlorite, which is a relatively inexpensive solution that releases free chlorine when dissolved in water.

Chlorine solutions can be generated on site by electrolysing common salt solutions. A solid form, calcium hypochlorite exists that releases chlorine on contact with water. Handling the solid, however, requires greater routine human contact through opening bags and pouring than the use of gas cylinders or bleach which are more easily automated.

The generation of liquid sodium hypochlorite is both inexpensive and safer than the use of gas or solid chlorine. All forms of chlorine are widely used despite their respective drawbacks. One drawback is that chlorine from any source reacts with natural organic compounds in the water to form potentially harmful chemical by-products trihalomethanes (THMs) and haloacetic acids (HAAs), both of which are carcinogenic in large quantities and regulated by the United States Environmental Protection Agency (EPA).

The formation of THMs and haloacetic acids may be minimised by effective removal of as many organics from the water as possible prior to chlorine addition. Although chlorine is effective in killing bacteria, it has limited effectiveness against protozoans that form cysts in water. Chlorine dioxide is another faster-acting disinfectant. It is, however, relatively rarely used, because in some circumstances it may create excessive amounts of chlorite, which is a by-product regulated to low allowable levels in the USA. Chlorine dioxide is made in water and added/ used in water to avoid gas handling problems; chlorine dioxide gas accumulations may spontaneously detonate.

Chloramines are another chlorine-based disinfectant. Although chloramine is not as strong of an oxidant it does provide a longer lastinge residual than free chlorine, and it not form THMs or haloacetic acids. It is possible to convert chlorine to chloramine by adding ammonia to the water after addition of chlorine: The chlorine and ammonia react to form chloramine. Water distribution systems disinfected with chloramines may experience nitrification, wherein ammonia is used a nutrioent for bacterial growth, with nitrates being generated as a byproduct.

Ozone (O_3) is a relatively unstable molecule "free radical" of oxygen which readily gives up one atom of oxygen providing a powerful oxidising agent which is toxic to most water borne organisms. It is a very strong, broad spectrum disinfectant that is widely used in Europe. It is an effective method to inactivate harmful protozoans that form cysts. It also works well against almost all other pathogens. Ozone is made by passing oxygen through ultraviolet light or a "cold" electrical discharge. To use ozone as a disinfectant, it must be created on site and added to the water by bubble contact.

Some of the advantages of ozone include the production of relatively fewer dangerous by-products and the lack of taste and odour produced by ozonation. Although fewer by-products are formed by ozonation, it has been discovered that the use of ozone produces a small amount of the suspected carcinogen Bromate, although little Bromine should be present in treated water. Another one of the main disadvantages of ozone is that it leaves no disinfectant residual in the water.

Ozone has been used in drinking water plants since 1906 where the first industrial ozonation plant was built in Nice, France. The U.S. Food and Drug Administration has accepted ozone as being safe; and it is applied as an anti-microbiological agent for the treatment, storage, and processing of foods. UV radiation (light) is very effective at inactivating cysts, as long as the water has a low level of colour so the UV can pass through without being absorbed. The main disadvantage to the use of UV radiation is that, like ozone treatment, it leaves no residual disinfectant in the water.

Because neither ozone nor UV radiation leaves a residual disinfectant in the water, it is sometimes necessary to add a residual disinfectant after they are used. This is often done through the addition of chloramines, discussed above as a primary disinfectant. When used in this manner, chloramines provide an effective residual disinfectant with very little of the negative aspects of chlorination.

9

Hotel Security Design

The demand for more secure facilities, coupled with computerised technology and its growing integration capabilities, is making access control and intrusion detection a science of its own. The design of a system incorporating the security functions far too often emphasises the technological aspects of access control and intrusion detection rather than the basic design considerations associated with the system's intended use. Security needs and requirements must be determined early in the project programming and definition process. Burglary, industrial espionage, shoplifting, riots, vandalism, assault, rape, murder, and employee theft are crimes that imperil lives and drive up the cost of doing business.

Designing a facility without security in mind can lead to expensive lawsuits, injuries, and retrofitting of protection measures after the facility is complete. As a result, the designer needs to factor basic security system design and integration considerations into the design. These include, at a minimum, the purpose and objectives of the security system, the physical and operational environment, and the anticipated complexity and responsiveness of the system to be employed.

Security concerns need to be defined by the owner, with subsequent assistance in formulating system objectives and design details provided by a security architect/engineer. With the proliferation of security devices, along with rapid advances in system technology, security planning requires specialists with a working knowledge not only of the devices themselves, but also of the various integration possibilities for joining discrete systems for increased facility monitoring effectiveness.

Electronic intrusion detection, perimeter protection, surveillance, and access control techniques are contributing elements in a total security system and design approach. Each technique has distinct technological and operational characteristics, and environmental reactions, along with differing requirements for installation and maintenance.

To justify the use of an electronic access control system, the owner will need to know what assets and areas are to be protected along with what the potential loss or damages will cost. Each security situation is unique; there are no package solutions. The type of alarm system needs to be defined, as well as the allowable false alarm rate tolerance. The proposed transmission system from sensors to alarms needs to be considered; for example, radio waves, hard wired, dedicated circuits, or multiplexed fibrw-optic systems. Weather, water surfaces, wildlife, vegetation, corrosive condition of acid rain, or salt are the main factors that affect the security system. Information is needed on topographic conditions of the site and human-made impacts such as physical structures, traffic patterns, and industry controls.

The security design process is a key element in the overall project development plan. Most designers perform their design and integration tasks according to specific phases. Generally, these phases of the design process include: survey and report; conceptual design; preliminary and final design; bid and construction; and, turnover and operation. It is imperative that the requirements for security systems be incorporated at the earliest possible phase of planning. Requirements for security systems normally result from the initial survey and report phase, are formally identified as functional requirements and are reflected in an initial security design solution in the conceptual design phase. These requirements are the principal responsibility of the owner/user to develop, and they form the basis for quality control and review of the more detailed phases of engineering and system implementation planning.

Establishing and baselining system requirements early on in the design process can allow the design team to avoid the costly oversight and disruptive consideration of security requirements at later phases of major design and construction. Each site or facility to receive a security system will offer the designer unique differences in local circumstances and conditions. As a result, the requirements for individual facility protective measures must be evaluated on a case-by-case basis.

Specific factors that need to be evaluated when designing integrated systems include: the mission criticality of the facility and its assets; the threats anticipated for each of the assets, including current threat assessments and owner concerns; the vulnerability and consequence of loss for each asset to be protected given the anticipated threats; local security response force capabilities; and design constraints such as monetary, operational, and environmental limitations.

Once the functional baseline of the system has been established, other considerations become the basis of selecting appropriate security measures. These include the physical and operational environment, the need for protection-in-depth, and the complexity and sensitivity of the subsystems to be employed. The system designer must consider these factors in the analysis of proposed security measures, including upgrade efforts.

Each type of security system is intended to perform a specific function within a total system design. Basic factors to be considered in selecting security measures include, but are not limited to, the physical environment, operational environment, and the need for protection-in-depth of critical assets. The end results of the failure of the designer to consider these factors are a non-responsive system, an ineffective system, and an unacceptable level of false and nuisance alarm occurrences.

A false alarm is an alarm indication that results from the malfunction anywhere in the system hardware or software between the outermost sensor and the control and display central annunciator. A nuisance alarm is an alarm condition that is caused by sensor system response to outside stimuli such as environmental conditions, vehicle traffic, electrical power line disturbances, electromagnetic interference, and vibration-causing machinery, to name a few. Both sources of system degradation, false alarms and nuisance alarms, demand that the designer carefully consider the physical environment and operational environment, as well as the most effective protection-in-depth schemes.

The state-of-the-art of electronic security systems presents a series of options for the designer that will result in the selection of best, acceptable, or unacceptable technology and other countermeasure options. In particular, sensor and CCTV elements are designed to perform within specific environmental parameters and failure to adhere to accepted application requirements for each technology will lead to degraded performance, excessive nuisance alarms, or both.

In addition to the real system performance costs associated with a degraded detection and assessment capability, hidden costs of such misapplication are in the real dollar cost of repair/retrofit and in the loss of owner confidence in the system. The security system designer needs to carefully analyse the physical environment to determine and document the host of physical environment variables that may adversely affect the performance of electronic components.

In the exterior physical security environment include the factors of wind, temperature extremes, fog, foliage, salt, rain/standing water, condition of fence fabric, location of underground utilities, and other environmental influences that would cause sensor and other technologies to not respond within specified performance limits. The selection and placement of interior sensors must consider the heating, ventilating, and air conditioning (HVAC) location; heat sources; transient light; vibration; moving machinery; dust; and moisture/humidity. The assignment and positioning of CCTV must consider the aspects of sun glare, even and sufficient distribution of artificial light, temperature, wind, and the monitoring location.

The most critical consideration for the security designer is that the initial requirements analysis phase of system design should identify all potential sources of environmentally generated stimuli which could adversely impact overall system performance. The subsequent preliminary design phase will then be able to accommodate these design constraints through the selection of the appropriate technology, combining technology with other measures and/or modification of the environment. Another aspect of the physical environment to be considered by the designer is the notion of security control through environmental design. This concept involves a review of the physical environment to be protected and the use of facility and site design concepts to reduce the inclination of the physical environment to support criminal behaviour.

Environmental design strategies include the use of natural access control through placement of walkways, natural surveillance through the elimination of unsafe areas, and the use of improved lighting. Included within the environmental design approach are concepts of individual territoriality, effective use of space, and manipulation of the natural environment to deter potential threats.

Operational issues place two types of constraints on the architect and engineer as designers: physical and owner-required. An example of the former is a facility perimeter that must adapt to site constraints, property availability, or usage. Owner-required issues include the need to compartmentalise certain operations, limitations on location and design of access control portals, and placement of handicapped access. Distinct owner groups must maintain their own separate operations that include their own safety, efficiency, and a variety of other mission performance criteria within which the security system must adapt. Each of these unique requirements may result in selection or rejection of specific security system solutions.

Rejection of a technology is usually due to an inability to operate effectively within the operational environment or as a result of a potential for impeding routine organisational operations. Specific examples of these instances include rejection of CCTV assessment in the manufacturing environment and rejection of access control portals at a key entrance gate.

Depending upon the criticality of the asset in terms of mission or replacement value, the security designer attempts to establish a series of integrated protective measures around the assets to be protected. The strategy of forming layers of protection is known as designing for protection-in-depth.

The purpose of the protective layers is to make it progressively more difficult for an intruder to reach critical targets and to escape undetected. These protection-in-depth schemes also build time delays into the intruder's path to the asset, calculated to allow for arrival of the response force and neutralisation of the threat before reaching the asset. Technology selection and placement are critical to forming effective protection-in-depth schemes and must be made in such a pattern as to maximise the potential that the intruder will pass through the desired detection pattern.

A well-conceived security system should detect penetration attempts as far away from the asset to be protected as is practical, and at several points along the path of the intruder to the asset. The area where the system detects an intrusion is defined as a zone or line of detection. A comprehensive system protecting highly critical assets may require multiple lines or zones of detection.

The security designer determines the number of zones to be implemented and their configuration according to the perceived degree of protection required to ensure a rapid response. Also considered are the possible intrusion schemes that might be launched against the defence and the neutralising capacity of the security forces.

The security system designer must constantly strive to make the probability of detecting and assessing the nature of an intrusion 100 per cent and the potential for nuisance and false alarms zero per cent. Both objectives in their extremes are ideals and most likely unattainable given our relevant inability to absolutely control the environment, technology limitations, and unexpected threat capabilities. Probability of detection of individual sensors and detection configurations is the ratio of the total number of successful test intrusion detections to the total number of attempted test intrusions. Probability of detection can be expressed in terms of individual sensors or as an indication of the complete security system, considering all of its individual components together.

Most commercially available interior systems individually claim a ;

of 0.95, while other sensors designed to operate in harsh or outside environments generally are rated to have a PD of 0.90 for each sensor. This latter rating is usually based upon tests of actual intrusions by relatively knowledgeable intruders into the sensor field in a controlled environment. A higher overall system rate can be obtained by combining sensors in a protection-in-depth scheme. Combining sensors in a protection scheme can increase the likelihood of intruder detection and correspondingly the probability of detection. In any event, PD ultimately needs to be evaluated as a system performance goal rather than as a measure of individual sensor performance.

The probability of successfully detecting an intrusion will depend upon the inherent performance of the component, the method and appropriateness of technology deployment, the type and number of sensors deployed, the environment in which the technology operates, the individual sensor PD, and the competence and knowledge of the intruder.

Security systems should be designed and installed to generate the absolute minimum number of nuisance and false alarms per unit of time. False alarms are differentiated from nuisance alarms in that the former are caused by non-intrusion internal phenomena inherent to the system, such as a malfunction, while the latter are valid alarms generated by physical stimuli or environmental phenomena. Careful equipment selection, system design, and effective installation can substantially minimise nuisance to an acceptable level. Since nuisance-alarms are so dependent upon controlling the environment or reducing the sensitivity of the sensing equipment and cannot be completely controlled in the typical installation, the technique of assessing alarm annunciations through CCTV or direct visual observation covering the sensor field is normally used.

The designer must perform the critical integration function of determining an acceptable level and mix of electronic, physical, and procedural measures that will work together to maximise intruder delay, detection, assessment, and speed of response. While this mix will be unique for each site or facility, cost trade-off analyses conducted during the initial design phase will force the selection of certain countermeasures against a perceived threat. Although nuisance alarm sources must be considered in an overall negative light, they nevertheless do provide an actual test of the system to respond to various phenomena.

All sources of false alarms should be eliminated from the system by the designer and installer, although it is often operationally difficult to differentiate between false and nuisance alarms. The security system designer needs to establish acceptable levels of nuisance alarm criteria and false alarm rates, and take particular note of these requirements in the design specifications, subsequent installation, and test of system components.

Integration Considerations

Access control systems in particular relied more on human-power than technology. In cases where technology was integrated with personnel and procedures for access control, managers were faced with reliance on complex processing systems that had limited applications and required major capital expenditures. Today, the security industry offers a wide assortment of capable protective technologies and integrated systems at affordable prices.

Integrated protective systems can include:

— guard personnel,

— responsive procedures for contingencies,

— detection sensors,

— automated access control elements,

— CCTV,

— fibre-optic communication and transmission lines, and

— multiplexed control and display equipment

Integrated security systems are designed to detect and communicate intrusions and other alarm conditions to a central control location for response.

The adequacy of the security force response depends largely upon the ability of the security command and control function to assess reliably the nature of the alarm, and to communicate the circumstances and conditions in the alarm zone to the available response force. The use of CCTV, which is tied into the sensor annunciation system, permits the security system operator to immediately view the alarming sector, to validate the alarm, and to communicate relevant information to the response force. The designer must consider the most cost-effective means to accomplish this system objective.

Integrated security systems can be used to reduce the cost of providing essential security services. Integrated systems permit more economical and efficient use of humanpower usually assigned to building patrols and fixed guard posts. Integrated intrusion detection and access control systems have become electronic extensions of the security organisation by permitting remote monitoring of critical locations at a lower initial equipment cost vs. continuing human-power expenditures. In addition, integrated security technology can be used in place of other physical security measures that cannot be employed because of safety regulations, operational requirements, appearance, layout, cost, or other reasons.

Security technology can augment guard personnel to provide additional protective measures at critical entry points or within a building's high security or sensitive areas. Technology can also provide increased protection-in-depth where the use of multiple protective measures for increased system reliability is considered essential by the owner.

The system designer should ensure that future expansion or upgrades, such as adding new alarm points and electronic access controls, and expanding CCTV coverage, are included in initial system designs and that future upgrades do not force the retrofit of costly control and display equipment. Most state-of-the-art alarm and video control systems are modularly expandable and permit future growth. The integrated system should have an expansion capability sufficient to accommodate modular additions throughout the lifecycle of the installed system.

The security system designer also must keep the system as simple as possible, and carefully consider the interaction of people and hardware. In particular, at the alarm control and monitoring location, it is important to know the operational limitations imposed on the system design in terms of operator sophistication and the inventory of functions to be performed while monitoring the alarm and display. System and component maintainability is also a critical concern for non-redundant items, as is the probability that an item can perform its intended function for a specified interval under stated conditions. As a common system descriptor, meantime-between-failure (MTBF) is a basic measure of reliability for repairable hardware items. MTBF is the mean number of life units during which all parts of the hardware item perform within specified limits, during a particular time interval under defined conditions.

Mean-time-to-repair (MTTR) is a basic measure of maintainability, defined as the sum of corrective maintenance times at any specific level of repair, divided by the total number of failures within an item repaired at that level. The designer must keep these two concepts in mind when preparing the initial and final security designs with specific technologies selected on the basis of these and other criteria.

Unless carefully specified in design and construction documents, system installers may often connect sensors in series to simplify the installation task and to reduce installation costs. This may result in the annunciation of each device in the series as one alarm at the control and display annunciator, without giving the console operator the benefit of knowing which device in the area is causing the alarm. This type of sensor integration is called daisy-chaining. The opposite is called point-for-point integration, where each sensor is wired separately to a common control unit and, upon alarm, the sensor is readily identifiable as the source of the alarm by the control operator. Where direct point-for-point annunciation is a design goal, care should be taken in designing and specifying the control network so that the control console will display an individual sensor zone, CCTV sector, or specific point, as well as facilitate troubleshooting and maintenance.

Different types of sensors may be annunciated separately by sensor zone so that the security system operator can differentiate between sensor types and location. For example, door contact switches would annunciate attempted entry from one approach, the microwave or infrared sensors would annunciate when the intruder enters the room, and the capacitance sensor would annunciate when the intruder attempted to penetrate a given asset. This has the added advantage of providing operator assessment of intruder progress across or through the censored area. At some level within the system, the identification of individual sensor alarms must be possible to enable maintenance personnel to expeditiously identify sensors for maintenance or repair. Wiring sensors individually to the control unit substantially eases troubleshooting, and reduces maintenance cost, as a trade-off against initial increased wiring costs.

The designer must ensure that the security system hardware complies with the applicable codes, standards, and regulations that are in effect for a specific site at the time the design is prepared. This includes safety and legal protective measures such as posted notices. Additionally, security system components located in areas where fire or explosion hazards may exist due to flammable gases or vapours, flammable liquids, combustible dust, or ignitable fibers must be made intrinsically safe.

Intrinsically safe components are those that are incapable of releasing sufficient energy to ignite a specific atmospheric mixture under normal operating conditions. Methods of accomplishing intrinsic safety include either limiting the level of voltage and current, or housing components within sealed conduit or enclosures that would prevent the release of hazardous energy. System integration of protective measures is the primary objective of the security system design process. The designer must effectively combine all physical protective measures with security personnel and procedures.

The designer's selection of which security measures are more effective depends upon several factors, e.g., the availability and capability of the security force to respond within a specific time, the value of the asset, the criticality of the mission, the capabilities of the adversary, budgetary constraints, and a host of other factors. These are all basic considerations factored into the design effort from the beginning. System integration is totally within the hands of the security manager as he or she ponders over the choices appropriate to individual asset protection schemes. Principal design considerations include the physical and operational environment, and the need for the designer to base his or her protection scheme on the need for protection-in-depth.

Integration and Security Design

The nature of threat is the key to security design and integration efforts, in many cases the consequences of loss for a small or medium firm due to even a medium-level threat can be catastrophic when a key business asset has been compromised. Security managers are becoming increasingly convinced that the best defence against dynamic threats and potential catastrophic loss is a fully integrated security programme that carefully and effectively blends architectural, technological, and operational elements into a flexible, responsive system.

The design and integration process is one approach that can be employed by security managers to effectively counter threats and substantially reduce risk or consequence of loss. The process is generic and requires that the manager overlay his or her own security problem in order to arrive at an effective design solution. Some security organisations place undue emphasis upon the selection and application of security personnel or equipment alone without equal consideration of the full range of options and countermeasures that comprise a totally integrated security system. Security managers must avoid the tendency to emphasise a single solution or approach and they must strive to achieve a virtually seamless mix of security countermeasures designed specifically to address anticipated threats and risks.

A security system is an integrated combination of barriers, technologies, personnel, and procedures designed to safeguard personnel, property, and operations. System objectives generally address deterrence, denial, detection, delay, assessment, and response options based upon a precise definition of threat and user requirements. It is essential that the security manager recognise that complete systems incorporate a wide range of measures to achieve stated objectives.

In the case of a fully integrated security system, protection objectives are achieved through the selection and integration of protective measures from the following range of subsystem options:

— Facilities, architectural barriers, and space definition to deter and delay the movements of an adversary.

— Physical security equipment designed to detect, assess, and, in some cases, respond to intrusion attempts and unauthorised activities.

— Communications and control and display networks to collect, integrate, transmit, and display alarm and other data for operator response and to control activities of the response force.

— Security personnel to conduct day-to-day security programme operations, management and system support, and response to non-routine events.

— Security procedures to guide security operations and provide overall security programme direction and control.

The essence of design is to invent an order or arrangement of components and details of a system in accordance with a plan. In all cases, whether for security or any other function, a system is designed for a purpose. In the case of security design, the plan is to select and incorporate the various physical elements, personnel, and procedures into a unified system that reduces and controls vulnerability based upon an identified threat.

The essence of integration is to make a whole by bringing together individual parts. For the security manager, system integration is the art of fusing security equipment, facilities, personnel, and procedures together seamlessly in a manner that produces proactive asset protection. The end result is a fully integrated security system that responds effectively to dynamic threats and risks during crisis conditions and, at the same time, functions imperceptibly during normal conditions. Whereas design results in the various security elements responding to a threat or risk, integration fuses them into a workable, day-to-day strategy for effective asset protection.

Facility and site protection plans are always based on the identification of critical assets requiring protection and the identification of appropriate countermeasures for each asset. Barriers, electronic hardware, personnel, and procedures are selected to interplay at key locations within the design scheme to form an integrated subsystem protection scheme. The system concept is formed through the collection of integrated approaches at each asset, facility, and group of facilities sharing a common boundary.

Given the diverse missions found in organisations, the integration of protective measures and resources does not involve a static set of environments. Since threat is normally dynamic at each asset or facility requiring protection, the fully integrated system concept must allow for various scenarios, system redundancy based on criticality, and collective management of available resources in order to achieve the best possible protective design solution.

The security manager is always the final authority

on system options based on requirements stated early in the process and resource constraints. Based on the approved concept, the system engineering and design phase brings the system through the various phases of design steps from preliminary to final design. The end result is a complete system solution. The integration function that follows the design phase is merely a design review phase where the final design and integration solution is formally reviewed by the security manager based upon previously stated requirements. This integration phase is absolutely critical for the security manager to be ensured that the integrated design solution addresses all stated requirements.

More importantly, design solution validation is essential before hardware is acquired and construction is begun. Once validated, the system is ready for the final phases of implementation and ultimate operation by the end user. Feedback on the effectiveness of the system, which is based upon the dynamics of threat and changing missions, is continuously fed into the front-end requirements phase.

The system design and integration process must be front-loaded in order to arrive at a valid security concept. This means the process cannot be expected to yield sufficient results unless it is based upon a thorough analysis of threats and risks, and the relative exposure of individual assets to these conditions. Thus, the requirements analysis phase is critical to develop an optimum system configuration and to determine the relative cost-effectiveness of various physical security options. Initially, assets that need protection are identified, and their criticality to the facility or organisational mission are determined. The attractiveness of these assets to potential threats and their likely modes of attack are evaluated.

Areas in which existing security measures do not

adequately address the threat are identified as vulnerabilities. Based on the results of the on-site requirements analysis, asset-specific countermeasures are applied at various locations on and around the asset to be protected. Selection of individual countermeasures is made by the designer based upon an initial statement of system objectives and functional requirements, such as detecting unauthorised entry and controlling access.

The designer and security manager must consider the full range of potential countermeasures, to include architectural barriers, intrusion detection, access control, and assessment subsystems, as well as procedural and personnel intensive countermeasure combinations appropriate to each asset. Finally, the security concept or design solution is reached through the selection of the best combination of individual, complementary countermeasures for specific assets.

The accumulation of the various countermeasure selections for each asset are considered collectively in terms of total protection afforded and potential for unnecessary redundancy. The overall concept for protection of all grouped assets is then factored into a cohesive design solution, and preliminary lifecycle cost estimates are prepared. The security manager is the final arbiter of which conceptual design solution is offered for more detailed consideration and design in the next phase.

Design solution documentation that forms the basis for subsequent engineering and detailed design includes basic schematic representations or drawings, basic level of information specifications, and a preliminary "order of magnitude" cost estimate of subsystem and overall system costs in equipment, materials, and labour.

System Engineering and Design

This phase uses the system's conceptual design as a basis

and results in a detailed engineering design solution. The security manager is responsible for providing the designer with an established system goal, a full set of functional requirements upon which the design can be based, and a complete system concept that clearly defines how the total system and its elements will function to counter identified threats and reduce vulnerabilities. These are all expected outputs of the initial conceptual design phase incorporated in a security plan. The engineering design consists of both a preliminary and final design.

The preliminary design defines the total project through construction and operation and includes preliminary design drawings, outline specifications, a design analysis, and a total projcct cost estimate. The final design results in complete design documentation to include detailed drawings, specifications, cost estimate, bid requirements, contract forms, and contract conditions. The engineering design also addresses and resolves all of the integration issues associated with the resultant total system and its key elements.

Apart from the identification of equipment and subsystem interface, the engineering design also addresses a concept of operations that describes in clear terms the interplay of personnel and procedures with equipment. The system designer leads a team effort that concentrates on the development of asset; facility; organisational; and site-specific protective measures to deter, delay, deny, detect, assess, and respond to a variety of threats. Typical protective measures detailed in the engineering design phase include architectural barriers, interior and exterior detection technology, closed circuit television assessment/ surveillance equipment and associated support lighting, data transmission and communication, alarm and signal field collectors, and annunciator equipment for control and display.

The security manager must consider appropriate

response procedures along with security force weapons and equipment sufficient to counter the design basis threat. These protective measures must be identified in terms of their individual characteristics and overall contribution to facility/asset protection from an integrated perspective. Considered individually, countermeasures likely offer little in the way of complete protection for critical assets.

A carefully chosen combination of measures keyed specifically to facility and site-unique requirements comprise a wholly effective, integrated approach to asset protection. Selection of the best measures is based on the designer's determination of individual and collective performance, reliability, maintainability, cost, and vulnerability reduction potential. The designer's principal function is to select the various components, elements and subsystems and integrate them into a complete system design. In all cases, selecting and balancing combinations of asset protection measures according to perceived threat and desired results are the key to design integration.

Integration is singled out as a major phase to emphasise the importance of reviewing and balancing the engineering design according to validated requirements and constraints before proceeding to the costly later phases of construction and operation. In effect, the integration phase is really a formal, detailed final design review elevated to a major phase in the process. While not normally recognised as a major design phase, system integration is an essential step between final design and implementation where the security manager validates the system design in accordance with previously established requirements. It is at this point that the security manager considers the adequacy of the complete final system design solution in terms of previously determined threats and vulnerabilities, the security manager's concept of security operations, economic and other constraints, organisational operations, and overall system requirements. In effect, system integration is really the final design review elevated to a major phase.

The integration phase confirms the primary objective of the earlier design process to incorporate the various subsystem elements with personnel and procedures resulting in an integrated approach to asset protection. During integration, each subsystem, along with its associated components, needs to be evaluated by the security manager and the designer according to its individual contribution to vulnerability reduction and contribution to the total system protection effort. Each measure offers trade-offs in terms of costs and benefits.

Subsystem integration reflected in the final design represents the culmination of choices appropriate to individual asset protection decisions. The end result of the engineering design phase is a completely integrated security system consisting of various subsystems and their associated elements, which collectively counter an adversary with a high degree of reliability an assurance.

Implementing the security system involves preparing facilities, acquiring hardware, installation, testing and evaluation, training, and establishing a comprehensive logistics and maintenance support system. In terms of eventual system performance, proper completion of the steps in this phase, namely, system installation, will to a large extent determine successful operation and responsiveness of the final system. It is at this crucial phase that the security system designer can lose control of the desired results. Project controls need to be exercised with respect to the design specifications to ensure quality control.

The security manager has overall responsibility for quality assurance, test, and acceptance issues. On-site quality control of system installation is essential to successful system performance. The designer plays a key role in this phase by carefully considering key installation activities when on-site inspection can confirm that design requirements are being met. The designer must be completely familiar with the devices being installed and ensure that all items, right down to cable connectors, meet the design specifications and are appropriate for the conditions and environment in which they will be used.

Quality assurance representatives are responsible for monitoring compliance with technical design requirements and they must be given the authority to stop the project upon determining that the system will not meet the requirements and objectives established at the beginning of the process.

The system operation phase involves the actual operation of the accepted system by the user organisation. Key aspects of this phase include preparing and submitting as-built drawings, and the final receipt of technical manuals for system operation and maintenance. A principal element of this phase is the assumption by the user of responsibility for system support. One pricing option involves the forming and training of a dedicated maintenance team to perform the routine preventative and troubleshooting procedures on a regular basis. Another option is to contract out all maintenance to a qualified firm. Regardless of the option chosen, all maintenance personnel need to understand system operation and be able to test, troubleshoot, and replace modular components and repair certain components.

In some cases, multiplex control and display manufacturers offer diagnostic software to troubleshoot system, subsystem, and component failures. All operational systems should be evaluated on a regular basis—at least yearly—based on a continuing threat and vulnerability analysis, and changes in organisational missions. System hardware should also be tested regularly to verify that system performance has not been degraded. Some experts recommend repeating original system-level acceptance tests semiannually. Lastly, sustained training of all system personnel, including operators, maintenance, and supervisory personnel, is mandatory.

Effective security system integration not only includes security hardware selection and application, but also must take into consideration existing procedures, architectural measures, and security resources. This requires a thorough understanding of the system design and integration process, as well as the roles and responsibilities of each member of the project team. Adherence to the phased steps of the process is critical to effective system design and operation.

After selecting assets deemed critical for protection, the security manager must systematically determine potential threats and their characteristics, the attractiveness of critical assets to threats, potential attack modes, and potential attack severity. Finally, with the aid of a project team that understands that the most effective, flexible, and economical security system is one that has an appropriate blend of personnel, procedures, and technology, an integrated security system can be designed.

Many security plans were established as the need dictated, without regard to centralisation and coordination. Many such plans resemble a crazy quilt affair. More often than not these plans need to be brought together in such a manner that the component parts complement instead of contradict one another. If the facility has no security plan, then the survey can establish the need for one and develop some or all of the following security services, most of which are commonly found in an industrial setting. By conducting a comprehensive survey of the entire facility—its operations and procedures—one can identify critical factors affecting the security of the premises or operation.

Pre-employment Verification

As a process, employment may begin with the search for an employee to fill a vacant or newly created position. The employment process may continue when applicants begin appearing in response to an advertisement or notice of vacancy. That process continues again when applicants formally apply, are considered, rejected, interviewed, tested, and hired. The employment process continues throughout the life. Of the employment, from initial job placement, to training, to motivation, to supervision, to discipline and to promotion. It extends literally to all aspects of the person's working life from the moment he views the announcement of a vacancy until he leaves the organisation. Employment is a continuum which ranges on and on for any given employee.

Therefore, when corporations proclaim that people are our most important resource they are not simply voicing PR gibberish. People, indeed, are the most important tool a manager has. Without them, he is totally dependent—until or unless total automation replaces us all. Employees, in some ways, may be likened to the guest. Without the guest the property simply cannot survive. So also without the employee the manager simply cannot function. Obviously given these facts, no small amount of planning, effort and attention must be given to the process of employment.

Pre-employment verification is considered by many experts to be the paramount one available—particularly against crime. Why should this be so? The answer is at the same time rather simple and rather astounding. Consider the entire array of crimes which might befall a guest: armed robbery, room theft, criminal assault, battery, to name only a few. In virtually every case, proximity to the guest-victim is a necessary ingredient. And who has more close proximity than the employee? While this question may seem cold-hearted and disloyal, it is a consideration with which all hoteliers must deal. Hoteliers must accept the fact that while employees are the most vital of all assets, they also constitute an often unrecognised threat on the protection management matrix.

The hotelier must be totally satisfied that the person finally selected for employment is the one most qualified, the one most appropriate, the one most suited, and above all the one most trustworthy. The hotelier, in other words, must do proper, extensive and systematic pre-employment verification. When our nation was predominantly rural with the majority of the population located in small towns and communities, the task of selecting the best qualified applicant was relatively easy.

Today, the prospective employer is faced with a myriad of difficult decisions when the prospect of employing a person must be faced. When properly accomplished, however, these early steps in the employment process allow for an eventual workforce which can be superlative. Failure, however, to effectively do pre-employment verification can result in untold difficulties ranging from needless lost time and effort to adverse effects on the bottom line, to and including tragic results.

The employment process, in its entirety, must conform to all laws and regulations. There are federal, state and local requirements which must be understood and complied with—and different requirements exist in different locations. Hoteliers must become knowledgeable about the laws which affect them in their particular locale. To do otherwise invites great difficulty and possible sanction. And these laws are changing virtually on a daily basis. Hoteliers must not only know and abide by these laws but keep continually aware of them and their changing status. It is equally critical to note that consideration of the employment process—particularly the pre-employment verification portion—is not something that is normally considered as being part of guest protection and reasonable care.

One major part of the protection begins with the property's employment process, particularly pre-employment verification. While this function may be and often is centred in the human resources department, it is indeed a property-wide consideration. Perhaps nothing is more important to the protection of the guest than the reliability of the employee—a consideration which begins with pre-employment verification.

Employment Application Form

Application forms are as varied in form and design as properties differ one from the other. They are alike, however, in that they often are the first clue that the hiring authority has in determining the qualifications of an applicant. While the form should be designed to elicit sufficient information to assist in the selection process, it should only include only those questions which tire pertinent to the job in question. Subjects to be avoided include inquiries regarding national origins, race, colour, political affiliations, religion, sex, marital status, economic status, and number of children. The components of the application form may vary somewhat but certain basic information is called for on virtually all of them. This includes:

— *Applicant's personal data section*: Full name, current address, telephone number and social security number.

— *Background data section*: Pertinent job-related personal background data which includes both education and experience.

— *References section*: Names of persons who can attest to his abilities, character, education and reliability.

— *Disclaimers section*: Normally in bold and clearly stated fashion immediately above the signature block, the applicant is informed of drug testing policy and policy of the property to engage in background verification including earlier employment criminal background and personal references. It should be stated that the property may use any or all job-related verification techniques which the property manager plans to utilise.

— *Accuracy verification and information release authorisation section*: Typical application forms include statements regarding acknowledgment of the applicant that the information supplied is complete and accurate to the best of his knowledge. Any deliberate falsifications, misrepresentations or omissions may be grounds for not hiring or for subsequent dismissal if hiring has taken place. This is normally followed by a request that the applicant authorise the property to verify all information.

The application form begins with a review of the application form itself.

— *Total form completeness*: Has the applicant completed every required blank and answered every required question? If not, the hotelier may wish to go no further but rather return it to the applicant for completion. For example, many application forms ask the question: "Have you ever been convicted of a felony?" Applicants may choose to ignore this question, often out of fear that disclosing such a history will disqualify them from consideration but fearful also of lying on the application. They decide instead simply to leave that question unanswered.

— *Specific question completeness*: Has the applicant addressed the totality of each question to the satisfaction of the hiring authority? For example, in the space requesting earlier employment job duties an applicant might indicate "supervised staff". This minimum response does not allow an ample amount of information from which to form even a preliminary hiring decision. The hiring authority needs to know, for instance, how many persons constitute "staff' what the applicant's duties as "supervisor" were; the extent of his authority, etc.

— *Continuity*: Has the applicant provided continuity of activity, for instance, in the section detailing earlier employment? Is there an unbroken time line or are there gaps which are unexplained? Often this may be an oversight and can be easily explained. Sometimes such gaps in the time line may be purposeful. For example, applicants who have periods of their life which they feel will be disqualifying in nature simply skip that time-frame and go on to the next. If an applicant had a period of employment from which he was dismissed for cause, he may feel that disclosing such a time or such background will preclude his hiring.

Clarify: If the position in question requires a degree of clear, concise writing skills, has the applicant shown such skills on the application form? Fore example, if the applicant is, for instance, applying for a protection officer position and the duties of that position require on-the-spot, clear and concise report writing, are such skills exhibited on the application form?

Interview

The interview should be conducted following processing the application form and immediately before the extensive pre-employment verification process. While the employment process is often centred in the human resources department, and preliminary steps conducted there, interviews by the person to whom the applicant will report directly are vital. In many cases, such supervisors may not have had the opportunity to learn and practise effective interview techniques. Such techniques need to be learned simply because if they are members of the management team then a part of management is the supervising of employees.

During the interview the interviewer has unequalled opportunity to observe the applicant first hand, and view and listen and almost have a sense of what the applicant is about. He can determine certain behavioural patterns such as communication ability, personal grooming standards, ability to listen and apparent ability to understand, alertness, and ability to be at ease. The application form can establish the basis for the formal part of the interview process. The interviewer can, and should, go over each item of the form individually, verifying the applicant's understanding of the query and the completeness of the response.

Particular attention should be given to the extent of the applicant's fitness for the job in question—his skills, experience, education and attitude. Related applicant characteristics may also be addressed such as interests, hobbies, and ambitions. The particulars of the job should be previewed. Discuss what the applicant will be expected to do, the hours involved, the tasks, and the environment. Only by a realistic and honest discussion of these factors can an applicant be expected to determine if he is interested. Interviewers must be taught that the subjects to be avoided on the application form must also be avoided during the interview.

Pre-Employment Verification (PEV)

Great care must be taken in the early stages of the

employment process. From the design and style of the job application form, to the processing of that form, to the interview process—all have been preludes to the possible decision to hire.

The Pre-employment Verification (PEV) is an integral and vital part of the employment process, one which can be of tremendous benefit to an employer. When overlooked, it can be tragic. There are lodging managers who feel apprehension about not only doing PEV but about the subject itself in our world of host-related endeavours. Doing a background check on a prospective employee seems to some as bad if not worse than the taboos surrounding our old world security. Not only is this position not defendable, it is counterproductive. When done correctly, there is nothing unethical, unlawful, or immoral about PEV.

Lodging managers who, as an excuse not to accomplish PEV, claim that the necessity of hiring an application immediately prohibits pre-employment verification. While the need to hire in an emergency is a dilemma, the answer to the dilemma is obvious. When time constraints demand immediate hiring, then it should be done. Immediately thereafter the pre-employment process should begin. To do otherwise can be a serious and tragic mistake. Failure to perform properly pre-employment verification prior to hiring or in the case cited above failing to accomplish it as soon as possible sets the scene for:

— Civil suits alleging failure to screen properly employees;

— A work force which is burdened with morale problems, knowing there are co-workers who should have been screened out prior to being employed;

— Higher than normal turnover in employment; and

— Low productivity brought on by a less than adequate work force.

PEV is a win-win-win situation. Not only does it help a prospective employer to validate job experience, education and qualification, it has a myriad of other advantages. A check of an applicant's criminal history, consistent with the law, may disclose convictions of a type which may cause further inquiry. In a review of an applicant's criminal record might disclose a conviction for forgery some years back and a subsequent sentence which was carried out. Such a record might not be a major consideration if the applicant was applying, for instance, for a chef's position. On the other hand, if the applicant was applying for a position of lifeguard, then multiple convictions for the crime of child molestation would certainly be of interest to the prospective employer.

The Motor Vehicle Department (MVD) records checking often provides a wealth of information. A review of MVD records in many states provides the correct spelling of the name, address, date of birth, and social security number of the applicant. Such data may be cross checked against the job application form to verify completeness and accuracy. Additionally, if the MVD review were to reveal multiple violations of local motor vehicle ordinances, then an applicant's desire to be the van driver might be questioned.

Review of workers' compensation records might reveal a disqualifying disability about which the hiring official was unaware and which might disqualify the applicant for the job.

Reference checks with persons having personnel knowledge of the applicant can be revealing. An example of a reference check revealing unexpected results was once experienced during a pre-employment exercise in a south-western state. The hiring official called the mother of an applicant since the applicant had listed her as a reference.

The position in question was one of bartender and the hiring official asked the reference (the mother) if she thought her son would make a good bartender. She replied, "Yes, indeed he would and it sure would be nice to see him on that side of the bar for a change".

Vital statistics, like drivers records, can be a great help in verifying much of the information on the job application form. It is not simply an exercise which replaces the other aspects of the employment process. It is a verification that the other portions are valid.

Pre-employment Verification Process

The methods of pre-employment verification process include face-to-face interviews, telephone checks, mail correspondence and the use of commercial firms which specialise in such verification.

i) *Face-to-face verification*: This method of PEV is often difficult or impracticable to perform. Particularly when the job opening is one which is relatively low on the pay scale and other methods of PEV are possible, this technique usually is not used. If however, the applicant is applying for a higher level position or if references are available from within the existing workforce, this method is often valuable.

ii) *Telephone verification checks:* The calls are usually quick and inexpensive. They are also less reliable than other methods. Many properties use a standardised checklist which the caller uses as a reminder to cover all needed and desired subjects.

iii) *Mail verification:* Use of the mails to accomplish PEV is inexpensive and can be useful. It is however quite slow. It is most useful when the information sought is lengthy and statistical in nature and not particularly time-sensitive or subject to interpretation.

iv) *Background verification firms*: In virtually every city a review of the yellow pages will reveal firms who specialise in PEV. These firms, often listed under employment or employee screening will, for a fee, perform the function of pre-employment verification.

The US National Employment Screening Services published a source directory for employee screening. *The Guide to Background Investigation* presents state-by-state brief summaries of what laws apply in each state regarding PEV.

ACCESS CONTROL, LIGHTING AND KEY CONTROL

Access control is designed to limit access. A locked or otherwise secured door to a storage shed limits access. Ease of access is lessened while not absolutely preventing the unauthorised entry into that building or room. Access control is designed to monitor access. A log-in sheet at a food-storage area monitors the unauthorised entry into that room. The controlling quality access control is designed to control access. An electronic access code used in conjunction with a touch pad to a restricted area controls the unauthorised entry into that area.

Access control is designed to otherwise influence access and the movement of people or vehicles. Perhaps the most obvious example of such successful influencing is the simple use of gender signs on restroom doors. It is obvious then from these and other examples that access control is a relative countermeasure. It is also complementary. That is to say, its effectiveness can be enhanced by its use in concert with other countermeasures and by adjusting the control features with the countermeasure itself.

While locking or otherwise securing the door of a storage shed provides a certain level of protection, the requirement that a roving protection officer intermittently

selecting a badging system. The issues for consideration include initial and replacement cost, the use for which the proposed system is anticipated, and the appearance of the badge itself.

The use of employee entrances can be an effective access control method. It offers several advantages:

— If properly designed and enforced, employee entrances can channel and restrict employees to desired designated areas.
— It can facilitate and strengthen time and attendance procedures.
— It can minimise exposure of employees to hazards.
— It can reduce employee theft.

In guest-room situations, particularly, employees should be encouraged and directed to encounter or report any person who has the appearance and mannerisms of being "out of the ordinary" or whose movements and body language suggest being lost, confused, or "suspicious". Obviously, if such a situation in any way suggests danger, the employee must be trained to call a predetermined person or department. When the employee is comfortable in a direct encounter, such should be encouraged. By reporting to predesignated persons or departments the appearance of persons who appear to be unauthorised, crime can often be deterred. In the event that a person or group is encountered who turns out to be authorised, the mere fact of having encountered them tends to "put them on notice" and the likelihood of subsequent in appropriate behaviour is decreased.

Key Control Process

The front desk, housekeeping and maintenance are the three departments most involved in the key control process. The "beginning" of the circular route is the front desk. This department, generally speaking, is the focal point of the circular path which the guest-room keys will take throughout the property. Training of the front desk staff in the key control policies and procedures is essential if success is to be realised. This training should be a continuing process. Inventory of guest-room keys should be a matter of course and on a regular and scheduled basis, at least once daily. The ideal time for such inventory is often immediately after check-out time and appropriate inventory forms should be completed promptly. Housekeeping, then should be placed into the inventory loop so that keys recovered by that department are considered. If re-keying, recording or rotation is appropriate, the affected guest-rooms absolutely should be placed out of service by management until this is accomplished.

Guest-room keys are to be issued to registered guests only, normally at the time of registration. A method of recording the number of keys issued should be adopted and additional authorised issuance, should also be noted so that reconciliation can be made upon check-out. Both positive identification and authority must be obtained prior to issuing additional keys. Additionally, guest-room numbers should never be audibly announced by the issuing front desk clerk.

If the departing guest indicates his key or keys have been left at the guest-room, he should be assured that is perfectly acceptable and that housekeeping will retrieve the key during cleaning. On the other hand, often the guest has his key in his pocket and a simple courteous comment will serve as a reminder. When the front desk is alerted that a situation has occurred which might impact from a protection standpoint on the key control process, corrective action is called for immediately. Such procedures would be a part of the overall key control procedure and a continuing part of the training.

Front desk responsibility normally extends beyond

guest-room key control into both master key and E key control. Both these types of keys should he inventoried on a regular basis, at least once daily. The ideal time for this inventory is often late afternoon when most of the master and sub-master keys have been returned to inventory. This recurring inventory, like the guest-room key inventory, should be appropriately recorded on an inventory form and properly stored according to established policy.

The housekeeping staff normally is the next department to become involved in the key control process. During the daily process of cleaning guest-rooms, room attendants will normally retrieve several keys which have been left, inadvertently or by design, by departing guests. Ideally a locked box securely attached to the housekeeping cart should be utilised to store these retrieved keys until delivery at the end of the shift. A responsible person should be assigned to transport all retrieved keys shortly after the end of the shift, back to the front desk so that they can be entered into the inventory.

Strict rules prohibiting the access of anyone to locked guest-room doors should be established and rigidly enforced. Room attendants should be instructed that requests from anyone to enter a locked guest-room door should be referred to the front desk or to senior management. Master keys should be secured on the room attendant's person at all times. Chains which allow both such security and required access are usually successful.

The maintenance department could be labelled as that point on the "circular" key-control route where all things begin. While from the guest's standpoint the front desk is where the process begins, in actuality, it is in the maintenance department that the process has its roots. This is normally where the initial production occurs with the cutting of guest-room keys from the stored key blanks. This awesome responsibility, the ability to duplicate virtually any guest-room key at any moment, causes special attention to be focused on the maintenance department.

Key-cutting machinery should be well stored, controlled, and access limited. This machinery should be stored in a secure area, either in a room to which access can be rigidly controlled or if this is not feasible, then sub-compartmentalised in a secured cabinet. Access to the controlled room or the secure storage location should be by designated persons only. Key blanks should be controlled by a designated level of management—often the chief engineer or maintenance department manager. Storing these blanks and securing them independently from the key-cutting device and limiting access to them by designated management personnel allows for an effective audit method for security purposes. A running inventory of these blanks provides for assurance of control.

Normally guest-room key duplication requests come exclusively from the front desk and are printed in multiples allowing copies to be maintained at specific locations along the production and issuance path. The procedure as well as the format of the key request should provide and insure control at all locations along the circular route. The request form should indicate the reason for the request.

Master and sub-master key reproduction requires special controls. Obviously a misplaced master or sub-master requires immediate attention, not only to replace the key but more importantly to re-key effected doors to which the misplaced master allowed access. Authority for such duplication and the adherence to quick and reliable re-keying should be vested in a predetermined level of management. Adherence to the required rapid re-keying in this situation is essential and should be audited on a frequent basis.

When a bellperson escorts a guest to his room, he should be certain that the guest-room key is functioning properly and that the guest understands how the key operates. If a bellperson assists a guest during check-out, the bellperson would remind the guest that the key is to be returned and that he can assist if that is desired. The retrieved key is then obviously returned to the front desk. Issuance of keys to the bell and valet staff should normally be controlled at the front desk.

Van and courtesy drivers should remind departing guests of the necessity of returning keys and offer to accept from them any guest-room key which might have been forgotten. A locked box, not unlike that suggested for the room attendant's cart, is useful on vans and courtesy vehicles. All employees, irrespective of position or department, should be trained in the importance of key control. They should be aware of key control discrepancies and proper response. Such events might include such circumstances as discovering misplaced keys or becoming aware of inappropriate issuance or "borrowing" of keys. Some properties employ a guest-room key deposit system. In such an approach, a nominal deposit is collected or announced during the registration process and then returned or eliminated from the billing process when the key is returned. There are at least two distinct advantages to this process:

— a reminder to the guest to return his key as well as an incentive to do so, and

— the system also provides a money stream to offset the cost of key replacement.

The principal disadvantage is the danger of poor guest relations. There is little doubt that this danger exists—guests often feel "put upon" when a deposit is required, feeling either that they are being mistrusted or that the property is taking unacceptable advantage of them. It is important, therefore, if a key deposit system is employed, that the front desk personnel be careful and thoroughly trained and scripted in the way the system is to be presented and carried out.

At check-out time, a soft approach should be used—courteously accepting the guest's explanation, for instance, that he "left his key in the room". Obviously, if a key deposit system is employed, it must be universally applied. Intermittent use, for example, when a "suspicious" guest is being processed is unacceptable. Finally, managers must understand that a key deposit system in no way is meant to replace a comprehensive and effective guest-room key control system.

10

Guest Protection and Safety Management

Confidentiality of the guest-room location is vital. No audible announcement of the guest's room number should be made at the front desk or at any location. When providing the key to the guest, he should be informed of the room number by the use of a card or key holder or some other nonverbal means. Obviously, when the bell staff is used, the room number again should never be verbalised but rather the bellperson should be informed of the room location in the same confidential manner by which the guest was notified.

When receiving inquiries regarding a guest, whether by phone or in person, the confidentiality must again be maintained. A guest's right to privacy is a vital and long-standing tenant of lodging and should never be violated. When a request is made for a room key by a person claiming to be an occupant of that room, positive identification must be made of that person prior to issuing a key. Standard identification methods should be established and used as appropriate.

The locking system utilised at the guest-room door is a major consideration in this countermeasure. Basically systems available to the hotelier fall into one of four general categories. They are key in knob, standard mortise locks, mortise locks with programmable cylinders and/or removable cores, and electronic lock systems.

Key-in-knob is a system in which the key channel is actually within and a part of the doorknob itself. It is activated by inserting the key directly into the knob and the channel. This is probably the least effective of all systems, is considered generally insecure and in fact is prohibited in some states as a hotel/motel guest-room locking system.

The word "mortise" means, literally, "a hole, groove or slot into or through which some other part of an arrangement of parts fits or passes". This system usually consists of a face plate, with the doorknob and an unconnected separate key channel on the exterior side of the door and a deadbolt arrangement on the interior side of the door. Mortise locks with programmable cylinders and/or removable cores allow for quick key combination changes. Electronic lock systems allow for a unique selection of keying combinations whenever a new guest is assigned to that room, whenever a compromise or key loss is suspected and whenever management determines that such action is warranted.

New and more sophisticated systems are reaching the market on a continuing basis and the choice for the hotelier is a difficult one. If there is a single rule-of-thumb to follow, it is that whatever system is chosen, it offers higher protection if the locking combination can be changed on a random or programmed basis whenever required.

Door and frame construction as well as attendant locking hardware should be of such quality and workmanship as to minimise the ease by which an intruder can bypass them by force. Obviously, the hinges should be located to preclude the pins being pulled from the exterior. Glass, either in the door or in a panel near the door, should be of such strength and of such configurations as to minimise the possibility of an intruder breaking it and reaching into the room and accessing the locking system. The lock bolt should be configured to minimise forceful entry and of such strength as to minimise being cut. Self-closing automatic locking devices should be standard.

Connecting room doors are those doors which are placed between guest-rooms to allow for access from one guest-room to another or to enlarge the rented space from one-room to two-or-more-room capacity. Historically, these doors often have been of lesser construction than the main guest-room door. In fact, the threat which is posed to the guest by inappropriate connecting room door design, maintenance or construction warrants special attention. Single connection door arrangements are strongly discouraged.

Instead, there should be two separate doors, each void of all hardware on the inside. In effect, then, there are two doors facing one another, neither with locking hardware and with space between them. On the guest-room side of each door, however, there should be provision for the guest himself to provide added self-protection. Only guests occupying both rooms simultaneously and in concert with one another or hotel/motel staff should have the ability to access both rooms.

View ports should be installed in the guest-room door. The exception to this guideline would be in the case of those door/room configurations in which adjacent glass panelling allows observation of anyone immediately outside the guest-room door. A minimum 200-degree viewing angle is considered acceptable. A second view port for disabled persons is recommended and is in fact required in rooms complying with the Americans with Disabilities standards. Secondary and additional protective equipment is appropriate on the main guest-room door, depending on the locking system utilised.

Many door locking systems have a double locking dead bolt and single action panic release features installed within the system.

Many states require the hotelier laws of that state to be posted prominently within the guest-room. The limits of liability in so far as the loss of personal belongings are normally shown and are posted so that the guest understands those limits. Also, normally noted on these postings are the considerations of safe deposit and property safekeeping facilities available at the property. All too often, however it is the hotelier himself who has not kept his knowledge current.

Announcements concerning what actions the guest ought to take in order to secure that door to the fullest extent possible should be posted on or near the back of the guest-room door. Use of the safety chain, if applicable, should be explained as should the use, if appropriate, of the dead bolt. All double locking procedures should likewise be explained. Use of the view port and methods of securing any connecting or sliding/ patio doors should also be addressed.

Personal injuries due to accidents occur more often in the bathroom than any other portion of the guest-room. Postings, therefore, regarding tub safety, use of any grab bars, slip-and-fall deterrent bathmats, etc. should be considered. If particular use of electrical equipment in the bathroom is desired, warnings regarding their use should be posted.

The guest-room telephone is more than a convenience. It can be, literally, a life-saving guest protection device. Consider posting prominently and distinctly on the phone faceplate a notation of the number to be called to summon help. Of even greater concern, obviously, is the system devised to both answer immediately and prioritise any emergency calls. Several methods are possible to accomplish this immediate handling of any emergency call. The emergency number can be channelled, like all operator calls, into a central switchboard. If this is the system chosen, care should be taken that when the emergency number is dialled, it has an extremely distinct ring—much louder perhaps or with a distinct tone.

Some hotel chains/properties have adopted a procedure whereby the guest is advised to dial an outside number such as 911 to request emergency assistance. Great care and planning are essential before such a procedure is established. Whatever method of immediate response is adopted, the recipient of the call, whether a front desk clerk, a switchboard operator or a security officer, must be trained and scripted in quick and accurate response. Many municipalities using the nearly universal 911 system have developed scripting which is quick and concise and makes misinterpretation or extraneous conversation of a minimal concern.

The use of a warning light which is activated along with the distinct ring adds greater assurance that the operator will note the call immediately and cease all other duties to respond to it. The emergency line might also be channelled into a continually manned security office, dispatch point or control centre. Again, the ringing apparatus and arrangement must be such that the ringing tone is clear, distinct and unique and is inevitably responded to immediately. Consideration should be given to installing a system so that the room number is displayed when a call is received. Automatic taping of the ensuing conversation is a plus.

The lodging industry is long past the time when it was felt that education of guests about threats and dangers and protection methods were contrary to the "host image". On the contrary, such announcements and notifications are now considered absolutely essential by most professional hoteliers.

The bell staff should be scripted and instructed in all protection aspects of the guest-room. They should direct the guests to the TV announcement, if there is one, even turning the TV on and to the particular announcing channel so that the guest gets an early opportunity to view and hear it. The bellperson should also call to the guest's attention the guest-room service directory and highlight the fact that there is a section regarding protection. Finally, the bellperson should mention the entire range of protection devices, techniques and announcements present in the room. He should discuss all subjects ranging from the use of the door devices, safe deposit system to advice about safety and fire protection.

Training of Guest Protection

Trained employees are the main resources for the success of any business. Manufacturing firms are virtually assured of failure without trained employees. Retail establishments have failed because they did not have trained employees. Public utilities, financial institutions, health care organisational, without exception, are highly likely to fail unless the personnel responsible for the product or the service which is intended to be delivered to the public are trained. In all service industries a significant number of employees apply and are employed with little or no previous formal education or training. Even those who arrive with some degree of basic skills are not knowledgeable or informed of the particulars and peculiarities of their new property environment.

The training process begins at the time the employee begins his employment and continues until lie leaves that employment is crucial to the success of the property, In literally every department, every manager must accept that fact. Property success will not evolve unless and until every employee in every department is afforded the process of training in guest protection. Such training is vital because the lodging industry has a high turnover rate. Such training is vital because the lodging industry employs such a high rate of previously untrained persons. Such training is vital because the lodging industry is experiencing, not unlike many other industries, rapid technological changes.

The three objectives designed to accomplish the training process are:

i) Teach employees to perform new and unfamiliar tasks.

ii) Assist employees in improving current skills.

iii) Assure that the guest will be protected.

The elements of training programmes which are useful and necessary to the lodging industry and various types of guest protection training methods are discussed here.

The highest level of management on a property has overall training responsibility. In most individual properties, this means the general manager. Often he assigns the responsibility to the human resource department, a unit usually well situated to oversee the plan. However, the actual conduct of training is often a vastly different concern and thus requires a vastly different approach.

Determining needs are the initial consideration of guest protection training—the preparing of a statement of training objectives. Such a statement allows for a common beginning point for all levels of employment from the prospective of management as well as the work force. A sample guest protection training objective can be read in following ways.

> This property is absolutely committed to the care and safety of its guests. Toward that commitment, every employee at every level in every department will receive sufficient detailed and documented training in the methods and safeguards of guest protection as is required.

Such training will be accomplished at the time of hire, at the time of promotion or transfer, and on an ongoing basis during the employee's entire tenure with the property.

Responsibility for guest protection training will rest with the human resources director who, in coordination with the protection management committee, will ascertain that specific tasking is assigned to each department as appropriate, validate that the training is accomplished and maintain training records.

Although initial entry guest protection training may be a part of the, overall new hire indoctrination programme, specific in-service guest protection training will be accomplished departmentally.

The entire scope of guest protection training will be reviewed at a minimum during every quality assurance review.

The programme can evolve from this statement benchmark.

Guest protection training needs survey. Training needs must initially be determined and this can be accomplished in several ways.

i) Determine guest's wants and concerns. There is no surer method of determining guest protection training needs than actually listening to the guest himself. By reading complaint cards, by having the staff listen and report comments received from guests and by successfully utilising guest comment cards, a significant amount of information may be gained.

ii) Determining what the line employees see as guest protection can be useful. Employees are usually the best source of information. They should be given not only the opportunity to voice their concerns, they should be urged to do so. If an employee sees a guest protection problem, then likely there has been a breakdown in the guest protection training programme.

iii) Determine the supervisory staff views as actual or potential guest dangers or problems. Usually by soliciting this assistance, department by department, the best results ensue.

iv) The general manager, during his periodic assessments of the property, should concentrate on those observable items which suggest changes or additions which are needed in the guest protection training programme.

Several methods are used in gleaning this data from several sources. Specifically, the conduit to and through the protection management committee should be fully utilised. Input from all levels of employees, input from guests, and input from vendors and contractors should filter through this committee. Appropriate corrective action then can be accomplished. Individual interviews are also used. This method is often valuable but it is time-consuming and expensive when compared to others. Group interviews allow opportunity in an open atmosphere for employees to make their views known. Questionnaires are used quite frequently.

Methods of Training

Organisation and implementation is the another major second step in the development of the guest protection training programme. It involves decisions regarding who will be trained, by whom, where and with what frequency. Training population should be a matter of policy that all employees, in all departments and at all levels will be trained in the specifics of guest protection. This policy should require that guest protection training be mandatory upon initial employment, upon transfer or promotion and on a scheduled basis throughout the career of the employee.

While the overall responsibility for training often lies within the human resource department, specific guest protection training is often best done within individual departments. One reason for this is that the department head is best equipped to manage training time and schedules. Another reason is because guest protection training should be departmentally threat-specific. Those threats which exist in one department may not exist in another and departmental concentration, therefore, for this training is usually advantageous. Still another reason is that the personalities, capabilities, and needs of individual employees are best known to management personnel in their individual departments.

Generally, training methods fall into two categories: group training and individual training. Both have advantages and disadvantages but both should be considered, not only individually but in concert with one another when planning a guest protection training programme.

Group training

i) *Lecture approach*: This approach includes any methods in which presentations before an assembled group are delivered. The lecturer may supplement his presentation with visual aids and often concludes with questions, answers and discussions. This method is often used for guest protection indoctrination training to new property employees. An agenda is set and several managers or departments make prepared presentations. This is the ideal time to introduce the property policy which stresses the absolute requirement that guests be protected at all times in all departments.

ii) *Role-playing approach*: The approach includes any of several approaches in which a scenario or circumstance is presented to the group and then roles are assigned or taken in order to demonstrate predetermined conclusions. Individuals in the group act, intermittently, as participants and observers and as observers provide feedback to those playing the participative roles. This approach is particularly effective when a trainer has a specific circumstance or setting to be explored.

For instance, in a group meeting within the housekeeping department, the executive housekeeper may decide to concentrate on the training of unauthorised access to a guest-room. The housekeeper may assign one employee from the group the role of the room attendant working in the guest-room hallway and assign to another employee the role of an unknown person who is also found in that hallway. The unknown person can be invited to think of all the reasons he needs to get into a room. The employee playing the role of the room attendant must conjure up appropriate responses to each of the questions. This type approach can be extremely useful not only as a teaching method but in identifying and isolating guest protection subjects about which the employee has questions or is indeed ignorant.

iii) *Behaviour modelling*: Behaviour modelling takes the approach that repeated behaviour under directed circumstances reinforces that behaviour. This process is geared to specific workplace situations. The training session typically begins with a discussion of the situation to be portrayed and a discussion of the expected learning objective. Behaviour modelling can be adopted into literally any department, often with the department head acting as the role model and performing exactly the behaviour desired, having the employees mimic this behaviour until there is satisfaction that the behaviour is well instilled.

iv) *Case study*: Members of the group are presented with a guest protection problem, preferably in written form, and are requested to discuss it, analyse it, and come up with solutions.

Individual Training Method

Individual training methods fall into three categories: on-the-job training, buddy system and coaching.

i) *On-the-job training*: This is an essential method of training best described as learning by doing. It is the most common of all lodging training generally and certainly the most common training method in so far as guest protection training is concerned.

ii) *Buddy system*: It is a true variation of the on-the-job training method and involves a one-on-one approach. An experienced employee who has been at the same property for an extended period of time is assigned to coach a new employee. Perhaps the most common example of the buddy system is that used in the housekeeping department when an experienced room attendant is assigned a new employee to coach.

iii) *Coaching*: Coaching is designed to address a specific desired change in behaviour. A front desk supervisor who is coaching a trainee can effectively monitor behaviour while that trainee completes the registrations and assigns the appropriate guest-room key. Should the trainee forget and verbalise the room number, the supervisor can take immediate action, recall that key, assign another one correctly and immediately coach the trainee on the desired and necessary behaviour.

Hotel Thefts

Many companies that include hotels go out of business due to employee theft and/or guest theft. The risk of liability for slander and/or ill-will that affects future business usually is seen as far outweighing the benefit of recovering the items believed to have been stolen. The security manager's first task is to assess the hotel's assets, determine which of these assets are vulnerable to theft, and then devise a programme that will reduce the risk. One helpful tool is to instruct the human resources department, while conducting employee exit interviews, to ask questions regarding employee theft, use of drugs, and so on. This technique usually will assist you with information to narrow down areas needing further investigation. The usual approach is to conduct a risk analysis of the property and its assets. This entails identifying the risk of loss and determining what measures may be employed to reduce or eliminate that risk.

In addition to the actual physical survey, the security manager should review all reports of loss for the previous year to assess where and possibly how items were stolen. This approach will help identify the most vulnerable areas of the hotel. Continue to conduct this survey as often as possible. This is done annually in most hotels; however, conducting a quarterly or even monthly survey would lead to the best results. The key to protecting assets is to obtain cooperation and assistance from all hotel employees. Security managers who think they can do the job by themselves are making a dreadful mistake.

Security is everyone's job. In fact, this slogan should be emphasised during an employee's initial orientation programme as well as in monthly departmental meetings. Successful prevention measures depend on a well-designed programme that involves input from all employees. The security manager can work with employees in a variety of ways.

— First, he or she should educate employees about the seriousness of theft and how it affects them.

— Second, she or he should attempt to develop employees' understanding of the problem in terms that they as members of the organisation can relate to and appreciate. For example, if it is made clear that all losses cut into the profitability of the property and that reduced profits, if severe enough, may result in lower wages or even laying off employees, the employees may realise that they too have a financial stake in the prevention of losses.

— Third, assistance from employees may be elicited by encouraging them to call and report suspicious people or circumstances and at least make an extra effort to secure valuables when leaving a work area (for example, securing tools in storage rooms).

— Fourth, it is essential that the security department maintain a good working relationship with all employees, avoiding morale problems created by poor communications and a lack of understanding. Employees suffering from poor morale are not going to be very concerned about protecting the assets of the employer.

— Finally, the security manager must work with all other department managers to get their input on solutions to the problem of losses.

Some security personnel may think that the solution to the loss problem is locking up and limiting access to the hotel's assets, but if a measure interferes with the normal operation of a hotel, it will be resisted and is a guaranteed failure. In fact, the security function will be viewed as less effective unless the solution recommended includes input from the departments affected by it.

Programme design is only half of the crime prevention task. The other half, which is equally important, is continuous improvement. The security manager should repeat the risk survey at least quarterly, if possible, to ensure compliance with the programme, and to discover any changes in the physical structure or the hotel operation that may negate the original plan. The programme must always remain flexible to meet the needs of the business. New and better methods should always be sought for improved preventive measures. When losses do occur, as they will, evaluate the loss and adjust the programme accordingly.

One reason why hotel managers are concerned about the theft of guest property is the potential impact on future business. Legal issues, most states have limited an innkeeper's liability to a fixed amount and generally that amount is not very high. A history of serious guest losses may, however, drastically affect the hotel's reputation and may also be indicative of other weaknesses in the security programme which could lead to more serious crimes. Investigation of such losses should include, first, an examination of the locking hardware on the room to ensure that it is working properly. This could be a problem because guests frequently may not close their door tightly when leaving or when running down the hall for ice or soda.

Second, determine which employees have access to the room under investigation and note them for further follow-up. If good records are kept, after a short while the same employee's name will begin to appear regularly. Once that is discovered, the investigation could focus more on that individual. Third, find out when the locks were last changed or rekeyed. There may be an overall problem with key control.

Finally, check for missing room or master keys that anyone could use to gain access to guest rooms.

Prevention of guest room theft depends primarily on employee and guest cooperation. Employee cooperation and assistance were discussed above and apply to guest losses as well. Guest cooperation is more difficult to obtain because of guests' transient nature, but can be achieved to a reasonable extent.

The type of cooperation sought is generally limited to two areas: use of existing risk-reducing equipment such as safe deposit boxes and in-room safes, and making sure guests close and properly lock their room doors either when they leave or go to sleep. Some hotels put small signs or fliers in guest rooms advertising the availability of safe deposit boxes and in-room safes, as well as directions on how to properly secure the door. Other hotels use the cable system on the room television to promote safety and security measures.

An employee's personal property, uniforms, and hotel equipment are subject to theft in locker rooms and work areas. Although the theft of such property is not generally seen as a liability problem, it should be of concern from the standpoint of employee morale. It is a well-known fact that poor employee morale will reduce productivity and will fail to promote the kind of cooperation needed by the security department to prevent other losses. The theft of any employee valuable should be treated with the same level of concern and priority as any other loss. The two most common areas for losses to occur are locker rooms and office areas. In locker rooms, the lockers must be equipped with adequate locks and a sound key control system.

Security also should check locker rooms frequently during their patrols. This should be done randomly whenever security personnel are in the immediate area or intentionally as part of the routine patrol. When time permits, each locker should be checked to ensure it is secured, in addition to seeing that it has regular maintenance and bringing problems of abuse to the security manager's attention. (In some areas it has also been common to put push-button locks on the locker room entrance door to ensure added safety and security to those employees changing in the locker room.) Such inspections also reveal health problems (e.g., pest control) and problems such as stockpiling of uniforms or other hotel equipment (banquet utensils, housekeeping amenities, etc.). Consistent with this approach is the need for a hotel policy on what may be kept in employees' lockers and the hotel's right to search them periodically (a two-person integrity search is recommended).

In office areas, the most frequent loss occurs when employees leave their handbags, wallets, backpacks, briefcases, or gym bags unattended in unlocked desk drawers or on top of desks. The security manager needs to be sure that desks can be locked, and encourage employees to use those locks to protect their personal property. Another common practice is for employees to leave an office door wide open to give a false impression that they are still working, when in fact they have left for the day. Yet in doing this, they may leave their personal effects in plain view for anyone to take easily.

Anytime someone is injured in the hotel or property is lost, security should conduct some form of an investigation. There are at least three advantages of a thorough investigation. First, the root cause of the problem hopefully will be discovered. If, for example, a guest became injured as a result of falling down a stairway, it is important to investigate the root cause of the fall. In such a case, the fall could be caused by torn or worn carpeting, poor lighting, lack of handrails, wet or slippery surfaces, or some factor inherent to the guest.

Some possible reasons for the guest to fall include intoxication, improper footwear, bifocals, or other mobility problems. The same issues are present when an employee is injured on the job. The second reason for a thorough investigation is prevention. By analysing the cause of a theft, for example, security can determine how the article was stolen and then develop preventive measures to avoid similar losses in the future.

The theft of food from kitchen storage areas is common to hotels and restaurants of all sizes. If investigation of this indicates that methods of inventory control are deficient, recommendations can be generated to implement better control and reduce further losses. The security manager who analyses all incidents and implements proactive procedures will prevent incidents of theft. However, employees are constantly developing new methods to steal which, when discovered, should be used as learning tools for security. New methods of theft are usually brought into a facility by a new employee who introduces that method to other employees.

The third benefit gained from an investigation also is related to future loss prevention. In a case of stolen property or drug dealing, for example, the simple process of questioning witnesses and suspects will create a deterrent to future crime. Routinely interviewing potential suspects will help establish an atmosphere of non-tolerance for crime.

Employees who may be guilty of wrongdoing, or who may have considered it, hopefully will be deterred from future activity if the impression is given that the hotel management will not tolerate misconduct. A timely and thorough investigation of every incident, requiring more than just an initial incident report, will enhance the department's image and will help develop an effective security programme.

Chasing suspects, making arrests, and testifying in court are also job responsibilities of a hotel's security staff. For many hotels, though, these activities often are ones of last resort when attempting to address the problem of crime and its associated losses. Although arrests may not be the preferred option of many hotels, they may be necessary and will occur in even the safest properties. Security managers, therefore, need to be prepared to deal with the problems generated by making arrests and prosecuting offenders.

If the hotel security staff will use special police powers or licences, it is essential that they receive at least minimal training in arrest, use of force, and civil and criminal law—including the limits of their authority, use of weapons, and the rights of the accused. In addition to training, security personnel need directions in the form of written policies and procedures. It is important to review the laws of the jurisdiction where the hotel is located to determine what restrictions may exist. For example, a state may limit the time that someone can be detained by a security officer. Most states will extend arrest authority of security officers who have been licensed as special police or deputised police to include offences for which an unlicensed officer may not arrest, e.g., shoplifting.

An arrest made without legal authority is invalid and likely to subject the officer and the hotel to civil liability. If handcuffs or weapons are authorised, additional training and policies will help ensure that proper practices are followed. A track record of successful arrests and convictions can enhance the security programme in the hotel. However, improper arrests, mishandled suspects, and unprepared testimony surely will result in acquittals and lawsuits.

A city or town that feels that a hotel cannot protect its employees or guests and their belongings may choose to fine the hotel or suspend its licence. Thorough investigations are necessary if a hotel security manager wants to prevent future loss from theft. Finally, most hotels will have a corporate policy covering arrests and prosecution. Any hotel manager unsure of these procedures should consult the hotel's corporate or local legal advisor.

Lodging Industry Laws

The roots of the entire legal system may be found in England. During the middle ages travel was not uncommon in that country. While significant commerce was difficult at best because of the conditions of the roads, travel by foot, horse and light wagon was at a surprisingly high level. In addition to the roads being in deplorable conditions, they offered another obstacle—they were infested with robbers, thieves and any number of other miscreants. Our common vision of Old England with numerous and thick forests is fairly accurate. It is true that these criminals used the woodlands as their bases and their protection.

As dangerous as travel was during daylight hours, darkness brought even more danger. The traveller knew well he had best secure himself for the night. He was limited in the amount of provisions he could carry, and with the added limitation of daylight movement, the traveller had to seek added protection and comfort. In answer to the needs and demands of the traveller, lodging establishments were developed and the hospitality industry as we know it today was begun.

The earliest establishments included religious houses which catered both to nobbles and to the poor. However, private homes constituted the majority of these establishments. They were converted in total or in part as temporary accommodations catering to the traveller's need for food, lodging, entertainment and protection. From these early homes came the inn. The inn, or public house, looked much like the private home from which it evolved. It centred, as did the private home, around the Great Room, where much of the life spent indoors was concentrated. Other parts of the inn were added as required, and private quarters were common for the owner and hoteliers. The majority of the inhabitants including servants, workers and various classes of guests gathered, entertained themselves, ate and eventually slept in the Great Room. Light was provided by candle and heat by a fireplace. And after the meal and at bedtime, the tables were converted to beds and the Great Room became a Great Common Bedroom. All this evolved from the private English home along the travel roadway.

When accommodation facilities advanced, inns began appearing which were being planned and constructed as just that—inns. More space was provided and in some cases somewhat more privacy was possible, for a price. Yet even with these advances, it must be assumed that the majority of travellers, along with their horses which were tended in adjoining stables, were expected to eat and eventually sleep surrounded by less than perfect conditions. They shared not only their sleeping quarters but many times their beds with strange fellow-travellers.

The land/home owner who opened his home to the traveller became an hoteliers as a businessman operating in this public arena. As such, his obligation became, as a public businessman, to serve all the public to provide food and lodging and protection. Restrictions, variances and peculiarities notwithstanding, such obligations exist today.

Laws are commonly used to explain and to defend their own actions and the actions of others. All law is dynamic, which is contrary to popular opinion that it is concrete and unchanging. Not only does the law move, but such movement is caused by and reflective of the evolution of the society it supports and attempts to influence. It is one's individual decision, as a private citizen, how little or how much of the law with which to become familiar. As a hotelier, however, it is imperative that he becomes familiar with that portion of the law which so deeply and severely affects our industry. Lodging law, like all law, is a living breathing entity which is constantly changing. To ignore it and those changes is to put oneself as a hotelier, in peril.

The laws by which the lodging industry is governed, came from old English common law—that system of legal thought which forms the basis for the laws which exist today in most states. While old basic common law has evolved greatly over the years by judicial precedent, and many exceptions apply, it cannot be overemphasised that protection of the guest is an absolute requirement.

A basic explanation of the law is in order, as it affects us as hoteliers. This is not to say that hoteliers are not governed or influenced by the criminal codes—on the contrary just as every citizen is held to those guidelines and restraints, so also are hoteliers. However, in your day-to-day conduct of lodging business, the civil aspects of the law are the ones with which you most often will come into contact. To state again for emphasis, the most vital civil law lesson which must be learned and practised by lodging professionals is that protection of the guest is an absolute requirement.

Loss Prevention Principles

A restaurant management can assess its crime risk by comparing the three expectations against crime-sensitive conditions, such as geographic location, ease of access to and from the premises, police support, characteristics of the clientele and the employees, hours of operation, amount of cash on the premises, and the adequacy of electronic/physical safeguards and procedural controls. A crime-sensitive condition that deserves close scrutiny is the characteristics of the hotel workforce. Dishonest employees commit internal theft and attract dishonest customers, poor supervisors and managers provide opportunities for crime and are seen by criminals as easy targets, inadequately trained employees fail to exercise controls that guard against crime, and drug-abusing employees steal to support their addictions and make mistakes that open the door to crime.

The best deterrent to robbery is to reduce the amount of cash available to the minimum amount necessary to conduct business. This means making frequent "bleeds" from the cash drawer and timely transfers of cash to the bank. Inattention to procedures is an open invitation to robbery. Many managers and employees who have been victims admit having violated one or more anti-robbery procedures. The rationale was that they believed it would not happen to them. The greatest threat to loss of money and inventory is from employee theft. Employees see and remember everything a manager does wrong or fails to do. Eventually, one or more of them may take advantage of these failures. While most employees are honest and trustworthy, at least a few are not. The dishonest employee is not easily identified and frequently goes to great lengths to appear reliable and trustworthy in order to take advantage of a careless or naive manager. The solution is to protect money, inventory, and other assets, and enforce controls in a fair and consistent manner.

Conventional wisdom says that 10 per cent of the people are totally honest, 30 per cent will steal if given the opportunity, and the remaining 60 per cent may be tempted to steal under the right circumstances. Our experience tells us also that three elements contribute to the commission of a crime: the need or desire of the criminal, availability to the criminal of the skills and tools needed to commit the crime, and the opportunity to act. The first two are difficult to control. Managers can attempt to control the desire to commit a crime by hiring honest people, but social and economic pressures can cause normally honest individuals to succumb to temptation. It is also beyond management's control to deny individuals the skills or tools that may be used to commit a crime. The only remaining recourse is to influence the opportunity to commit the crime.

Physical safeguards, procedures, and accountability are necessary controls in reducing the opportunity to commit crime, especially internal theft. Studies have shown that internal theft rests on three conditions: the employee feels a need to steal, the employee sees an opportunity to steal, and the employee rationalises the stealing. Loss can be considerable even when only one employee takes advantage of an opportunity to steal.

It is virtually impossible for a manager to absolutely ensure that every employee will be so personally honest that theft will not occur. Neither can the manager control employee rationalisations about theft because rationalising is very human and to be expected. The manager can, however, exercise a great deal of leverage in eliminating the opportunity to steal.

The concern of supervisors and managers for protecting the employer's assets is expressed in a multitude of actions that include orienting new employees concerning expectations of honest behaviour, providing employees with initial and refresher training designed to prevent crime, insisting on strict adherence to loss control procedures, and most of all, in personal behaviour that reflects integrity. Integrity means more than just being honest. It means doing the right thing and this applies to the quality of work as much as it does to the protection of assets. It should be no surprise that there is often a strong correlation between a smoothly operated restaurant and a respect for assets.

The key to successful crime prevention is employee involvement. Employees need to be empowered to help in protecting assets in much the same way they are empowered to improve customer service. Despite the demanding work schedules typical of restaurant operations, management must set time aside for educating employees in crime prevention and allowing them to contribute their ideas and efforts. Employees who are members of an opening or closing team need to be made aware of the robbery risks, they need to understand why it is necessary to leave as a group, and to appreciate that their individual safety is ensured when doors are locked and entry access is controlled during non-serving hours.

Honest employees will come forward and report theft because they do not wish to work in a dishonest environment. The reality is that honest employees will usually just quit without explaining why. When management actively involves employees in efforts to rid the workplace of crime in all its forms, crime decreases and workers gain both the satisfaction of being contributors to the common effort and the ease of mind that comes with working in a safe and secure environment. Research findings suggest that over half of the businesses that fail do so because of employee dishonesty. Loss from theft is paid from net profits and has a great impact on restaurant profitability.

In addition to internal theft are the many loss-producing outcomes associated with robbery, burglary, vandalism, and personal injuries and property damage suffered by employees and customers. The value of a crime prevention programme is impressive when its costs are weighed against the costs of loss and the severe impact of such losses on profit. Employees and managers working together can significantly reduce their exposure to crime and make their workplace safer and more secure.

Risks and Countermeasures

The restaurant industry is divided into concept segments,

such as full service, fast-food, sit down, carry out, etc. Each segment is confronted with a different set of risks. Establishments that are open during late evening hours have a higher degree of exposure to robberies, drug activity, and violence than is the case for establishments that close during early evening hours. Other factors, such as geographical location, clientele, and whether drinking alcohol occurs on the premises, will determine the risks. As a result, security programmes in the restaurant industry vary widely and reflect the unique risks associated with the nature of the business.

The risks commonly characteristic of restaurant operations are:

— robbery,

— violence directed against customers and employees,

— employee theft,

— burglary, and

— drug and alcohol abuse.

The last two are the least significant because they are controllable to some extent and the losses they produce are significantly lower than the first three. Robbery, violence, and internal theft are significant because they impact heavily in two critical dimensions: injury and death, and loss of assets. Robbery is most often committed with the aid of a lethal weapon and is accompanied by stress and fear on the part of the robber and the victim, thereby creating a potential for serious injury or death. Further, because many robbers are under the impairing influence of a drug or alcohol, or are seeking funds to satisfy a craving, they are likely to act violently.

A more disturbing fact is that the robber will kill people in order to eliminate them as witnesses. This fact has implications in the restaurant industry for two reasons. First, many robbers will frequent a restaurant one or more times before the robbery in order to work out a plan. The robber may realise during the commission of the crime that a restaurant employee may be able to provide information leading to arrest. Second, many robbers are former employees of the restaurant and they are known to their former co-workers. The motive for violence is built into the situation and carries over to customers who may be in the establishment at the time of the crime.

Violence can involve disputes among employees, among customers, and between employees and customers. It can also involve indiscriminate acts by street gangs and drug dealers whose internal disputes are often settled in parking lots. Indicators of gang-related problems at a restaurant are gang graffiti on rest room walls and the wearing of gang colours by employees. A waitress who is a gang member's girlfriend can attract to the restaurant gang members who bring with them the kinds of violence peculiar to gang activities. Gambling, prostitution, and drug selling are crimes that incite violence, and the persons involved often coordinate their activities from public telephones at restaurants.

On-the-job drug abuse by employees engenders disruptive, if not violent, behaviour, and because drug abusers are drug buyers, the sellers of drugs are attracted to restaurants that employ abusers. Persons who sell drugs are not limited to that criminal activity alone and may see on the premises an opportunity to commit other crimes, such as robbery and theft. The presence of a manager in the dining room/service area has been found to be effective in defusing and controlling potentially violent situations.

Employee theft is the most frequent criminal event facing a restaurant operator. The reasons are pretty obvious: cash attracts thieves and most restaurant sales are cash transactions, and employees have the greatest opportunity to steal because they have access to the assets and are familiar with the operation. The focus of successful restaurant operators is toward hospitality, which implies trust, openness, and a positive outlook. Many operators place too much trust in those individuals responsible for cash and inventory. If this trust is not tempered with the proper controls even the most reliable employee may eventually succumb to the temptation to steal. One of the most frequent methods of employee theft of cash is by manipulating sales transactions. Both mechanical and electronic cash registers can be manipulated to disguise a theft.

Bibliography

Bleser, David M., "Security Training; Cost Effective or Not?" Unpublished study, University of South Carolina, 1995.

Brislin, Ralph F., *Effective Report Writing for Security Personnel*, Boston, MA: Butterworth-Heinemann, 1994.

Broder, J.F., Risk Analysis and the Security Survey.

Chocolates for the Pillows Nightmares for the Guests: The Failure of the Hotel Industry to Protect the Travelling public from Violent Crime- Kenneth Lane Prestia.

Cote, Arthur E., *Fire Protection Handbook eighteenth edition*, National Fire Protection Association, March 2000.

Crowe, Timothy D., *Crime Prevention Through Environmental Design*, Boston, MA: Butterworth-Heinemann, 1991.

Dalton, Dennis R., *Security Management: Business Strategies for Success*, Boston, MA: Butterworth-Heinemann, 1995.

Dorothy Rabinowitz, "The Hostage Mentality", Commentary, June 1977.

Fischer, Robert J., *Introduction to Security*, 4th ed. Stoneham, MA: Butterworth Publishers, 1987.

Guide to Hotel Security- Denis C. Hughes.

Hotel Protection Management- the Innkeeper's Security Guide to Guest Protection & Reasonable Care-Raymone C., Jr Ellis.

Halon Disposal, *Ozone Protection*, Australian Government Department of the Environment and Heritage (Australia), Retrieved on 2006.

Jenkins, B.M., *Terrorism and Personal Protection.*

Lender, Mark E., and Martin, James K. *Drinking in America*, New York, NY: Macmillan Publishing Co., 1987.

Lodging, Monthly, New York, NY, July 1994.

Morn, Frank, *The Eye That Never Sleeps: The History of the Pinkerton National Detective Agency*, Bloomington, IN: Indiana University Press, 1982.

Private Security: Report of the Task Force on Private Security, Washington, DC: National Advisory Committee on Criminal justice Standards and Goals, 1976.

Salmen, John PS, *Accommodating All Guests: The Americans with Disabilities Act and the Lodging Industry*, Washington, DC: The American Hotel & Motel Association, 1992.

Security Management, A Special Access Control Supplement, Arlington, VA: ASIS, November 1990.

Security, Monthly Des Plaines, IL: Cahners, July 1994.

Sennewald, Charles A., *Effective Security Management*, 2nd ed. Stoneham, MA: Butterworth Publishers, 1985.

Victoria Marina, "Siege Leaves Mark on 2 Hostages", Los Angeles Times, May 20, 1979.

Walsh, Timothy J., *Protection of Assets Manuals*, Santa Monica, CA: The Merritt Company, 1991.

Index

Notes

Notes

Notes

Notes